News and Politics

News and Politics critically examines television news bulletins – still the primary source of information for most people – and asks whether the wider pace and immediacy of 24-hour news culture has influenced their format and style over time. Drawing on the concepts of mediatization and journalistic interventionism, Stephen Cushion empirically traces the shift from edited to live reporting from a cross-national perspective, focusing on the two-way convention in political coverage and the more interpretive approach to journalism it promotes.

Challenging prevailing academic wisdom, Cushion argues that the mediatization of news does not necessarily reflect a commercial logic or a lowering of journalism standards. In particular, the rise of live two-ways can potentially enhance viewers' understanding of public affairs – moving reporters beyond their visual backdrops and reliance on political soundbites – by asking journalists to scrutinize the actions of political elites, to interpret competing source claims and to explain the broader context to everyday stories. Considering the future of 24-hour news, a final discussion asks whether new content and social media platforms – including Twitter and Buzzfeed – enhance or weaken democratic culture.

This timely analysis of *News and Politics* is ideal for students of political communication and journalism studies, as well as communication studies, media studies, and political science.

Stephen Cushion is a Senior Lecturer at the School of Journalism, Media and Cultural Studies, Cardiff University. He is sole author of *The Democratic Value of News: Why Public Service Media Matter* (2012) and *Television Journalism* (2012), and co-editor of (with Justin Lewis) *The Rise of 24-Hour News Television: Global Perspectives* (2010, Peter Lang) and (with Richard Sambrook) *The Future of 24-Hour News: New Directions, New Challenges* (Peter Lang, 2016).

Communication and Society

Series Editor: James Curran

This series encompasses the broad field of media and cultural studies. Its main concerns are the media and the public sphere: on whether the media empower or fail to empower popular forces in society; media organizations and public policy; the political and social consequences of media campaigns; and the role of media entertainment, ranging from potboilers and the human-interest story to rock music and TV sport.

For a complete list of titles in this series, please see: www.routledge.com/books/series/SE0130

Praise for *News and Politics*:

"*News and Politics* combines the solidity of a well-researched monograph with the accessibility of a well-written book for students and academics alike. Based on content analysis, Stephen Cushion provides a broad-brushed *and* fine-grained account of the many ways in which British television news has changed in recent times. He shows how the fixed-time bulletins have been adapting to the faster-paced reporting styles of 24-hour news. He identifies the sources, manifestations and consequences for political reporting of the rise of inter-pretive journalism, in which specialist correspondents become central actors in the construction of news. Serving seemingly as authoritative analysts and judges of political events and standpoints, do they, Cushion asks, broaden citizens' understanding of political reality or tell them how to think about it? He judiciously considers the application of these trends to the currently fashion-able concepts of the mediatization of politics and journalistic intervention into it – proposing significant modifications of them. In all this, Cushion is remarkably up-to-date in the analytical and empirical literature. And he has an equally remarkable gift for clarifying complexity."

Jay G. Blumler, Emeritus Professor of Public Communication,
University of Leeds

"Anyone trying to understand how the nature of television news has changed to adapt it to the needs of today's faster-paced 24/7 media environment must read this book. Using the example of concrete practices in the UK, US and Norway, Stephen Cushion demonstrates the far-reaching relevance of these changes for journalists, politicians, audiences and academics. It's an extremely well-informed, original and compelling analysis of shifting news logics. He con-cludes by relating his findings to a wider 'Buzzification' of news and asks what this means for our democracy. Impressive."

Frank Esser, Professor of International and Comparative
Media Research, University of Zurich

"For anyone interested in the changing form, structure and style of television news journalism, *News and Politics* should be considered required reading. Focusing in particular on whether political news coverage has become more live, interpretive and mediatized, it both confirms and challenges findings in previous research, and will thus surely provoke further research and scholarly debate."

Jesper Strömbäck, Professor in Media, Communication and
Journalism, Mid Sweden University

News and Politics

The Rise of Live and Interpretive Journalism

Stephen Cushion

Routledge
Taylor & Francis Group

LONDON AND NEW YORK

First published 2015
by Routledge
2 Park Square, Milton Park, Abingdon, Oxon, OX14 4RN

and by Routledge
711 Third Avenue, New York, NY 10017

Routledge is an imprint of the Taylor & Francis Group, an informa business

British Library Cataloguing in Publication Data
A catalogue record for this book is available from the British Library

Library of Congress Cataloging in Publication Data
Cushion, Stephen.
News and politics : the rise of live and interpretive journalism / Stephen
Cushion.
pages cm. – (Communication and society)
Includes bibliographical references and index.
1. Television broadcasting of news. 2. Television broadcasting of news–Great
Britain. 3. Broadcast journalism–Political aspects. I. Title.
PN4784.T4C873 2015
070.1'95–dc23
2014035412

ISBN: 978-0-415-73988-7 (hbk)
ISBN: 978-0-415-74471-3 (pbk)
ISBN: 978-1-315-72764-6 (ebk)

Typeset in Sabon
by Taylor & Francis Books

Printed by Ashford Colour Press Ltd

Contents

List of Figures and Tables

Figures

Tables

Acknowledgements

I would like to acknowledge the support of a number of different people and funding streams involved at various stages in the development and writing of this book. Cardiff's Undergraduate Research Opportunities Programme (CUROP) funded students in 2012 and 2013 to help code the thousands of news items that inform this book. This included Richard Thomas, Rachel Lewis and Hugh Roger. I really appreciate the time and effort that went into monitoring and quantifying so much television coverage. Richard Thomas, in particular, enthusiastically watched hours and hours of television news reporting, considering in meticulous detail the words of political editors, such as Nick Robinson, Tom Bradby and, his personal favourite, Andy Bell. Richard also helped organize a cross-national collaborative project, involving the UK, US and Norway. I would like to thank Toril Aalberg for leading the Norwegian team of researchers, and Mari Nesbø and Annicken Sørum for coding the Norwegian television news bulletins. I am also grateful to John Huxford for recording the US material and sending it to the UK.

Researching retrospective television news is a difficult and costly exercise. A £1000 impact award from Cardiff University in 2013 – based on a project about BBC reporting of devolved politics co-managed with Justin Lewis – made it possible to fund archival research into BBC and ITV news during the 1990s and 2000s (many thanks to Justin for letting me have all the prize fund!). I appreciate the help of Greg Philo and Colin Macpherson for hunting down the footage I needed in the Glasgow Media Group's archive and sending it to me so quickly.

Finally, I would like to thank Routledge for publishing the book and for dealing so smoothly with the production of it. Natalie Foster was really enthusiastic about commissioning *News and Politics*, and I am very grateful to the series editor, James Curran, for supporting the book.

Introduction
From mediation to mediatization

The relationship between news and politics is considered intrinsic to democratic life. After all, news is routinely made up of political actors and parties, a place where their decisions, actions and motivations are most likely to be featured. Since most people in advanced Western democracies rely on the news to understand the world, politics is largely understood by what appears in it, whether learning about a new health policy, an imminent war happening or a politician resigning. Of course, citizens can personally interact with their elected representatives at town halls, say, or constituency surgeries and campaign events. Or by other means, such as writing, emailing or "tweeting" their thoughts and concerns to politicians.

But while there are opportunities for citizens to meet and greet politicians, for the vast majority of people politics remains a largely mediated experience, something they do whilst watching television, listening to the radio, reading the newspaper or browsing online. More recently, citizens have been encouraged to participate in news formats, be part of this experience and inform news content, such as being an audience member of a TV programme, writing a letter to a newspaper or commenting upon a Facebook wall. Yet again the vast majority remain satisfied with watching, reading or listening to the news, rather than making or shaping it. In other words, most citizens in advanced Western democracies live in *mediated democracies*, engaging with and being informed about politics by competing news outlets. Put simply, most citizens rely on the news to tell them what is happening in the world of politics.

The ability for news outlets to control and influence how politics is mediated has been brought into sharper focus by scholars over recent decades and is reflected by their respective book titles. So, for example, *Mediated Politics* (Bennett and Entman 2001) and *Mediating Politics* (Washbourne 2010) explored – from a range of perspectives – how contemporary political communication is shaped by an ever-expanding landscape of mainstream and alternative media. *Mediated Access* (McNair *et al.* 2003), meanwhile, examined political debates in broadcast news programming and how they are structured to allow audience members to participate. *The Mediation of Power* (Davis 2007), by contrast, focused on political and media actors, unpacking the forces that construct the presentation of politics. Likewise, *The Mediated Presidency* (Farnsworth and Lichter 2006) charted the relationship television news has had in representing past presidents of the United States (US). And there are many, even broader inquires, from *Mass-Mediated Terrorism* (Nacos 2007) to *Mediated Cosmopolitanism* (Robertson 2010), that have interpreted political issues through a mediated prism. Taken together, all these studies and many more aim to understand how politics is defined by an increasing range of news media.

However, in more recent years it has been claimed the term *mediation* has only limited conceptual use and application. As Lundby (2009a: 13) observed, mediation is a "general concept applied to acts and processes of communication with technical media ... [but] will not, in the long term, transform institutional practices and modes of social interaction". Likewise, Mazzoleni (2008) has argued that defining "politics as 'mediated' is a simple truism, in that communication and mass media are necessary prerequisites to the functioning of political systems". In other words, mediation is viewed as being a more descriptive than analytical concept, scratching at the surface of media power and influence. To gain a deeper insight, it is argued a more holistic grasp of the relationship media have with key institutions in society is required.

As a consequence, the concept of *mediatization* has gained greater purchase in academic debates. It is used to explore the antecedents of media power and influence in respect of impacting or transforming wider society in areas such as religion, art, culture, politics, fashion or marketing (see Hepp 2013a; Hjarvard 2008, 2013; Lundby 2009b). This is in recognition of the suffusion of media culture into almost every facet of people's lives and routines, taking on the role other institutions previously had in building social relationships. As Livingstone (2009: 5) has pointed out, "today ... the media not only get between any and all participants in society but also, crucially, annex a sizeable part of their power by mediatizing – subordinating – the previously-powerful authorities of government, education, the church, the family, etc". But in exploring the mediatization of different aspects of society or culture, it can be sometimes difficult to ascertain with any kind of substance where and how a mediatizing process has taken place, meaning the concept can appear somewhat elusive, a broad historical transition *rather than something empirically transparent*. Indeed, Livingstone (2009: 5) has cautioned that "The question of how far the power of traditional authorities has in fact been annexed by the media is an empirical one as yet unresolved".

The aim of *News and Politics* is to shed empirical light on *mediatization* debates by examining the changing nature of news and, more specifically, political reporting over recent decades. In doing so, the intention is to enter into debates about the mediatization of politics, an increasingly popular scholarly pursuit in journalism studies and political communication studies that, put broadly, interprets how far media shape how politics is practised (Mazzoleni and Schulz 1999; Strömbäck 2008). It is viewed as a necessary conceptual tool to understand the changing political landscape because, as Mazzoleni (2008) has pointed out, "politics and the way it is performed and communicated have been widely affected by the rise of mass media between the nineteenth and the twentieth centuries. Such media-driven influence in the political environment is the core of the concept of mediatization." This influence manifests itself in an underlying media logic, a driving force that – it is claimed – alters the behaviour of political actors and coverage of political news. Media logic, in other words, is shaped by the norms and routines of journalists as opposed to the principles and priorities of politicians. Moreover, it is driven by a media format subject to professional, commercial and technological demands that, taken together, influence the practise of politics (Altheide and Snow 1979; Esser 2013a).

The primary focus taken in this book is to explore a specific format of news – the television news bulletin, the most consumed form of news in most countries spanning many decades – and to empirically ask whether its underlying logic has changed the way news generally and politics specifically is reported over time. However, when interpreting media logic, 'the media' tend to be viewed as a singular force, rather than a medium that offers multiple ways of influencing the process of mediatization. Or, put differently, a shared media logic exists. And yet, as Lundby (2009a: 113) has suggested, "The sweeping concept of 'media logic' hides ... the constraints of specific formats and the transformations that are shaped in concrete social interactions and communication processes". In respect of understanding a shared logic in news media, there are of course competing and contrasting ways in which the structure, form and style of journalism operate to produce, amongst other things, political news. But this is largely accepted in the mediatization of politics literature because, as Strömbäck et al. (2011) explain, mass media is seen as a system or institution. They suggest that while "different media organizations and their formats, practices and contents constitute the building blocks of this overall system ... the sum is greater than its parts, and the norms and logic(s) that govern the media overall are considered more important than what distinguishes one media over another" (Strömbäck et al. 2011: 162).

This book argues that this approach to interpreting news media coverage of politics limits our understanding of how the process of mediatization can impact on the media itself *over time*. For if only *one* media logic is used to interpret the changing nature of political coverage it prevents competing *logics* from being theorized that operate simultaneously across and between different media outlets and systems. Or, put another way, it means the media cannot be subject to the process of mediatization. Of course, proposing the media can mediatize itself has more than a faint whiff of tautology. After all, how can the media mediatize itself? But in the chapters that follow the premise of the book rests on the fact that the culture of news production and presentation has *itself* undergone significant changes over time. This is not to imply media have independently changed. Far from it, since changes in media can be explained by a multiplicity of external influences: in the stock market, for example, in state regulation, technological advancements, consumer preferences and public attitudes. Understood from this perspective, this book argues that the process of mediatization can be applied to specific media formats – including television news bulletins – in order to interpret whether their underlying logic has been influenced by broader journalistic influences and changed the way in which politics has been reported over time.

The next chapter will explain in more detail how the concept of mediatization will be applied to television news bulletins. While debates in mediatization tend to deal with media influence generally, the approach taken in this book will be to *identify empirically what changes have emerged on a specific format of television news – fixed time evening bulletins – and to examine, in detail, political reporting.* In so doing, the study is primarily informed by empirical studies that have explored the *mediatization of politics in media content.* For now the relationship between television news, politics and competing media logics is introduced.

Television news, politics and media logic(s)

Reading newspapers was a principal way many people became informed about politics and public affairs prior to the twentieth century. Whilst cinema goers at the beginning of the century could enjoy newsreels, radio soon established itself as the medium of choice from the 1920 to the 1950s. It was, after all, the first to deliver live news into people's homes and workplaces. In the latter half of the twentieth century, however, radio was soon supplanted by television, the box in the corner that has become the focal point of most people's living room. Moreover, it has continued to be the dominant media well into the twenty-first century. Despite the rise of online news, television news has remained the primary source of information for most people in advanced Western democracies. In the United Kingdom (UK), for example, over three quarters of people – 78 per cent – indicated they regularly watched television news, a far greater share than watch, read or listen online, in newspapers or on radio platforms (Ofcom 2013). Whilst different newspapers offered a degree of editorial choice, up until the late 1980s into the 1990s most countries had just a handful of television channels to choose from. These channels thus became highly influential, and many countries issued strict licence agreements to ensure journalism was subject to public interest tests and conformed to high standards of journalism (Cushion 2012a). Political reporting, in particular, is subject to close regulation. Whereas newspapers are free to editorialize, most broadcasters today have to follow legal guidelines to ensure their journalism is, in some form, objective, impartial or balanced.

Needless to say, as television developed it delivered a distinct range of news and current affairs programming. Indeed, the genre of television has become increasingly hybrid, with different formats today blending together news, comedy and entertainment, such as *The Daily Show* in the US or *10 O'Clock Live* in the UK (Cushion 2012b). The focus of this book, however, is on one of the earliest forms of television news programming, fixed time television *news bulletins* or newscasts as they are more commonly known in the US.[1] Conway (2009: 4) has defined bulletins as "*a regularly scheduled program dedicated to the promotion of the top stories of the day and important issues for the audience, utilizing visuals, words and audio in a format not directly copied by another medium*" (Conway 2009: 4; his emphasis). In many countries bulletins have become the flagship news programme, a 20–30 minute continuous flow of news, sports and weather. Moreover, they have become a permanent fixture in many television schedules, a familiar point in time to catch up with what happened in the world that day. Aalberg *et al.*'s (2010) analysis of TV programming (1987–2007) in six advanced democracies – the US, the UK, Belgium, the Netherlands, Sweden and Norway – established that TV bulletins continue to be scheduled at peak airtimes. This was notably the case in countries where a strong public service broadcast environment existed, since channels were legally bound to schedule programming at different slots and at times when viewing figures would remain relatively high. In the US, by contrast, the more deregulatory culture has meant the major networks – ABC, CBS and NBC – can schedule their evening 6.30pm bulletins at the same time, making viewers pick between them and reducing pluralism in the process.

Of course, television news bulletins have had to withstand serious competition not just from rival television formats, but an ever-expanding media marketplace and fast-changing new technologies that extend the immediacy of journalism. For the advent of dedicated 24-hour news channels in the 1980s into the 1990s, and then the growth and expansion of online news and social platforms into the twenty-first century, has put pressure on 'old' formats – such as television news bulletins – to keep up with their pace of delivery. Whereas audiences can now access news at the flick of a switch or the tap of an app, for some people fixed time bulletins might appear an anachronistic format, a dated service asking viewers to patiently wait until they are supplied the day's headlines.

And yet, for all the competition and technological breakthroughs, fixed time television news bulletins continue to be the major source of news for many people. As one recent UK study of international news consumption empathetically stated, "TV bulletins still rule. In spite of all the discussion of the merits of online, of social media, of interactivity, choice and convenience, it was clear that more people got their news of these big international events from the main bulletins at 6pm and 10pm on BBC One than from the BBC website" (Sambrook 2013). Likewise, in the US, *The State of the News Media 2013* confirmed "network news – and especially the evening newscasts that attract a combined audience of about 22 million Americans each night – has remained an island of stability in an otherwise rapidly transforming media environment" (The Pew Research Center's Project for Excellence in Journalism 2013).

As well as competing with digital and online platforms, the rise of news channels on satellite and cable channels have threatened the relevance of fixed time television news bulletins. After all, why wait for a news service when there is a menu of rolling news channels instantly available? But while significant breaking news events – typhoons in the Philippines, say, or terrorist attacks in Boston – generate huge spikes in viewer demand for 24-hour news channels, in day-to-day, routine consumption bulletins continue to attract the largest audience share. In the UK, for example, Sky News and the BBC News Channel attract averagely weekly audiences of 83,000 and 136,000 respectively. BBC bulletins comparatively attract somewhere in the region of 4 to 5 million viewers, a little less for ITV (3 to 4 million) and under a million for Channels 4 and 5 (cited in Barnett *et al*. 2012). Interpreting these figures, Barnett *et al*. (2012) concluded that, "despite the growing influence of 24 hour news channels among certain sections of the news-committed audience, neither is significant as a mass viewing platform and their impact on the overall UK audience has remained relatively minor". Although rolling news channels have been part of the broadcast mix in the US for far longer than in the UK with a greater choice of cable news programming, they have not collectively challenged the monopoly of fixed time bulletins. *The State of the News Media 2013* found "network evening news is still a popular news source ... In 2012 ... more than four times as many people watched the three network evening newscasts on ABC, CBS and NBC than watched the highest-rated shows on the three cable news channels (CNN, Fox News and MSNBC) during prime time" (The Pew Research Center's Project for Excellence in Journalism 2013). Meanwhile, in Australia, bulletins can sometimes attract the highest audiences of any television programming despite the rise of Australian news channels in recent years. According to Channel Nine's national news director, Darren Wick, the "6pm [bulletin] is still a record of the day where everything is summed up. It's still a chance for people to sit down, take it in and assess ... I think people need that handbrake on the day" (cited in Kalina and Murfett 2012).

But while the emergence of instant news – whether on digital, online or dedicated television channels – has not necessarily replaced or supplanted viewers from routinely watching fixed time bulletins, the impact of rolling news journalism is arguably more systemic than immediately apparent. For in the age of convergence – where journalists move from one medium to the next, from television, radio to online – the culture of journalism, the occupational routines and norms, professional values and beliefs could have impacted on the production, format and presentation of 'old' formats. Of course, cross-nationally and between media systems there are different levels of convergence, professional identities and environments that bring different journalism cultures. As Hanitzsch (2007: 369) explains, journalism culture relates to "a particular set of ideas and practices by which journalists legitimate their role in society and render their work meaningful". In other words, age-old journalism norms and routines long practised in fixed time programming could have changed, or at least been modified, to legitimize values of immediacy and speed evident in the wider culture of journalism. Or, put differently, competing media logics may have influenced the underlying logic of evening television news bulletins.

Whilst the impact of the 24-hour news cycle has been interpreted in the context of how politicians behave and respond (explored further in Chapter 7), less attention has been centred on whether 'old' news formats have changed and adapted to 'new' media over time. Of course, it is easy to find impressionistic observations or sweeping statements about the changing character of news media. Most of which paint a pessimistic picture of deteriorating journalism standards, with little supporting evidence – echoing what McNair (2000: 10) calls the "narrative of decline". Thus, the '24-hour news cycle' is often invoked in an abstract way, characterized broadly without always empirically nailing down its impact on media content. The intention of this book is to offer both systematic and longitudinal evidence of whether the '24-hour news cycle' has changed the form, structure and style of *evening television news bulletins over time*.

For while the logic of the rolling news age privileges values of speed and immediacy, fixed time television news bulletins have a logic to the contrary. Rather than covering "news as it happens" – as many news channels now claim – bulletins have historically sought to convey the day's news (Conway 2009). In other words, the logic of an evening bulletin involves gathering, editing and packaging news for viewers over the course of the day, whereas a rolling news logic strives to deliver news immediately and on a continual basis. The studies drawn upon in this book were all designed to empirically assess whether and to what extent evening television news bulletins have adapted their logic to converge with the broader culture of instant broadcast, digital and online news media.

In doing so, debates about mediatization will be entered into, since – as previously explained – it is possible to explore how competing media logics can impact on specific media formats over time. For while television bulletins have remained the most consumed form of news in most advanced Western democracies – despite the expansion of multi-channel television and online news – whether their format has become more aligned with its competitors has not been subjected to sustained or longitudinal enquires. This book examines how far television journalism generally and political news specifically have conformed to a rolling news logic. Or, put another way, it asks whether there has been a mediatization of news and politics in television news bulletins over recent decades. The logics underpinning the research design of fixed and rolling news will be unpacked in greater detail in the next chapter, as will the specific methodological details. For now, a general introduction to the scope of the book is necessary, explaining the overarching aims and objectives, the sample, timeframe of the study and a brief introduction to the chapters that follow.

Scope of the study

The book draws on a number of quantitative content analysis studies supplemented with more qualitative analysis of television news. To analyse the form, structure and style of bulletins over time, the book will be informed by the concept of journalistic interventionism. This concept has primarily been used to examine political journalism during election campaigns in order to evaluate the "discretionary power" of the media (Semetko *et al.* 1991: 3). Whilst journalistic interventionism and how it will be applied in this book will be more fully explained in the following chapter, broadly speaking it refers to the extent to which journalists intervene in the campaign or follow party political agendas. By examining television news bulletins in detail, the book will interpret different television conventions – edited packages or live two-ways, for example – as journalistic interventions. For they help to convey the character of journalism, explaining why and how stories are covered. By examining coverage over time, the book will interpret the editorial direction of bulletins over recent decades.

So, for example, a story about a new health policy could be covered in a number of different ways. A reporter could put together a lengthy edited package with a range of sources drawn upon to inform it. Or a political correspondent could explain the policy in a shorter live piece to camera outside No.10 Downing Street or the White House. A studio discussion could be generated or it could be left to the television anchor to narrate the story. Put another way, by analysing the type and nature of journalistic interventions over time, the media logic of television news bulletins can be interpreted to assess whether they have maintained their own editorial character or been influenced by the broader culture of journalism. Have, for instance, bulletins embraced some of the values of 24-hour news culture, asking reporters to cover news with routine updates about the latest story? Or have bulletins remained committed to delivering largely edited news, drawing on external sources and packaging together news throughout the day?

To explore the changing nature of television news, UK bulletins will be examined between 1991 and 2013. The evening bulletins of the BBC and ITV will take the central focus, since these broadcasters have historically shared the largest audiences and have arguably wielded the biggest influence on UK television journalism. Whilst the BBC is a wholesale public service broadcaster, ITV is a commercial public service broadcaster. The competition between the two has defined – since ITV began broadcasting in 1955 – the genre of fixed time bulletins in the UK (Cushion 2012b). However, Channel 5, another commercial public service broadcaster, will be analysed and compared with the BBC and ITV in more recent years.

But UK journalism will not be exclusively examined and considered representative of all television news bulletins. As Dimitrova and Strömbäck have rightly argued, "scholars should be careful not to assume that findings regarding television news in one country apply elsewhere" (2010: 499). In particular, the US network 6.30pm bulletins – ABC, CBS and NBC, all wholesale market-driven broadcasters – will be analysed generally and more specifically about how politics is reported. The book will also draw on a study of Norwegian evening news bulletins – NRK, the main public service broadcaster, and TV2, a commercial public service broadcaster – in order to compare coverage with the US and UK (Cushion, Aalberg and Thomas 2014). Whilst the US and UK have had rolling news channels operating for many decades, in Norway dedicated domestic 24-hour news channels are in their relative infancy. In other words, comparisons can be made between countries with a deeply ingrained culture of rolling news and countries where its presence is relatively new to television journalists. In doing so, the competing logics of rolling and fixed time bulletins can thus be compared and contrasted. The media systems in each country provide another comparative dimension to the book: while the US has wholesale market-driven broadcasters (ABC, CBS and NBC), the UK and Norway have wholesale public service broadcasters (BBC and NRK) as well as mixed commercial public service broadcasters (ITV and TV2).

In comparing television journalism cross-nationally and between media systems, the aim is to contribute to ongoing debates in comparative research related to journalism studies, political communication and communication studies more generally. Comparative research prevents national studies and theories from being generalized, and enhances a greater international understanding of where differences between counties emerge and, perhaps more importantly, why. As Blumler (2012: xi) acknowledged, "comparative research is not merely desirable but scientifically essential ... both to test the applicability of generalizations about communication phenomena beyond their milieu of origin and to establish how surrounding structural and cultural conditions may impinge on and shape these phenomena".

The book examines thousands of news items over more than two decades and considers, in detail, the structure, form and style of television news bulletins cross-nationally. In addition, the book will draw on a wide range of national and internationally comparative quantitative and qualitative studies in order to more broadly interpret the prevailing trends of television news and the changing culture of journalism. Overall, this book delivers a systematic and longitudinal examination of television news bulletins over recent decades. It asks whether evening bulletins have been influenced by the wider culture of journalism by adapting a rolling news logic with greater use of live conventions and instant analysis. Or whether they have maintained a fixed time logic by maintaining largely edited conventions and relying on external sources to convey the day's news. Drawing on the concepts of mediatization and journalistic interventionism, the following chapters will interpret the degree to which these competing media logics have been subscribed to over time in television news generally and political reporting specifically. In doing so, television news will be compared across national journalism cultures and between media systems, developing comparative analysis that can evaluate how far television news has become mediatized, if at all, and to consider not just the reasons why but the wider implications for journalism and democracy.

Chapter 1 begins by exploring the birth of television news bulletins and how they evolved in the post–World War II decades. It will consider how the format of news bulletins has changed and matured up until the 1980s, a point in time when rolling news channels were launched and a new era of television journalism began. For while bulletins have been a long-standing television news format operating in most advanced democracies for more than 60 years, they have faced considerably more competition over recent decades with always on, 24/7 platforms. Fixed time bulletins, the chapter will discuss, face an existential challenge, since not only can dedicated television news channels bring news to viewers instantly, but online and social media can deliver news at the flick of a switch or the tap of an app. In doing so, it will be suggested that this could put pressure on how contemporary fixed time bulletins operate, encouraging them to adapt their logic to keep pace with the broader journalistic culture of rolling news. In order to interpret whether there has been a change in media logic, the concepts of mediatization and journalistic interventionism will be introduced and understood in the context of studying television news generally and political reporting more specifically.

Chapter 2 then begins the more empirical focus of the book, longitudinally exploring whether the conventions of television news have changed over recent decades. It contextualizes previous studies examining the form, structure and style of television news bulletins, developing a broader discussion about key trends and developments of news over recent decades. It then introduces the main UK study informing the chapter, drawing on the concepts of mediatization and journalistic interventionism to interpret the degree to which routine conventions and practices have changed the way television bulletins have reported what is happening in the world. Wholesale and commercial public service broadcasters – BBC, ITV and Channel 5 respectively – will be compared and contrasted. Overall, the chapter asks if fixed time news bulletins have increasingly adopted or resisted the journalistic logic of rolling news – quickening the pace of news, going live and being interpretive – into the new millennium.

Chapter 3 then more specifically considers the changing nature of political reporting over recent decades compared to news generally. It begins by engaging with the latest scholarly debates related to the mediatization of politics and then explains the distinctive analytical framework taken in the book. In doing so, a study examining UK news bulletins over two decades is drawn upon using standard indicators in mediatization studies – of soundbites, imagebites and journalistic visibility, for example – before considering new ways of measuring political news in edited and live conventions. It builds on the analytical framework of the previous chapter to more closely examine whether bulletins – once again comparing wholesale and commercial public service broadcasters – increasingly resemble the format and style of 24-hour news media in how they report politics. Overall, the chapter asks how far television news bulletins have subscribed to a media logic – adopting journalistic values prevalent in the wider culture of news, such as producing live and instant news coverage – or how far they reflect a political logic, where the actions and voices of political actors remain central to coverage.

Chapter 4 offers a cross-national assessment of television news, with bulletins in three countries – the US, UK and Norway – systematically compared, each with different levels of commercial and public service obligations. The need for greater comparative communication research is discussed in the context of different media systems and political identities. Drawing on a cross-sectional analysis of evening bulletins in each country, the chapter asks if the wider culture of journalism has impacted on the format and style of coverage. While rolling news has been a long-standing influence in the US after CNN began broadcasting in 1980, and to a lesser extent in the UK with Sky News launching in 1989, the first dedicated 24-hour news in Norway is less than a decade old. The extent to which fixed time news bulletins resemble 24-hour news channels cross-nationally, in other words, could be seen to represent the wider influence of instant rolling news conventions. The second half of the chapter takes a closer look at evening bulletins in the US and UK, considering their form, structure and style, in particular when reporting the world of politics. It interprets the comparative differences between bulletins by the contrasting media and political environments of both countries. The US's more interventionist and commercialized broadcasting environment – conditions widely seen to enhance the mediatization of politics – will be compared to the UK's public service regulated broadcasters.

Chapter 5 puts live two-way reporting under greater scrutiny. As previous chapters will demonstrate, this convention has become a more prominent feature of evening bulletins into the new millennium and arguably represents the most interventionist way of reporting politics. While previous studies have painted a broad quantitative picture of live two-ways, the focus in this chapter will be on more qualitatively interpreting the role of the live two-way, analysing its form and style in the reporting of politics. It considers previous studies exploring the role of live two-ways – in routine periods of time, during military conflicts and on 24-hour news channels – asking if its use is distinctive in fixed time bulletins. This will include exploring how edited political news is different to live two-ways, the way politicians are sourced, the interpretive nature of journalists as well as the ideological prism through which politics is understood by reporters. Overall, then, the aim of the chapter is to make an evidence based judgement about the normative value of live two-ways in political reporting.

The sixth chapter brings together the key findings of the previous chapters, interpreting the significance of each in light of relevant debates about mediatization and journalistic interventionism. It then turns to how television viewers understand and engage with politics and public affairs, considering whether live two-ways and a generally more journalistic-centred style of television news reporting – trends identified more broadly as delivering greater mediatization and interventionism throughout the book – strengthen or weaken democratic culture. By way of conclusion, the final part of the chapter considers how future mediatization studies should be constructed, engaging with the most recent scholarly critique of the concept. It is suggested that the concept of mediatization could – if clearly designed and operationalized – act as a future yardstick to empirically measure the evolution of evening bulletins or other specific media formats over time. In other words, is the logic of fixed time bulletins becoming more – or less – reliant on immediacy and interpretation to keep pace with rival online and social media? While fixed time evening bulletins have adopted some of the values of rolling news culture, it is argued their future role could be better served by resisting the speed of the news cycle and focusing on how to put issues and events into better context for viewers.

The seventh and final chapter moves beyond the primary focus on evening television news bulletins and the mediatization framework by considering the future of news in the context of broader changes in society and communication. It examines the relationship changing 24/7 platforms have with people's everyday lifestyles, their use of communications and the changing culture of politics. The value of new content and social media platforms will be interpreted, in particular the role they play in 24-hour news culture. In doing so, the chapter will develop a sustained analysis of Twitter and BuzzFeed, two increasingly popular platforms that communicate information in different ways that challenge the one-way flow of power previously held by the mass media. Overall, the chapter considers the wider impact new content and social media platforms have had on the information environment. And asks – if this is the future of news – in what ways will it enhance or weaken democratic culture?

Note

1 Whilst television news bulletins are more commonly known as newscasts in the US, they will be referred to as news bulletins throughout this book. However, bulletins refer to the same type of fixed time news programme (e.g. ABC, NBC and CBS 6.30pm newscasts).

Chapter 1

Interpreting news conventions as journalistic interventions

Exploring the changing nature of television journalism and political reporting

Introduction

In March 2013 the BBC moved into a new £1bn multi-media newsroom at Broadcasting House in central London. The aim – in the BBC's own words – was to put as many journalists "under one roof ... where they sit alongside colleagues who handle the essential live and breaking news content as it comes in and alongside the television, radio and online production teams".[1] Of course, BBC journalists had previously moved between mediums – to report live for the news channel, to offer opinions on evening television bulletins, to blog some analysis online or tweet the latest update to the story – but the new £1bn newsroom strikingly delivered what is known as media convergence, more fully integrating news services between different media. While perhaps not on the same scale, the BBC is not alone in converging its newsroom. In different parts of the world, broadcasters into the twenty-first century have increasingly connected competing platforms of journalism in order to more efficiently produce news output.

Since journalists are less likely to be confined to one medium, the culture in which they practise journalism appears to be changing and becoming more fluid. After all, journalists today routinely multi-task, producing news in different media, formats and styles. In doing so, this raises questions – often overlooked by commentators or scholars as the spotlight turns to the latest media technologies – about whether the journalistic practices of 'old' formats of news have changed and adapted to a new environment of news making. Or if they have resisted pressures to conform to the shared culture of news production and maintained their practices and principles.

The aim of this chapter – and overall purpose of the book – is to establish how these questions can be explored in respect of television news bulletins, a long-standing format that has been operating in most advanced democracies for more than 60 years. Over recent decades, however, its *raison d'être* has been threatened by a more competitive and faster-paced news culture. For television time bulletins – whether morning, lunch time, early or late evening – appear

at fixed time slots in the schedules, programmes that deliver an update on the day so far. Whilst television channels have always run unscheduled 'news flashes' or what are more commonly known as 'breaking news' bulletins today, these are extremely rare and reserved for major events, such as a terrorist attack or during election time. Up until the late 1980s, or even – for some countries – well into the 1990s, it made sense to punctuate the schedule with fixed time bulletins. In the analogue age, after all, television was in a period of programme scarcity, with limited space to schedule everything from the news to comedy, soap operas and other entertainment-based formats.

But since then there has been a rise of dedicated 24-hour news channels, of rolling online news and more recently social media platforms. Thus, fixed time television bulletins operate in a far more competitive media environment – beyond just radio or newspapers – where audiences no longer have to wait to see the news, they can switch channels, go online or tap an app for an immediate update. All of which, needless to say, puts considerable pressure on television news bulletins, prompting existential questions about their role and purpose in supplying news in a far more accelerated and immediate culture of news consumption and wider journalism practice. To put it another way, the media logic of fixed news bulletins could have changed over recent decades as competing logics – from news channels, online and social media platforms – push television journalism in a potentially new and faster-paced editorial direction.

This chapter will begin by exploring the birth of television news bulletins and how they evolved in the post–World War II decades. It will consider how the format of television news altered and matured up until the 1980s, at which point the media environment changed markedly. New competition from an ever-expanding media marketplace has put pressure on how contemporary television bulletins operate and their underlying logic. In order to interpret whether there has been a change in media logic, debates about mediatization will be introduced and understood in the context of studying television news bulletins. In doing so, the analytical framework used to interpret the mediatization of news and political reporting will then be explored, drawing on the concept of journalistic interventionism. The chapter will propose new theoretical and empirical lines of inquiry, with the final section methodologically explaining the research design shaping the many studies drawn upon throughout the book.

Overall, this chapter will introduce the overarching analytical framework for interpreting whether television news bulletins have become mediatized over recent decades used throughout the book. However, each chapter will provide more specific details and wider context about *how* news is analysed and interpreted between media systems and journalism cultures cross-nationally in light of debates about mediatization and journalistic interventionism.

The birth and evolution of television news: establishing routine conventions on evening bulletins

When news was first broadcast on television in the 1940s, its routine conventions and practices bore little resemblance to contemporary news bulletins. For radio had been the dominant medium for several decades and its mode of address – connecting aurally with listeners – was difficult to easily reconcile with the format of television. After all, television is a visual medium, making it a challenging prospect for journalists of this generation to juxtapose both audio and images in the presentation of news. NBC aired a scheduled television bulletin in 1940, for example, but it was exactly the same as its NBC radio network broadcast. Likewise in the UK, where – according to Crisell (2002: 98) – "between 1946 and 1954 the BBC offered no television news as such, merely a late night evening relay of the radio news during which viewers were obliged to stare at a single photograph of Big Ben". The BBC – the monopoly broadcaster at the time – had experienced radio producers who were reluctant to compromise their practices and principles to accommodate the medium of TV. When a more conventional bulletin was aired in July 1954 it still had the hallmarks of radio rather than television, since a newsreader remained out of shot and narrated over images and film.

It was in the US where news conventions and practices suited to the medium of television were pioneered. Conway (2009) has argued that CBS news in New York City was the first to visually experiment with television news bulletins in the 1940s. But it was not until the 1950s that more generic television news conventions began to emerge on different broadcasters. So, for example, while CBS had more than a dozen presenters of the news between 1944 and 1948, after this point in time the concept of the television news anchor was established and popular personalities – Walter Cronkite, say, or Dan Rather – became permanent fixtures on bulletins ever since (Conway 2007). The 1950s into the 1960s witnessed the rise of television news anchors, who – according to Meltzer (2010: 31) – became "the face, the identifying signature of the news broadcast, and signified that television had changed the expectations of what it meant to be a journalist". In other words, television news bulletins had acclimatized to the visual potential of the medium, with anchors placed at the centre of the narrative. Not only did they narrate one story to the next, they controlled the live flow of images and filmed packages.

Not every country so readily embraced the personality-fused role of television news anchors. In the UK, for example, "presenters", "announcers" or just "newsreaders" were – and sometimes are today – used to describe the equivalent of a US television news anchor. In the minds of the British political establishment, these labels conveyed a more detached position from which to narrate the news, curbing the possibility of any personal views or bias in broadcasting (Robinson 2012). It took ITV – a new commercial broadcaster – to shake up the format of UK bulletins. Whilst the BBC had employed an anchor just prior to ITV's arrival, it was pressure from the commercial channel that made anchors more central figures in UK bulletins, creating a less formal mode of address and enhancing a new visual style. So, for example, ITV news brought "an unprecedented quantity of film in its bulletins and incorporated as much informed comment as possible to give viewers better perspective" (Crisell 2002: 98). This was, of course, a period when video recorder equipment became more widely used by broadcasters.

Despite ITV's intervention into television news in the 1950s, according to Nick Robinson (2012), the BBC's political editor, bulletins remained qualitatively different to today's format. In his book, *Live from Downing Street: The Inside Story of Politics, Power and Media*, he observed at this point in time that "there were no satellites to deliver live broadcasting from anywhere at the drop of a hat; no lightweight cameras recording sound as well as pictures; no sophisticated graphics, and, of course, no colour" (Robinson 2012: 122). Moreover, he continued:

> Bulletins were ... much shorter than they are now, around ten to twelve minutes long. Largely silent film had to be brought to the studio – in the case of international news, this meant shipping it back from abroad – and developed before commentary, sound effects and, perhaps, music were added. Foreign reports did not carry the voice of the reporter: they were read out by the studio presenter or a specialist 'commentary reader'. Journalists never spoke to camera and appeared only occasionally when asking a question ...
>
> The first reporter ever to broadcast live from Westminster was ... Roland Fox. He used a tiny purpose-built studio near the Palace of Westminster ...
>
> For many years to come most political reports on BBC TV news would be provided by a man sitting in that little studio, staring into a camera and reading from an autocue controlled with a foot pedal. ... [W]ith cameras banned from the Commons there were rarely any pictures, and reports were largely free of commentary, analysis and explanation.
>
> (Robinson 2012: 122–23)

Robinson (2012) describes a history that is largely shared by television news bulletins internationally. For television news bulletins were constrained by technology, with live reporting limited to particular locales and editing packages considered highly cumbersome and time-consuming. At the same time, journalistic editorializing was not widely part of coverage – partly, of course, due to strict impartiality laws in many countries – and cameras prevented politics from being televised either live or in an edited format in Parliaments, Senates and Congresses. Televising their main legislative chambers in the US and Canada began in the late 1970s, in the UK it was 1989 and a year later for Australia. In other words, many television news bulletins around the world matured in the post–World War II decades without the opportunity to televise political institutions. Political soundbites of this era – where politicians talk on screen uninterrupted – were far greater in length. This was not only due to the comparatively unsophisticated editing equipment of that era – with interviews conducted live – but the relationship between journalists and politicians, which remained less adversarial and more deferential compared to later decades.

However, the character of television news bulletins became more distinctive in the 1960s and 1970s. As journalists became more familiar with juxtaposing sound and images, different kinds of news events were covered in new and pioneering ways. Meanwhile, television news anchors became more confident, more at ease with the format and began to stamp their own identity on individual bulletins. Television was also fast becoming the medium of choice. According to Crisell (2002: 100), 24 per cent of people in the UK chose television news as their principal source of news in 1957 – behind both radio and newspapers – but by 1962 52 per cent did, a majority of the population. Television news has not only maintained its popularity since then, it has increased it substantially to over three-quarters of the population more than a decade into the 2000s (Ofcom 2013).

Of course, the rising level of popularity and journalistic advancements in television were made easier as technology became more sophisticated, with improvements in editing equipment and live broadcasting. So, for example, when John F. Kennedy was shot in 1963 the US network bulletins could replay the footage with journalists live on-hand to interpret the reaction. By the end of the 1960s bulletins could broadcast in colour and many extended their length to convey events that could be captured on film or reported live. The BBC's 9pm evening news bulletin began in 1970 and remained until 2000, at which point it moved to 10pm. 1pm and 6pm television news bulletins were introduced in 1986 and 1984 respectively (both have remained since). In other words, in the 1980s fixed time television news bulletins – at lunchtime, early and late evening – became permanent slots in the weekday schedule.

Indeed, throughout the 1980s technological breakthroughs changed how broadcasters operated. There was, according to Nick Pollard (2009: 116) – a former executive producer at ITN in the 1980s – "very little 'liveness'" at the beginning of the decade, due to two factors: the technical equipment and lack of time within a 25-minute bulletin format. While satellite technology was improving, it was at this point costly and had to be limited to specific time slots in mostly urban developed countries (Pollard 2009: 117). This meant, in effect, live broadcasts remained reserved for big events at locations where equipment could be shipped and set up in advance. At the same time, however, the 1980s brought the first rolling news channel, CNN, at first an American domestic channel, but then an international one when CNNI launched in 1985. Initially the channel was perceived as amateurish, reliant on limited resources, raw images and live reporters pontificating at length on camera (Cushion 2010). Compared to the network bulletins – which had now mastered packaging edited film and sound together, along with anchors that followed carefully crafted scripts – 24-hour journalism produced a messy and somewhat frenzied format. But CNN's ability to instantly go live – during a failed presidential assassination or the launch of a space shuttle – gained journalistic traction. Indeed, it was the live reporting of the first Iraq war (1990–91) that put CNN on the global map. As argued elsewhere, this event can be seen as the "coming of age" for 24-hour news channels – the first of three overlapping phases – for it demonstrated the potential of live news to instantly communicate news around the world (Cushion 2010). The second phase of rolling news channels can be characterized as an era when national and international news channels attempted to emulate CNN's influence and generic conventions, as live and breaking news coverage became accepted journalistic wisdom. While a third phase and ongoing of rolling news has more hybridity in its journalism – with more regional and local news channels broadcasting – CNN's generic footprints remain imprinted on the way most 24-hour news channels operate (Cushion and Lewis 2010). But dedicated news channels were not the only format in competition with fixed time bulletins.

By the end of the twentieth century, 24-hour news channels were also operating with rolling online news competitors. As Internet penetration levels increased from the 1990s into the 2000s in many advanced Western democracies, more dedicated online news and blog sites emerged. While this gave rise to many alternative news websites, more than a decade into the twenty-first century the evidence suggests that it is legacy news sites – previously existing mainstream media – that have become the most popular sources and today wield the most online influence (Curran *et al.* 2012). In other words, well-established broadcasters – from the BBC to ABC – have morphed much of their content online, another vehicle for 24/7 rolling news. It has also granted specialist broadcast journalists – political, economic and business editors – the space to blog their views and verdicts on the latest events. This has been enhanced more recently by social media platforms, another place for immediate news and analysis. As Chapter 7 explores, Twitter, in particular, has become the signature tool to communicate not just a breaking news story, but to deliver instant analysis (in less than 140 characters).

Thus, the media environment television news bulletins had grown up in post-1950 changed markedly over the past 20–30 years. For television news bulletins today exist side by side with the pace and immediacy of 24-hour news channels, online news and social media platforms. As a consequence, many broadcasters who supply fixed time bulletins have converged their journalism on different mediums, pooling resources and integrating newsrooms. In doing so, the journalistic culture of news-making has become more fluid, with journalists moving between platforms and different formats. But what is less clear is how far old news formats have been influenced by new media and the emphasis on delivering live breaking news, instant comment and analysis. It is claimed, for example, that newspapers – an even older medium than television news bulletins – have responded to 24-hour news channels by morphing into viewpapers, delivering more opinion and speculation, since they cannot keep up with the pace of both dedicated news channels or online platforms. Put differently, it is suggested that newspapers have adapted their format and style in order to become more comment driven rather than simply reporting the 'facts' about an issue or event (Franklin 1999).

This book similarly explores the impact of rolling broadcast news and online news over the last 20–30 years. But the focus is on examining the changing form, structure and style of evening television bulletins. For, as already acknowledged, fixed time bulletins have historically had a different media logic when compared to instant news offered on dedicated 24-hour news channels, online and social media platforms. Before outlining how these competing media logics will be interpreted within the research design informing this book, it is first necessary to introduce debates about mediatization and how the concept of media logic can help measure whether and how fixed time bulletins have changed over recent decades. While debates about mediatization have explored media influence from a wide range of perspectives, the approach taken in this book proposes new theoretical and empirical lines of inquiry. The concept of mediatization thus needs some introduction and wider contextualization before it is applied.

Entering into mediatization debates: interpreting competing media logics

Mediatization is an interdisciplinary concept used to broadly interpret the influence the expanding media market is having on different aspects of society and culture (Hepp 2013a; Hjarvard 2008, 2013). For Lundby (2009a: 1), it signals "societal changes in contemporary high modern societies and the role of the media and mediated communication in these transformations". Whereas mediation conveys the prism through which the media paint the outside world, mediatization represents a far more radical intervention and transformation, since it is used to assess fundamental changes in a wide range of spheres such as marketing, culture, religion, fashion, art and politics (Lundby 2009b). Hjarvard (2008) argues mediatization is a process that can help chart the extent to which social and cultural activity has not only become influenced by media but dependent on it. In other words, mediatization represents a modification of behaviour brought about by the media in some form. Schulz (2004: 98) uses mediatization as an analytical concept to represent four processes media can change: 1) to extend communication; 2) to substitute social actions and organizations; 3) to amalgamate social activities beyond media; and 4) to accommodate media logic by shaping various actors and institutions in society generally. In short, mediatization debates broadly relate to whether and to what extent the media acts as an agent of change in society, with the 'strength' of mediatization varying across different nations due to a wide range of social, political and economic factors.

When interpreting any shifts in society or culture, debates in mediatization have been hotly contested spanning several academic disciplines, generating competing evaluations about the role and the degree to which the media shape contemporary life. According to Hepp (2013b), mediatization research can be broadly split into two camps: an "institutionalist" and "social constructivist" tradition. The latter tends to focus on media generally – from mobile phones, the Internet, television and newly emerging digital technologies – and to consider how different forms of communication impact on people's social and cultural everyday experiences and perceptions (see also Hepp 2013a). The former tends to understand the media as an autonomous institution, with research exploring how they shape other institutions, such as politics and religion (Hjarvard 2013). In recent years, there has been considerable debate about the virtues and values of each approach that go beyond the scope of this book (Couldry and Hepp 2013).

The approach taken in this book is primarily informed by the "institutionalist" tradition of mediatization research (Hjarvard 2008: 210). This is generally where the disciplines of journalism studies and political communication have entered into mediatization debates in recent years. Couldry and Hepp (2013: 196) have argued this tradition treats "media more or less as an independent social institution with its own set of rules". These rules broadly follow what has been termed "media logic": an underlying logic in the way media act or behave. According to Hjarvard (2013: 17), it has been "used to recognize that the media have particular modus operandi and characteristics ('specificities of media') that come to influence other institutions and culture and society in general, available to them". In making sense of this term, many scholars turn to Altheide and Snow's book, *Media Logic* (1979), which first proposed how specific media formats – including, for example, the news bulletin – draw on familiar production criteria in order to produce content. It has, moreover, become a way of delineating how media formats predominantly behave in terms of their format, style, mode of address and grammar. In Altheide and Snow's own words, "Format becomes a framework or a perspective that is used to present as well as interpret phenomena" (Altheide and Snow 1979: 10).

In more recent years, the concept of media logic has generated considerable debate in mediatization literature. Scholars have questioned the uniformity of a singular media logic, when the concept of mediatization stresses the ever-expanding presence and diversity of the media marketplace (Couldry 2008; Hepp 2013a; Landerer 2013; Lundby 2009b). An all-powerful shared media logic is thus often rejected, since competing mediums offer multiple ways of influencing the process of mediatization. Perhaps Couldry (2008: 378) is most vociferous, arguing it would be difficult to imagine a "single 'media logic', as if they all operated in one direction, at the same speed, through a parallel mechanism and according to the same calculus of probability". However, he concludes the value of media logic becomes more persuasive when applied to a specific format, since it can be theorized and empirically interpreted more coherently. More recently, Couldry (2012: 144) has suggested that the mediatization of politics "is arguably the clearest example of a sector where something like a 'media logic' is at work: in the day-to-day operations of policy generation, policy implementation and public deliberation".

How media logic can be theorized and empirically understood will be returned to, but first a brief context to the mediatization of politics is necessary. For how scholars have previously interpreted the mediatization of political content informs the research design taken in this book. Debates about how far media shape the behaviour and actions of politics can be traced back decades (Blumler and Kavanagh 1999; Mazzoleni 1987; Semetko *et al.* 1991). But it was Mazzoleni and Schulz's (1999) article, "Mediatization of Politics: A challenge for Democracy?" that arguably initiated widespread attention about the concept and how an underlying media logic shaped how politics is reported. Since then a number of important conceptual and empirical studies have emerged, all attempting to clarify the relationship between media and politics (Brants and van Praag 2006; Kepplinger 2002, 2007; Schulz 2004).

However, Strömbäck's 2008 article, "Four Phases of Mediatization: An Analysis of the Mediatization of Politics" has arguably brought most conceptual clarity to ongoing debates. Focusing on Western democracies since World War II, the four overlapping phases reflect the multi-dimensionality of mediatized politics. If the media are the predominate source of political information for citizens – which speaks to most Western democracies today – a first phase is met. How independent the media are from political institutions is the second phase. In this phase, according to Strömbäck (2008: 237), the media "now make their own judgments regarding what is thought to be the appropriate messages from the perspective of their own medium, its format, norms and values, and its audiences". Taking this further, a third phase results in political news being conditioned in order to fit into preconceived journalistic norms and routines. Conversely, if political institutions and actors attempt to adapt to a media logic, to modify their behaviour and actions, finally a fourth phase of mediatization is met.

Phases two to three are the central focus of this book, since they relate to the degree to which news conforms to their own media logic or a political logic. A political logic is seen by Esser (2013a) as prioritizing the actions of politicians and their institutions in three ways: producing policy, publicizing their actions and highlighting how polity influenced the conduct of political affairs. How far political news conforms to this logic, in other words, confirms how far a political logic is subscribed to in news coverage. Esser's (2013a) news media logic, by contrast, comprises three constituents: the norms and routines of professional criteria, the commercial imperatives of news selection and the technological possibilities of conveying news. These are examined in more detail further below, but in respect of reporting politics, they broadly reflect whether news media conform to their own judgements about political affairs or abide by – as just outlined – a political logic. Landerer (2013) has suggested media and political logics do not theoretically or empirically capture the behaviour of media or political actors. As such, they could be more distinctively defined as being normative and market logics when interpreting the mediatization of politics. A normative logic is when media seek to inform and engage citizens about the policies of political actors, thus serving both a public and policy logic. A market logic, by contrast, is preoccupied by maximizing profits/ratings whilst political actors secure an electoral logic of winning votes, thus serving a commercial and electoral logic (Landerer 2013: 248–49).

Overall, then, while the concept of media logic remains important to the mediatization of politics debates, scholars have recently been retheorizing its use and application. As Hepp (2013b: 4) observed, "exponents of the institutionalist tradition are rethinking the concept of media logic". So, for example, Esser's framework when interpreting mediatization of politics (2013a: 159) has recently referred to a *news media* logic, "a singular institution because its constituent organizations are structured similarly to achieve similar goals". His three constituents – professional, technological and commercial – taken together "casually influence the culture of news production in individual media organizations and in media institutions as a whole" (Esser 2013a: 167). While acknowledging media formats have competing forces shaping their production, Esser (2013a: 160) argues that the "rules and norms that govern the media taken as a whole are often more important than what distinguishes one media company, outlet, type, or format from another". In other words, this institutionalist approach compares the logic invested in politics with the logic invested in the media in order to make assessments about how far politics is mediatized.

If the aim is to develop a way of exclusively measuring a political institutional logic over a media institutional logic, working with this framework delivers the necessary comparative conclusions. However, this book is not only interested in exploring how far a *singular* media logic triumphs over a political logic. The aim is to explore how far competing media *logics* have influenced a specific news format over time. As previously argued, fixed time television news bulletins operate according to a different logic in television journalism – such as dedicated 24-hour news channels – but also from the prevailing culture of more instant online and social media platforms. How news generally and political news specifically is delivered in fixed time bulletins could have thus changed over recent decades as more rolling and immediate forms of journalism operate side by side and compete in the wider culture of news. In other words, in order to interpret how a specific media format – the evening news bulletin – has been influenced by broader changes in journalism, applying a catch-all media logic cannot reveal *how* news or political reporting has become mediatized.

Whilst acknowledging, at first glance, the tautology behind the process, the mediatization of news can reveal how competing logics – including Esser's (2013a) professional, technological and commercial characteristics – modify specific journalisms. So, for example, Kammer (2013) has identified a mediatization of online news according to whether news websites have become more in tune with mainstream media by adhering to market pressures, encouraging audience interaction and de-skilling the work of journalists. All of which, he argued, demonstrated how online "journalism is increasingly subordinating itself to the imperatives of the media institution and the media logic it sustains, thereby changing the institution's very professionalism" (Kammer 2013: 141–42). Likewise, Strömbäck and Dimitrova's (2011: 30) study of comparative of US and Swedish election coverage concluded "that the mediatization of news content may be moderated by national journalism cultures, political news cultures and political communication cultures." In particular, they found the US's more commercialized media environment helped shape a greater degree of mediatized election news coverage.

Indeed, internationally comparative research in mediatization of politics has become what Esser terms a neo-institutionalist approach. For cross-national comparisons can, in his words, help "distinguish different path-dependent models of institution-formation, different regulatory cultures of media policy, and different institutional arrangements ruling the media-politics inter-changes" (Esser 2013a: 161). This book will draw on studies that compare evening bulletins in different news cultures, media systems and political institutions in order to make sense of the characteristics that shape the degree to which news generally and political news specifically has become mediatized. So, for example, a driving force behind the mediatization of politics has been a shift towards a more commercialized media landscape over recent decades, a conformity to a market logic (Esser 2013a; Landerer 2013; Strömbäck 2008). Since this book will compare fixed time bulletins in highly market-driven media environments – in particular, the US – with countries where a strong public service broadcasting culture exists – in the UK and Norway, for example – the proposition that enhanced commercialization is a key explanatory variable for greater mediatization of media content can be empirically tested.

Having now introduced how this book will enter into debates about mediatization, it is now necessary to methodologically explain the overall research design shaping it. The next section will therefore interpret how the concept of mediatization will be applied to fixed time television bulletins generally and to political news specifically.

Methodological framework for studying fixed time bulletins and political reporting: interpreting journalistic interventionism

In exploring the second to third phase of Strömbäck's (2008) mediatization of politics – the degree to which political news is modified by journalistic norms and routines, above that of politicians – scholars have empirically devised measures to examine how far media and political actors appear in election coverage. For elections represent a critical moment in any democracy when political parties compete for attention, with the media either reporting what they say (following a political logic) or deviating from their agendas (following a media logic).

The concept of media interventionism is important in this context, since it relates to how far journalists intervene when reporting what is happening in the world (Hanitzsch 2007). Whilst it can be applied to a wide range of contexts, of most relevance to this book is how interventionism has been used in political reporting cross-nationally. This broadly relates to what Semetko et al. (1991: 3) termed the "discretionary power" of journalists in an analysis of US and UK election campaign coverage in the 1980s. More recently, Strömbäck and Esser (2009: 217) refer to media interventionism as "a media-centred political reporting style in which, increasingly, journalists and media actors become the stories' main newsmakers rather than politicians or other social actors" (Strömbäck and Esser 2009: 217). Blumler and Gurevitch (2001: 381–83) outline five macro system factors that can enhance or impede journalistic intervention during elections. Interventionism is reduced if 1) politicians are held in high esteem, or 2) if journalists consider politics intrinsically important. Conversely, interventionism is increased if 3) political parties are highly professionalized, 4) media competition is heightened, responding to the audience rather than politicians' needs and 5) politics is reported by commercial media as opposed to public service broadcasters. In other words, understanding the political culture and media systems of different countries can point towards how interventionist journalists might be during an election campaign.

In light of this conceptually, Strömbäck and Esser (2009: 219) consider media interventionism to act "as an engine of the mediatization of politics". They argue that media interventionism is "crucial for a full understanding of how, and through what venues, the media shape news content according to media logic" (Strömbäck and Esser 2009: 219). Journalism studies and political communication scholars have long developed ways of empirically measuring how far a media and political logic shape campaign coverage (Dimitrova and Strömbäck 2010; Esser 2008; Grabe and Bucy 2009; Hallin 1992a; Hopmann and Strömbäck 2010; Semetko et al. 1991; Strömbäck and Dimitrova 2011; Takens et al. 2013; Zeh and Hopmann 2013). Chapter 2 will unpack these studies and the variables tested in detail, and apply some of them to UK evening television news bulletins between 1991 and 2013. But for now Strömbäck and Dimitrova's (2011) study is worth considering in more detail, since it draws on the concept of media interventionism to compare the degree to which US and Swedish election coverage was mediatized.

Their content analysis builds on previous theorizing and empirical measures used in election studies to systematically quantify the degree to which journalists' or politicians' contributions shape campaign coverage (Strömbäck and Dimitrova 2011). These included the length of political sources, what are known as soundbites; the role of journalists in terms of their on screen visibility, whether they – or a political actor – concluded a campaign story or if they talked over a politician's speech or comment; whether the overall frame of news portrayed substantive issues or a strategic game or horse-race story; and finally the journalistic style of coverage, describing politics or actively interpreting it. All of which, it is argued, are quantitative variables designed to measure the "degree of media interventionism and the extent to which media content is shaped to suit the media's formats, production routines, news values, and needs, suggesting the close linkage among theories of media interventionism, media logic, and mediatization" (Strömbäck and Dimitrova 2011: 36).

While several chapters in the book will test some of these measures and more besides in respect of political coverage in evening bulletins over recent decades, the intention is to also explore *specific variables that capture the characteristics of changing conventions and practices of television news*. For it could be argued that the research design underpinning many mediatization of politics empirical studies appear more preoccupied with how far political actors verbally or visually appear in media coverage, whereas a greater focus could be placed on examining the form, structure and style of specific media formats, such as in fixed time news bulletins. Strömbäck and Dimitrova (2011: 44) agree their election variables quantifying media interventionism "are not by any means the only possible indicators, and through further theorizing more indicators should be identified, integrated, operationalized, and tested". Whilst they developed some measures that considered the editing style or form of television coverage of politics, the research design in this book is specifically geared towards characterizing the nature of routine television news conventions and considering them as journalistic interventions.

The theoretical framework of media interventionism and the empirical measurement of journalistic intervention in previous academic studies have been conceptualized largely by understanding how the media report election campaigns cross-nationally. By contrast, the approach taken in this book is to consider how both theoretically and empirically journalistic interventionism can be understood and operationalized in routine television coverage not just in politics but news generally. After all, politics today operates in a 24-hour news cycle, an age where the "permanent campaign" shapes the motives and behaviour of parties beyond just election time (Blumenthal 1980). Thus, journalistic interventions can be displayed during policy announcements, diplomatic meetings, conference speeches, budget days and so on. Moreover, the concept of journalistic interventionism does not necessarily have to be consigned to political reporting, since journalists could routinely intervene in *all* news from crime, education and health to business, wars and entertainment. Moving beyond election time might also enable a wider range of actors from being examined – beyond the main political parties – such as citizens, think tanks, police officials, business leaders, charities and military forces. In other words, understanding television news and how politics is reported can be interpreted beyond the typical institutional actors that predominate over the course of a campaign (Blumler and Cushion 2014; Cushion 2012a). Indeed, audience studies exploring how people understand politics and public affairs have long suggested knowledge and attitudes tend to be cultivated over many months if not years *in between* elections, rather than just over a campaign period (Philo and Berry 2004; Lewis 2001).

To develop an understanding of how the structure, form and style of fixed time bulletins have changed over recent decades in respect of all news and political news especially, the use of routine conventions will be examined and reinterpreted as journalistic interventions. Television news conventions – from edited packages to live two-ways – will be treated as conscious editorial decisions, judgements made by editors and journalists about how a story could – or should – be reported. All of which, of course, is contingent on the news media logic shaping coverage at the time, such as the bulletin's professional criteria, its technological capabilities and the commercial pressure it faces reporting certain stories or covering them in particular ways (Esser 2013a). As this chapter has shown, having initially been influenced by conventions in radio broadcasting, television news bulletins developed a more distinctive character in the post–World War II years. By the early 1990s many fixed time bulletins had been operating for approximately 40 years. The analysis in this book is thus focused on how television news bulletins may have changed in the years they have been in competition with new dedicated 24-hour news channels, online news and social media platforms.

In order to interpret the changing nature of television evening bulletins, the book draws on a range of different content analysis studies supplemented with qualitative textual analysis of coverage, particularly of political reporting (Cushion and Thomas 2013; Cushion 2014a; Cushion, Aalberg and Thomas 2014; Cushion, Lewis and Roger 2014; Cushion, Roger and Lewis 2014). In these and other studies of television news conducted over recent years (Cushion and Lewis 2009; Cushion *et al.* 2009a, 2009b; Cushion *et al.* 2012; Lewis and Cushion 2009) extensive piloting was carried out to explore the typical conventions used in television news coverage. Eight distinctive categories were identified and organized according to whether it was a convention largely pre-edited or live (see Figure 1.1 for each operational definition). While each convention will be more thoroughly discussed throughout the book, it is important at this stage to explain the conceptual framework used to describe how these conventions were reinterpreted as journalistic interventions. And how, more broadly, they can methodologically characterize the changing nature of television news generally and political news specifically.

The types of journalistic intervention selected over time can help to interpret whether bulletins have maintained a fixed time logic (continuing to rely on pre-edited news conventions) or deviated towards a rolling news logic (relying on more live news). Or, put differently, they can be used to support or challenge the proposition that there has been a mediatization of television news bulletins. As previously acknowledged, in their original formations fixed time

Pre-edited news	
Reporter package	An edited packaged report is produced typically by a reporter on location
Anchor only	Anchor narrating a story with no background visuals (still pictures or moving images)
Anchor image	Anchor narrating a story with a still picture
Anchor package	Anchor narrating a story with moving images or edited graphics
Live news	
Anchor/live reporter two-way	An anchor interacting with a live reporter outside the studio
Reporter live on location	A live reporter outside the studio without any interaction with anchor
Anchor/reporter live studio discussion	Reporter and anchor in same studio discussing a story
Studio discussion	A discussion within studio involving anchor and other guests (sometimes including reporter) .

Figure 1.1 The code frame used to analyse different conventions and the types of journalistic interventions
(Adapted from Cushion and Thomas 2013)

bulletins were "*a regularly scheduled program dedicated to the promotion of the top stories of the day*" (Conway 2009; his emphasis). Rolling news, by contrast, brings "news as it happens". So, for example, Sky News boasts it "covers breaking news whenever – and wherever – it happens", whilst the BBC News Channel claims to bring news "24 hours a day, as it breaks, whenever it breaks".

The different logics can thus be operationalized according to the different journalistic interventions. Pre-edited television news conventions (see Figure 1.1, in the column under 'Pre-edited news') are tightly scripted, subject to close editorial oversight and monitoring. Edited packages, for example, typically rely on a journalist investigating the background to a story over the course of a day, drawing on external sources and taking the time to carefully produce it. As Nick Robinson (2012: 364), the political editor of the BBC, has explained: "Normally a TV report takes at least an hour to edit. If I want it to be really good, or the story is particularly complex, I sometimes allow an hour's editing for every minute on screen, which means a four-minute report takes four hours to cut". Meanwhile, anchors generally follow a script – a teleprompter – with editors thus able to more carefully articulate a news story. They can of course supply a live update to a story, but again this can be somewhat scripted before an anchor delivers the news.

Live journalistic interventions (see Figure 1.1, in the column under 'Live news'), by contrast, cannot be policed as robustly or editorially controlled as pre-edited news. Of course, live reporters may know broadly what they want to say and the questions an anchor might ask them. But journalists are also asked to improvise and respond to fast-moving events 'on air' without always knowing for how long. This was aptly captured in the title of former ITV political editor John Sergeant's (2001) autobiography *Give Me Ten Seconds* – a reference to the time afforded to him by his production assistant before he is expected to wrap up his live report. In other words, live journalistic interventions are more fluid than edited news.

An edited political news package, for example, tends to be less interventionist than a live two-way, since it is likely to be informed by external sources – typically from competing political parties – with the aim of constructing 'balance'. Live two-ways, by comparison, can be theorized as being more interventionist, since they place journalists at the centre of the narrative, typically asked to offer a perspective or update to a story. In summary, this book will examine television news over time by comparing the different types of journalistic interventions, e.g. is news delivered in a largely pre-edited and tightly scripted format (Figure 1.1, under 'Pre-edited news') or is news increasingly reported live and in a more improvised format (Figure 1.1, under 'Live news'). While eight distinct conventions have been operationalized, different chapters sometimes group live and edited conventions together. For example, anchor items are always grouped together, but the specific operational definitions in Figure 1.1 have been kept to indicate that anchor-only news can convey stories slightly differently (adopting roles future research projects could explore further).

By understanding conventions as journalistic interventions the aim of the book is to interpret how far television news has been influenced by a journalistic logic of news-making, rather than relying on external actors to shape coverage. Hence, studies exploring the mediatization of politics have been drawn upon, since they have been designed to specifically compare the degree to which media actors influence coverage compared to political actors. To move debates on, however, the research design in this study focused on how the structure, form and style of television journalism has changed over time. In breaking down every type of television news convention, the aim will be to assess the purpose and value of journalistic interventions routinely employed by bulletins in recent decades, exploring whether their editorial practices resemble the format of dedicated news channels or 24-hour journalism more generally. Or, put differently, the book will interpret how far television bulletins have become mediatized, adopting or resisting values inherent in rolling news culture. This process of mediatization is conceptualized in Figure 1.2, which indicates how

Figure 1.2 Interpreting the mediatization of news generally and politics specifically (Adapted from Cushion and Thomas 2013)

different journalistic interventions will be interpreted in fixed time television bulletins and the degree to which they are mediatized.

Whilst interpreting the conventions of fixed time bulletins over time will be a key part of understanding whether news has changed – and become mediatized – over time, the book will also explore the nature of journalism from a wider range of perspectives. So, for example, it will examine the type of news reported (from health, business and crime to sport to politics). The purpose of live news will be subject to close analysis, considering whether the aim is to bring 'the latest' update/development to a story, to report from a specific location/backdrop or for journalists to deliver analysis/interpretation. The use of sources – or soundbites – over time will also be carefully examined, considering for instance how politicians are represented visually and aurally. In doing so, the relative degree of journalistic interventionism can be measured, examining how far politicians appear in news compared to journalists. This will be explored by studying the visibility of journalists, how they convey the views of political actors and more broadly how they report the political world. All of these different aspects of news coverage will be introduced at greater length at relevant points in each chapter.

The book draws on thousands of news items from 1991 to 2013. The empirical data informing this book has been subject to rigorous intercoder reliability tests to ensure news was accurately and consistently coded. All studies drawn upon had high intercoder reliability scores. The sample of television news explored longitudinally throughout the book will focus on BBC and ITV, early evening bulletins in the UK. However, more contemporary coverage will also include analysis of Channel 5 news in the UK, ABC and NBC in the US (both broadcast at 6.30pm) and NRK's 7pm and TV2's 9pm bulletins in Norway. These three advanced democracies were selected for their comparative broadcast systems. Broadly speaking, the US's market-driven broadcast system is radically different to the more public service broadcast model in the UK and Norway (Cushion 2012a). However, there is some evidence to suggest UK television news has adopted an increasingly downmarket agenda on UK commercial television news (Barnett *et al.* 2012). According to Hallin and Mancini's (2004) comparative study of media systems, the sample selection can be described as containing a strong Corporatist (Norway) and Liberal (US) model, with the UK hovering somewhere in between. The differences between the wholly public service broadcasters (BBC and NRK), commercial public service broadcasters (ITV and TV2) and wholly commercial broadcasters (ABC and NBC) will be explored throughout the book. In the chapters that follow, the differences between broadcasters in each country will be explained in detail along with a broader discussion about comparative media system research (Hallin and Mancini 2004). In addition, a wide range of external empirical studies will inform each chapter in order to help explain and interpret the changing nature of television news bulletins internationally.

The next chapter focuses on the mediatization of news generally. It first contextualizes previous empirical studies, examining the changing form, structure and style of television news bulletins over time. It then draws on a longitudinal study of UK evening bulletins, asking whether edited and live conventions shaping bulletins have changed from 1991 to 2012 and exploring the wider implications of how journalists interpret the daily news agenda.

Note

1 Quote taken from the BBC website: available online at www.bbc.co.uk/mediacentre/latestnews/2013/tv_news_move.html (accessed 2 December 2013).

Chapter 2

Embracing or resisting a rolling news logic?

Understanding the changing character of television news bulletins

Introduction

Over the last 20 to 30 years, fixed time television bulletins have operated in a far more competitive journalistic culture, where news is delivered instantly on dedicated news channels, rolling websites and most recently social media platforms. Fixed time bulletins, in this context, appear somewhat antiquated, a relic of the analogue age before the advent of always on, 24-hour news provision. Rather than having a menu of news served at a set time, most people can now instantly serve themselves whatever diet of news they want on broadcast, online or social media platforms. As an Economist (2011) special edition about the future of online news enthusiastically exclaimed, contemporary news is "a far more participatory and social experience. ... Readers are being woven into the increasingly complex news ecosystem as sources, participants and distributors". But for all the ostensible choice, freedom and immediacy of media in the information age – as the Introduction highlighted – fixed time bulletins continue to be the most popular format of news consumption in most advanced democracies, defying predictions that scheduled news will die off.

And yet, whilst bulletins have remained resilient in the face of new competition, what is less clear is how they have adapted and responded to the new pace set by rolling news platforms. As far back as 1987, one US newspaper predicted "the first phase of an adjustment by the networks to a harsh new reality – a life-or-death struggle for survival in a changing news-delivery environment co-inhabited by newspapers, specialized magazines, radio and TV news bulletins, 24-hour cable and radio news services, satellite transmissions to local stations, and video-cassette recorders" (Unger 1987). More than a decade on, a UK television journalist – Alasdair Reid (1999) – commented that "Many of us grew up with television that dictated an 'appointment to view' approach to news – all of which looked pretty much the same. It is inevitable that the convenience and relevance we demand from all other consumer choices will have to be reflected in news coverage". Although there has been much speculation and excitement about the new media age (see Curran *et al.* 2012), less attention has been paid to how 'old' formats of news have changed such as television bulletins.

This chapter will draw upon a systematic content analysis study exploring UK television evening bulletins between 1991 and 2012 and explore the changing conventions – the different types of journalistic interventions used to convey news – in this period of time (Cushion, Lewis and Roger 2014). As previously acknowledged, over recent decades the media environment has radically changed: in the UK – and Europe – the first dedicated 24-hour news was launched, Sky News, in 1989, followed by the BBC News Channel in 1997 and ITV News Channel in 2000 (although it only lasted until 2005, whereas the other two news channels continue today). At this point 24-hour news channels were also able to be internationally accessed – with the arrival of multi-channel television in the late 1990s – along with a growing presence of online news in the 2000s and, more recently, the arrival of social media platforms such as Facebook and Twitter. In other words, this chapter will be able to empirically trace whether fixed television bulletins have embraced or resisted the values of 24-hour news in routine coverage.

The chapter begins by explaining the comparative focus of the study before reintroducing the analytical framework shaping it, including the different types of journalistic interventions examined. In doing so, it will draw on the concepts of mediatization and journalistic interventionism – already outlined in Chapter 1 – to help explore whether the use of routine conventions and practices have changed in evening bulletins over recent decades. Previous studies exploring the form, structure and style of television journalism will also be engaged with in order to develop a broader discussion about key trends and developments in news into the new millennium.

Interpreting the changing nature of television news bulletins over time

The analysis of UK television news begins by longitudinally tracking coverage of BBC and ITV bulletins between 1991 and 2012. A total of 2,040 journalistic interventions were examined over the sample period. Four different periods of time – in 1991/2, 1999, 2004 and 2012 – were systematically examined over three weeks (excluding weekends). The sample dates were selected to broadly cover the last 20 to 30 years or so and in consecutive weeks at periods of time when Parliament was in session. Needless to say, the aim was to sample moments in time when routine politics was reported. However, the specific dates were partly shaped by availability, since it proved extremely difficult to obtain retrospective television news. So, for example, 1991/2 was sampled because no complete three-week period was accessible in each year. Over this period of time the format and scheduling of bulletins changed. ITV's bulletin in 1991 began at 5.40pm and lasted approximately 15 minutes. However, the length of the bulletin increased in 1999 to approximately 25 minutes and moved to 6.30pm. A decision, incidentally, related to the regulatory conditions of ITV's licence agreements in order to ensure news was delivered at peak time (6–10.30pm). BBC's 6pm bulletin remained the same over the sample period, lasting approximately 25–30 minutes. In 2012 Channel 5's 5pm bulletin of approximately 25 minutes was also included. However, no archive material of Channel 5 could be located. Whilst the duration of each bulletin is different between years and broadcasters, the comparative analysis is primarily based upon *the proportion of time* dedicated to different aspects of coverage.

The selection of three different broadcasters allows some comparative analysis between their relative balance of commercial and public service commitments. While all UK broadcasters are required to be legally impartial, there are significant differences between how the BBC, ITV and Channel 5 editorially operate and are regulated. The BBC can be described as a wholesale public service broadcaster because it is funded entirely under a licence fee (in the UK) and is robustly regulated by a separate body (the BBC Board of Governors until 2007 and currently by the BBC Trust). It is therefore ostensibly free from commercial constraints, although inevitably the pressure to remain relevant and popular – maintaining public support for the universal licence fee – fosters indirect market pressure.

ITV and Channel 5 meanwhile are commercial public service broadcasters regulated by more 'light-touch' regulation (the ITC up until 2002 and currently by Ofcom). Both have a mix of market-driven and public service duties, but the regulatory baggage is arguably different between the two broadcasters. ITV has historically held significant public service broadcasting responsibilities since its launch in the 1950s (even if these have decreased in recent decades) and is considered more influential than Channel 5, attracting, on average, a far greater share of viewers. The licences of both broadcasters – in respect of their provision of news programming – also indicate ITV's public service commitments remain stronger.[1] Channel 5, for instance, only has to deliver national news programming in peak time hours, compared to ITV which is legally required to air both national and regional television news programming. Whilst ITV has attempted to renegotiate the scheduling of news – to accommodate more popular genres such as feature films – the regulator has intervened. In 1999, for example, ITV's 10pm bulletin was allowed to temporarily move to 11pm. After viewing figures dropped rapidly, however, the broadcaster was required to reinstate its original 10pm slot.

ITV's long-standing public service commitments and higher audience ratings thus bring greater regulatory oversight than Channel 5. For the newest commercial public service broadcaster – only launched in 1997 – appears less susceptible to political or regulatory pressures. This was witnessed during Channel 5's takeover by Richard Desmond in 2010. The chairman of the culture, media and sport committee, John Wittingdale, stated that "Richard Desmond [the new owner of Channel 5] has the freedom to produce a station that's economically viable. If he wants to do something slightly different then that's fine, but there are still some [public service] obligations" (cited in Conlan 2010). In respect of Channel 5's news bulletins, scholars and media commentators have identified a more informal reporting style and tabloid news agendas (Barnett *et al.* 2012).

The channel also runs the earliest evening news bulletin at 5pm (compared to BBC's 6pm, ITV's 6.30pm and Channel 4's 7pm slots). Perhaps as a consequence of both its style and timing, Channel 5 viewers represent the highest proportion of DE demographic groups of all news bulletins, e.g. the lowest social economic viewers. Thus, whilst Channel 5 has the lowest overall audience share of early evening news viewers (approximately 700,000 as opposed to 3.4 million on ITV and 4.4 million on the BBC), an Ofcom (2012) review of the channel's licence obligations indicated the broadcaster brings distinctive public service value, attracting audiences who do not typically consume news.

Overall, then, the sample selection of different UK bulletins allows bulletins to be compared according to their relative degree of public service obligations. The BBC, of course, are the most public service driven, Channel 5 the least, since it has more regulatory autonomy in its news format and style, with ITV hovering somewhere in the middle. As previous chapters have explained, the concept of public service broadcasting has been a crucial part of the development of UK television news (Cushion 2014b). But since recent decades have witnessed an increasingly market-driven media sector and more lightly regulated environment, concerns have been raised about deteriorating standards in the agenda and reporting of television news. This chapter will therefore be able to shed empirical light about the changing nature of coverage over recent decades on public and more commercially driven broadcasters. This comparative dimension between public service broadcasting and commercial media is developed in greater depth in Chapter 4, with comparisons between UK and US television news brought into sharper focus. The main US television networks, for example, are entirely market-driven and subject to far less regulatory oversight.

As Chapter 1 explained in detail, the primary focus of the book – and this chapter – is to explore the changing nature of routine conventions shaping television news bulletins. Whereas many scholars and commentators principally focus on news agendas such as asking whether more trivial forms of entertainment have replaced more serious public affairs news (Franklin 1999), the predominant aim of this inquiry is to also understand *how* information is conveyed by television news journalists. The concept of journalistic interventionism was introduced and explained previously as a means of measuring the "discretionary power" of journalists in making sense of everyday news (Semetko *et al.* 1991: 3). In doing so, it was explained how routine conventions would be reinterpreted as journalistic interventions. To recap, journalistic interventions such as deciding the format of a news story – whether, for example, it should be reported live or be pre-edited – will be systematically examined in order to understand the changing character of evening bulletins.

Moreover, underpinning this analytical framework will be the attempt to ascertain whether recent decades have witnessed a change in the logic of fixed time bulletins towards a more 24-hour service of instant news. If it is the latter, it was argued, it could be seen to represent a mediatization of television news bulletins, since the influence of rolling news logic could be seen to be having a systemic impact on fixed time evening bulletins. After all, since the inception of evening bulletins, the format – and underlying logic – has broadly sought to reflect the day's news. In doing so, television journalists typically spent the day gathering news, interviewing sources and editing a package together to be broadcast for evening transmission. Rolling news logic, by comparison, involves reporting news more instantly and spontaneously, with more live reporting as opposed to edited packages, and regular updates and interpretation from journalists about the latest event or issue. To summarize, then, in understanding the changing form, structure and style of television news over recent decades the following chapter will explore whether television news bulletins have resisted or adopted a rolling news logic in their routine conventions.

Understanding the form, structure and style of television news bulletins

To interpret whether the character of television news has changed over recent decades, four types of journalistic interventions were identified to reflect the different types of conventions used to convey a particular story. Or, put differently, conventions were operationalized in order to be able to interpret whether television journalism had maintained or moved towards a rolling or fixed time logic. First, an edited package – typically involving a reporter out on location, interviewing sources and filing a pre-recorded item. Second, an item exclusively presented by an anchor, either presenting straight to camera or narrating over a still picture or moving images. Third, an item based within a live studio format either involving just the anchor and reporter or also a guest. Fourth, a live two-way between anchor and reporter out on location or just a reporter talking to camera. A shift towards the latter two interventions will be interpreted as an editorial adaptation of 24-hour news conventions whereas the former two would reflect a resistance to rolling news logic.

It has widely been claimed that the pace of journalism has quickened over recent decades. Changing technologies and the broader influence of rolling news culture – the 24-hour news cycle – has meant news can be published or aired almost immediately. Writing about the 1980s, for example, Hallin (1994: 117) suggested the "character of the evening news [had] ... changed substantially. Its pace has come to resemble more closely the pace of the rest of commercial television, with 10-second soundbites and tightly packaged stories". Whilst there is longitudinal evidence demonstrating politicians appear less often on television news (Hallin 1992a) – a point explored in Chapter 3 – there is less sustained empirical research systematically tracking the changing structure of television news.

Winston's (2002) comparative analysis of the UK's early and late evening bulletins on BBC and ITV examined the length of stories in 1975 and in 2001.

Table 2.1 Average story lengths in early and late evening UK television news bulletins in 1975 and 2001 (minutes and seconds)

	1975	*2001*
BBC early evening	1m, 15 secs	2m, 13 secs
BBC late evening	1m, 40 secs	2m, 5 secs
ITV early evening	1m	2m, 5 secs
ITV late evening	1m, 35 secs	2m, 13 secs

(Adapted from Winston 2002)

Contrary to popular wisdom, the study found the duration of stories had increased overall, a finding perhaps related to the early evening bulletins having doubled in overall length. In so doing, as Table 2.1 indicates, the average story length of early evening bulletins on both ITV and BBC significantly increased, demonstrating – according to Winston (2002: 12) – "a tendency to deal with fewer items at greater length whatever the overall duration of the bulletin."

Harrison (2000) has also examined the average story length of UK television news bulletins between 1993 and 1996. Again, rather than measuring conventions – the focus of this study – it was the length of individual stories being compared. As Table 2.2 shows, with the exception of ITN News at Ten – which already had the lowest average story length – all bulletins reduced the time spent on individual stories. While the reduction of story length is relatively small, the longitudinal study was only three years long. Nevertheless, Harrison suggested that the drop could be "of some concern if it results in less information being transmitted or indicates a long term trend" (Harrison 2000: 165).

More than a decade later and a longer term decline in the length of television news items can be empirically confirmed. As Table 2.3 shows, the length of BBC conventions reduced by a half (from an average time of 2 minutes and 1 second in 1991/92 to 1 minute and 39 seconds in 1999, 1 minute and 31 seconds in 2004 and just 1 minute and 5 seconds in 2012). ITV, by comparison, shortened

Table 2.2 Average story length of UK television news bulletins between 1993 and 1996 (minutes)

Programme	*1993*	*1996*
ITV's 12.30pm News	2.0	1.6
BBC's One O'Clock News	2.2	2.1
ITN's 5.40pm News	1.5	1.3
BBC1's Six O'Clock News	2.2	2.0
BBC1's Nine O'Clock News	2.1	2.0
ITN's News at Ten	1.4	1.6

(Adapted from Harrison 2000)

Table 2.3 Mean length of journalistic interventions in BBC and ITV early evening television news bulletins 1991–2012 (minutes and seconds)

	1991/2		1999		2004		2012		
	BBC	ITV	BBC	ITV	BBC	ITV	BBC	ITV	Ch.5
Edited									
Reporter package	2m, 15 secs	1m, 42 secs	1 m, 59 secs	2m	2m, 18 secs	2m, 12 secs	2m, 19 secs	1m, 27 secs	2m, 3 secs
Anchor	27 secs	23 secs	22 secs	24 secs	25 secs	28 secs	20 secs	23 secs	24 secs
Live									
Anchor/reporter two-way/live location	1m, 46 secs	1m, 5 secs	1m, 15 secs	1m, 8 secs	55 secs	44 secs	47 secs	1m	35 secs
Anchor discussion	/	/	1m, 4 secs	1m, 35 secs	/	1m, 20 secs	57 secs	52 secs	38 secs
Total N	199	136	223	142	233	205	325	285	292

(Adapted from Cushion, Lewis and Roger 2014)

by a third (from 1 minute and 33 seconds in 1991/2, 1 minute and 40 seconds in 1999, 1 minute and 33 seconds in 2004 and just 59 seconds in 2012). But a closer inspection of the changing form and structure of television news reveals that the relative length of different news items shortened most strikingly in live as opposed to edited journalistic interventions (see Table 2.3).

In particular, the average length of two-ways have declined, notably on the BBC from 1 minute 46 second to just 46 seconds. On Channel 5 – the most commercially driven of the three bulletins – the average length was little more than 30 seconds. This raises questions about how far reporters can meaningfully convey or analyse a story within such a limited time frame. Moreover, the length of a reporter's contribution appears almost like a soundbite – a theme explored below and in subsequent chapters.

More generally, to what extent has television news shifted from edited to live reporting in television bulletins over successive decades? Winston's comparative analysis of evening bulletins in just a week during 1975 and 2001 gives a useful snapshot. After excluding edited packages (explaining why data does not add up to 100 per cent), Table 2.4 shows that the role of anchors – or newscasters as he labels them – has fallen on all bulletins. But the major finding is the enhanced role of the "standupper" (Winston 2002: 15) – another term for what has been defined as a live two-way in this book – which did not really exist and was hard to compare over time. Making his observations in 2001, according to Winston (2002: 15) the standupper represents "American-style payoffs, where the newsperson gives his or her name and location, are now the norm. In 1975 such payoffs were rare … A major contemporary technique, unknown in 1975, is for the newscaster in the studio to encourage correspondents on location in live interviews to update packages".

More than a decade on – examining coverage over three weeks from 2001 to 2012 – a more gradual decade-by-decade shift towards the use of live two-ways

Table 2.4 Percentage use of news conventions (excluding edited packages) in early and late evening UK bulletins in 1975 and 2001 (by time)

	Newscaster (Anchor)	Correspondent in studio	Standupper (live two-way)	Total % (excluding edited packages)
BBC early evening 1975	26	8.3	N/A	34.3
BBC late evening 2001	11.7	2.5	6.9	21.1
ITV early evening 1975	24.5	13.4	N/A	37.9
ITV late evening 2001	14.8	0	6.30	21.1

(Adapted from Winston 2002)

Table 2.5 Percentage use of journalistic interventions in BBC, ITV and Channel 5 early evening television news bulletins between 1991–2012 (by time)

	1991/2		1999		2004		2012		
	BBC	ITV	BBC	ITV	BBC	ITV	BBC	ITV	Ch.5
Edited									
Reporter package	95	89.4	89.1	89.9	79.4	73.7	67.9	63.3	63.7
Anchor	2.8	1.4	3.5	4.1	6.8	0.6	18.6	19.9	21.2
Live									
Anchor/reporter two-way/live location	2.2	9.3	7.1	5.4	13.8	17.6	10.8	14.1	14.9
Anchor discussion	/	/	0.3	0.6	/	8	2.7	2.8	0.2
Total N	199	136	223	142	233	205	325	285	292

(Adapted from Cushion, Lewis and Roger 2014)

can be evidenced (see Table 2.5). The role of anchors has also been enhanced substantially.

Most striking was the greater role of anchors on ITV news – an increase from just 1.4 per cent of airtime in 1991/2 to 19.9 per cent in 2012 – meaning their on screen presence rose by 14 times. Similarly, BBC anchors rose dramatically from 2.8 per cent in 1991/2 to 18.6 per cent in 2012. Meanwhile, Channel 5 left marginally more broadcast time for anchors in 2012 than the BBC or ITV (21.2 per cent). Today's news bulletins thus feature anchors for about a fifth of airtime on a typical television news bulletin. However, despite anchors being on screen for far longer, the average length of news items has remained remarkably consistent (20–23 seconds). In other words, it would appear news anchors today narrate many news items within a bulletin at a rapid pace, which again raises questions about how informative journalists can be within such a limited time span.

But the enhanced role of anchors might not just represent a faster pace of news delivery by conveying more (shorter) items within a bulletin. For the television anchor has arguably become a significant actor in UK television news bulletins and taken on a more active role similar to US evening newscasts. As Chapter 1 explored, it took some time for television news to adapt its journalism to a visual medium and include on screen presenters either conveying stories or introducing packages (Conway 2009). In the US this trend began first, with strong journalistic personalities emerging and becoming household names – Walter Cronkite, for instance, or Dan Rather – making anchors an intrinsic part of evening bulletins. In the UK, by contrast, the reluctance to informalize television news bulletins and risk undermining the impartiality of broadcasting by having a personality shape it appears to have been relaxed (cf. Montgomery 2007). Moreover, many anchors – Natasha Kaplinsky (BBC, Channel 5 and ITV), Dermot Murnaghan (BBC, ITV and Sky News), Sian Williams (BBC), Sophie Rayworth (BBC), for example – appear on television beyond their role in bulletins (whether presenting documentaries, quiz shows or participating in reality TV programmes). Writing from an Australian perspective, Bainbridge and Bestwick (2010: 205) have observed a similar trend and suggested anchors have morphed into "marketed newsreaders", celebrity-like figures that encapsulate not just the bulletin but the channel promoting them.

In considering the changing nature of other journalistic interventions over recent decades, the role of anchors interweaving different types of conventions throughout a bulletin is also changing. So, for example, whereas in the early 1990s anchors were primarily introducing reporter packages (which will be addressed next), today they engage in live two-ways and discuss issues with guests or fellow journalists *within* the studio. Interestingly, Montgomery's (2007) impressively detailed textual analysis of television news suggested a relatively clear distinction in the presentation of bulletins and 24-hour news formats. He observed that

> the role of the presenter/anchor on the dedicated news channels depends more upon unfolding the events through interview with correspondents, commentators or 'newsmakers'. Their role is less scripted [than half-hourly news formats], more improvised, and more of a question of blending together, in the real time flow of broadcasting, the voices that are drawn upon to make up the news (Montgomery 2007: 60–61).

However, it would appear that television news anchors have, over the last twenty years, increasingly begun to resemble the practices of their counterparts on rolling news channels embedding different types of conventions into a live, dynamic and improvised format – a point returned to at the end of the chapter.

Before exploring the shift towards live journalistic interventions, it is necessary to reflect on the decline – of about a quarter of total coverage – in airtime allocated to edited reported packages. For viewers of television news over several decades, reporter packages represent the most familiar way bulletins communicate what is happening in the world. While approximately two-thirds of UK bulletins' airtime today remains accounted for by reporter packages – although slightly higher for the main public service broadcaster, the BBC – the reduction in the use of this convention has arguably changed the character and purpose of television news bulletins into the 2000s. Edited packages are, after all, the longest standing convention of television news, typically featuring a journalist out on location, investigating a story, interviewing sources, writing a carefully prepared script and editing it for evening news consumption (Robinson 2012). Of course, improvements in editing equipment – allowing reporters to self-edit material more easily away from the studio – means edited news can be packaged together much closer to when a programme airs. But reporter packages represent a different type of journalistic intervention compared to live reporting, which is a convention that allows a journalist to project more of their own voice into a news story (see Chapter 5).

Reporter packages, by comparison, typically draw on external sources to inform a news story and are ordinarily subject to greater scrutiny by an editorial team prior to being broadcast. As a consequence, a script shaping a reporter package – as opposed to a live two-way – is more diligently informed by editorial production values, such as balance and accuracy. In other words, reporter packages undergo a more rigorous editorial process than live reporting and conform to a set of familiar codes that structure its presentation and style. As many practical television news textbooks explain (Ray 2003), reporter packages typically involve standard editing conventions from establishing shots, interviews, pieces to camera, cut aways, vox pops, use of graphics and other stylistic devices. Indeed, these have become so entrenched in the discourse of television news they have attracted attention in parody sketch shows. Charlie Brooker's BBC programme, *Screenwipe*, for example, offered a cynical appreciation of a TV news reporter package:

> Before long a standard news report established itself, one that is immediately recognizable to anyone. Me, has this report [adopting sarcastic tone]: it starts here with a lackluster establishing shot of a significant location. Next a walky-talky preamble from the auteur pacing steadily towards the lens, punctuating every other sentence with a hand gesture and ignoring all the other pricks milling around him like he's gliding through the fucking Matrix before coming to a halt and posing a question 'what comes next?' Often something like this – a filler shot, something designed to give your eyes something to look at while my voice babbles on about facts. Sometimes it will slow down to a halt, turn monochrome and some of these facts will appear on the screen one by one.

But while reporter packages have become a familiar feature of television news – inviting the kind of parody Brooker supplied – close textual qualitative studies of bulletins over recent decades have observed a change in how news is communicated. So, for example, Ekström (2000: 487) has suggested television news has moved from delivering less information towards conveying more "attractions" and "storytelling" within packaged reports. He writes:

> The communication strategies associated with storytelling and attractions both differ from those associated with the journalism of information in that they put greater emphasis on form than on content. The formats and techniques used to achieve excitement, drama and spectacular and fascinating content are applied to fiction as well as non-fiction.
>
> (Ekström 2000: 487)

Likewise, scholars – notably in the US – have suggested some of the generic conventions of television news storytelling have become intertwined with entertainment programming (Caldwell 1995; Glyn 2000; Hallin 1994). As Caldwell (1995) sets out in *Televisuality: Style, Crisis and Authority in American Television*, the style of news in the 1980s into the 1990s drew increasingly on the visual and stylistic production values of fictional populist genres. In other words, it has been observed that the changing form of a reporter package has had an impact on its informative value over recent decades. How far audiences have, in fact, become less informed due to the changing presentational styles of reporter packages remains an open question. Chapter 6 considers the evidence of viewers' expectations, understanding and interpretation of changing television news formats.

It is thus difficult to reach a clear quantitative conclusion about the changing *presentational characteristics* of either BBC or ITV television news. Over the two decades of analysis, both bulletins witnessed a number of revamps, such as rescheduling the time of broadcast, redesigning the studio set and graphics illustrating news or appointing new editors or anchors to the programme. Perhaps the most striking presentational format change in recent years was the emergence of Channel 5's news in 1997. For several decades television news anchors presented behind a desk, but Channel 5 asked its presenter, Kirsty Young, to roam around a studio. Despite attracting considerable controversy at the time, competing broadcasters soon followed suit and today anchors move freely around the studio to present news items, most often in front of a video wall explaining a story. Indeed, the greater role of anchors in routine television news bulletins has already been evidenced (see Table 2.4).

But while there have undoubtedly been changes to the semiotic make-up of television news – subtle shifts from the codes identified by Hartley (1982) several decades ago – it is arguably the underlying structural changes to journalistic conventions that have changed *how* news is conveyed. Put differently, despite all the stylistic and presentational changes to the format of reporter packages, the steady decline of them as a routine convention prompts bigger existential questions about how the medium informs and contextualizes news stories in the future. For reporter packages still offer the longest mode of communication (compared to live or anchor-only presented items). In doing so, the ability for journalists to edit together a substantive package and draw on a range of actors to inform a news story has gradually been reduced and replaced by shorter items delivered by anchors or live reporters. While subsequent chapters compare and contrast different types of journalistic interventions more closely, for now attention is paid to the rise of live reporting. For the delivery of live and instant news has been a broader development in online or rolling news journalism over the last two decades, but it would appear to be a routine part of today's fixed time television news bulletins.

The rise of live news and immediacy in political reporting

It has been widely observed that contemporary broadcast journalism is increasingly shaped by live news reporting. As Chapter 1 explored, over the course of the twentieth into the twenty-first century more mobile and sophisticated satellite equipment enabled broadcasters to report live from journalists first-hand locally and internationally. In practice, of course, broadcasting live in routine or remote locations – outside the White House, say, or in war-torn countries – continues to bring journalistic challenges and drain financial resources. But the opportunity to go live has increased over recent decades, broadly since CNN broadcast the first live images of the Gulf War in 1990, triggering the arrival of many other dedicated news channels (Cushion 2010). A decade or so on and the arrival of the Internet meant journalists increasingly work in real-time, breaking stories online, and more recently tweeting the latest news or reactions. As a consequence, scholarship about the journalistic culture of "going live" (Seib 2001) has grown exponentially, inviting critical reflection about the purpose and value of reporting news instantly.

Whilst the relative merits of live reporting in routine broadcasting have generally been debated – in textbooks or in more scholarly inquiries, by journalists or media commentators – there is little quantitative evidence exploring how far it informs everyday news agendas (see Winston 2002). Historically, research into live television is centred on what Dayan and Katz (1994) labelled "media events" – significant moments in time such as the first landing on the moon or a royal wedding. However, more recently it has been suggested these ceremonial types of events are less visible in live broadcasting due to greater coverage of disruptive events related to terrorist attacks, wars or disasters on more flexible television schedules. Thus, scholars have placed greater emphasis on making sense of these dramatic broadcast news events. So, for example, Raymond (2000) carried out a detailed discourse analysis of live broadcasters' interpretation of the 1992 civil disturbances in Los Angeles. Or, in the aftermath of recent terrorist attacks, many scholars have unpacked in detail how breaking news coverage was first framed and made sense of by journalists (Nacos 2003; Reynolds and Barnett 2003; Zelizer and Allan 2002). But beyond atypical moments – of disasters, acts of civil unrest or during wartime – little systematic or longitudinal research has been conducted to empirically trace how far over recent decades live news shapes the way news is routinely conveyed.

Of the few studies exploring the degree to which live reporting shapes contemporary journalism, it is dedicated 24-hour news channels that have been brought into sharpest focus. Lewis and Cushion (2009), for example, identified that both the BBC News Channel and Sky News had substantially increased the amount of time spent on breaking news coverage between 2004 and 2007. They used the moniker 'breaking news' to interpret how far coverage was shaped by the latest news item or development. However, breaking news coverage was not always 'live' or spontaneous, since many items were pre-planned and highly predictable. Live breaking news could include stories straight from the wires without a journalist on location to report or bear witness to ongoing events. Moreover, there was little agreement about what was tagged as 'breaking news' between channels, implying live instant news was used more to punctate rolling news agendas, rather than to break any meaningful journalistic scoops. Similarly, Livingston and Cooper (2001) found live reporting conventions had become increasingly part of CNNI's routine coverage during the 1990s. They identified that live news was not necessarily being used to report spontaneous news stories. Utilizing new technologies, instead live news was being used to enhance event-driven news of international news stories, such as the ongoing conflict in Kosovo. In other words, the selection of live news on rolling news channels did not appear to challenge long ingrained norms and routines of reporting, since CNN continued to rely to a large extent on elite sources to shape news selection.

Tuggle and Huffman's (2001) content analysis of 24 local television news stations in 1998/9 offers greater insight into the degree to which conventional bulletins – or newscasts – are driven by live reporting. After all, rolling news channels have 24 hours of news to fill compared to conventional bulletins lasting 20–30 minutes. They established that the volume of live items exceeded that of reporter packages in every station examined. However, they further suggested that in over half of all live items the journalistic rationale for going live was not justified. Particular criticism was reserved for the 'donut' convention – where a reporter briefly introduces a package on location without adding much value to it. In summing up, their final conclusion was damning:

> Broadcasting live from a scene where little or nothing is happening may distract from rather than add news value to the story. Many practitioners and media critics decry the use of "black hole" live shots and these data show that live reports of this type are far more common in many markets than taped reporter packages.
>
> (Tuggle and Huffman 2001: 343)

"Black hole", in this context, refers to journalists at the scene of a story but reporting live without anything happening in the background. The motivation for live news, in other words, appears a more commercial pursuit – to inject visual excitement into a story – rather than something anchored by journalistic purpose. More recently, Casella (2013) has tested this proposition by interviewing news directors and senior reporters in US television news stations about the purpose and value of live reporting. Four justifications for reporting live news were established. First, for breaking news. Second, editorial necessity, since journalists needed to be on the scene to gather and investigate information about a story. Third, news presentation, with reporters able to mix with locals and convey more accurately what is happening on the ground. Fourth, publicizing the identity of the station, with live news able to showcase the brand of the news corporation. However, senior reporters in the sample rejected the third and fourth expectations due to it being difficult – to quote Casella (2013: 374) – "to promote a sense of immediacy in an event that ended long before news time, and that news managers do not always take advantage of adding context or reporter credibility to live shots". A point of agreement, however, was the growing influence of and reliance on technology to help facilitate live reporting.

The study drawn upon in this chapter builds upon previous academic literature examining live broadcasting and, moreover, empirically confirms that live news has gradually increased on UK television news bulletins between 1991 and 2012. As Table 2.4 showed, the overall proportion of live news increased on both BBC and ITV evening bulletins over successive decades. In particular, live two-ways became an increasingly used convention. Montgomery's (2007: 119) analysis of broadcast news describes the two-way as a "short exchange live from the studio with a correspondent at the scene". On the BBC a sixfold increase in live news was evident, from 2.2 per cent to 13.8 per cent between 1991 and 2004. ITV, meanwhile, doubled the amount of live news – from 9.3 per cent to 17.6 per cent – which, in 1991/2, was five times greater than the BBC. While the proportion of time spent on live two-ways fell marginally in 2012 on BBC and ITV, the commercial broadcasters – ITV and Channel 5 – relied to a greater extent on the two-way convention than the main public service broadcaster, occupying just under 15 per cent of airtime compared to 10.8 per cent on BBC news.

Before taking a closer look at live two-way news (as Chapter 5 does in detail), Table 2.4 also showed a new live convention – the studio discussion – became a more significant feature of television news bulletins into the 2000s. Whereas live two-way reporters appear out on location, the exchange between anchor and reporter is within the confines of the studio. Patrona (2012: 158) has described this convention as "a new form of broadcast news interaction, where prominent journalists engage in live conversation on a designated news story". Indeed, senior journalists with specialist knowledge appeared – including science, medical, media, international, home affairs and economics editors – on both BBC and ITV in order to discuss relevant stories with the anchor face to face. The mode of address was – as Patrona has observed – largely conversational, a dialogic form of communication scholars have observed is increasingly apparent more generally in broadcasting over recent years (Montgomery 2007). So, for example, an anchor may sometimes refer to the journalist in the studio on a first-name basis (e.g. "our Hugh has the latest").

But while the proportion of airtime devoted to studio discussions has increased post millennium, the average length of them has declined over time (see Table 2.3). By 2012 the mean length of studio discussions was under a minute long, with Channel 5's averaging just 38 seconds. How far journalists can thus meaningfully add to the discussion within such a limited timeframe is highly debatable – a point brought into sharper focus in Chapter 5. While the studio discussion convention only represented a small proportion of all airtime in the 2000s (with the exception of Channel 5, which relied exclusively on live two-ways), it reinforced a post-millennium swing towards greater live news in evening news bulletins.

The focus and discussion in this chapter so far has been on exploring the general shift from edited to live news in UK television news bulletins over recent decades. But beyond the shifting form and style of television news, the relationship between changing conventions and the news agenda has not yet been established. Put differently, does a greater supply of live news privilege particular types of stories – in crime, politics, say, or business – compared to edited news? So, for example, Lewis and Cushion's (2009) analysis of breaking news stories on 24-hour news channels discovered that – contrary to popular wisdom – most of it was made up of soft news compared to the news agenda more generally. Crime, for example, was the most reported breaking news story, allowing live reporters to supply regular updates on proceedings outside a courthouse. Likewise, Tuggle and Huffman's (2001) study of local news bulletins found more than half of live news was made up of entertainment (21.7 per cent), sports (18.3 per cent) and human interest (16.7 per cent). In accounting for this, they argued: "It is not surprising that feature news (entertainment) was the most frequent topic in live reports, because events such as the state fair, the peanut festival, and preparations for a concert are taking place in the late afternoon during news time" (Tuggle and Huffman 2001: 342). This perhaps reflects a highly localized news agenda, with live reporters representing the community.

A UK national television news bulletin, by contrast, has a far wider agenda to fulfil, including addressing international news stories. Prior to the new millennium both broadcasters – notably the BBC – featured relatively few live news conventions (as Table 2.4 indicated). In 1991/2, for example, the BBC conveyed just a handful of live items (on stories about the media, defence, war and foreign affairs and the monarchy). Whilst twice as much time was spent on live news on ITV, a range of largely hard news topics was reported, such as stories about politics, European affairs, religion, science, international summits, terrorism, health and business, the monarchy and sports.

Table 2.6 Percentage use of journalistic interventions in political news items in BBC, ITV and Channel 5 early evening television news bulletins 1991–2012 (by time)

Politics news	BBC				ITV				Ch. 5
	1991/2	1999	2004	2012	1991/2	1999	2004	2012	2012
Edited news									
Reporter package	100	83.6	66.1	65.5	81.5	86.1	68.8	51.4	53.9
Combined anchor	/	2.9	5.2	15.4	/	2.1	/	19	15.4
Total edited news	100	/	/	80.9	81.5	/	68.8	70.4	69.3
Live news									
Anchor/two-way/reporter live	/	13.5	28.7	16.3	18.5	11.9	27	24	30.7
Anchor discussion	/	/	/	2.8	/	/	4.2	5.6	/
Total live news	/	13.5	28.7	19.1	18.5	11.9	31.2	29.6	30.7
Total N	19	30	19	88	8	17	28	53	57

(Adapted from Cushion, Lewis and Roger 2014)

In other words, unlike local news the national bulletins appeared to report live political affairs.

On both channels, live political reporting increased substantially into the new millennium. In 2004 more than a quarter of political news on the BBC's bulletin was reported live compared to close to a third on ITV. While the BBC's live coverage of politics marginally declined to a fifth of all political news in 2012, ITV's coverage was largely unchanged at approximately 30 per cent. Channel 5, meanwhile, conveyed the most live news reporting related to politics – driven entirely by live two-way reporting (compared to the live studio discussions on BBC and ITV especially). Indeed, live two-ways have become an increasingly central part of political reporting – and news generally – over recent decades on all channels. Since live reporting is arguably the most interventionist approach to reporting, Chapter 5 is dedicated to exploring this convention and examining how it is used in political coverage. For edited political news packages on the BBC and ITV have gradually been sidelined as more news is delivered by live reporters.

Moreover, it would appear political news is, above all, the topic most likely to be covered live when it is compared to other possible genres. Of course, this needs to be understood and interpreted in the context of how much political news is covered generally between the broadcasters. Take 2012, for example, politics represented close to a quarter of all news on the BBC – 23.2 per cent of airtime – whereas for ITV and Channel 5 it occupied approximately half of this proportion (13.1 per cent and 12.5 per cent respectively). Crime was covered the most on Channel 5 (19.4 percent), and to a similar degree on ITV and BBC bulletins (14.9 percent and 15.3 percent respectively). The third most reported topic was news about business (5.9 per cent on BBC, 7.8 per cent on ITV and 4.1 per cent on Chanel 5). When each topic was broken down by the convention used to cover it, Table 2.7 reveals that political news was reported live to a greater extent than crime or business coverage.

Indeed, edited packages made up just over half of all political news on the commercial broadcasters – 10 per cent less than how news is typically reported (see Table 2.3). The BBC, by contrast, supplied close to two-thirds of political

Table 2.7 Percentage use of journalistic interventions by the top three topics in BBC, ITV and Channel 5 television news bulletins in 2012 (by time)

Politics	BBC	ITV	Channel 5
Edited news			
Reporter package	65.5	51.4	53.9
Combined anchor only, image and package	15.4	19.0	15.4
Total edited news	80.9	70.4	69.3
Live news			
Anchor two-way	16.3	24.0	30.7
Reporter live	0	2.8	0
Anchor-reporter discussion/studio discussion	2.8	2.8	0
Total live news	19.1	29.6	30.7
N=	88	53	57

Crime	BBC	ITV	Channel 5
Edited news			
Reporter package	60.7	65.3	56.2
Combined anchor only, image and package	30.1	22.8	22.6
Total edited news	90.8	88.1	78.8
Live news			
Anchor two-way	7.6	6.0	21.2
Reporter live	1.6	0.9	0
Anchor-reporter discussion/studio discussion	0	5.0	0
Total live news	9.2	11.9	21.2
N=	56	43	62

Business	BBC	ITV	Channel 5
Edited news			
Reporter package	57.1	55.3	60.3
Combined anchor only, image and package	15.5	21.9	19.7
Total edited news	72.6	77.2	80.0
Live news			
Anchor two-way	12.8	13.1	14.3
Reporter live	1.8	0	0
Anchor-reporter discussion/studio discussion	12.8	9.7	5.7
Total live news	27.4	22.8	20.0
N=	20	23	12

(Adapted from Cushion and Thomas 2013)

coverage by edited packages. However, live news still occupied almost a fifth of all political news on the public service broadcaster, compared to roughly 30 per cent on Channel 5 and ITV. Live news was largely composed of two-ways and was used as a convention to a greater extent comparatively than in business or crime reporting. On Channel 5 live political reporting was only covered using the two-way convention. The degree of journalistic interventionism in routine coverage of news, in other words, was enhanced when UK national bulletins reported politics. The next chapter explores the changing nature of political reporting in more detail, longitudinally tracing political news with non-political news between 1991 and 2013.

Overall, this chapter has shown so far that as live coverage has increased over recent decades on UK national television bulletins the form and structure of news has changed. For television news spends more time conveying live two-way exchanges between anchor and reporter. However, these exchanges have gradually shortened over time, prompting questions about the journalistic purpose of live news and how news is increasingly delivered in today's media environment. Moreover, since the analytical framework for this book is concerned with exploring whether television bulletins have become increasingly interventionist and mediatized over recent decades, it is necessary to analyse how journalists convey routine coverage. Four categories were thus developed to convey the *primary* purpose of live reporting (outlined in Figure 2.1). First, to introduce or summarize an edited package (similar to a donut as Tuggle

Live reporting related to edited package
1. General introduction/summary to an item – when a live reporter either introduces or summarizes an edited package, offering little additional information relating to updating viewers about the latest news, offering analysis about a story or relying to a great extent on the location/backdrop.

Live or location reporting
2. Latest news – if a reporter adds new information not supplied by the news anchor or in an edited package
3. On location – if the location/backdrop of the reporter is used to help inform the news story
4. Interpretation – if a reporter provides interpretive analysis or delivers judgements about a story

Figure 2.1 The primary value of live reporting in television news bulletins (Adapted from Cushion and Thomas 2013)

Table 2.8 Percentage of the primary purpose of journalistic interventions in live reporting in BBC, ITV and Channel 5 television news bulletins 1991–2012 (by frequency)

	BBC				ITV				Ch. 5
	1991/2	1999	2004	2012	1991/2	1999	2004	2012	2012
Latest news	40	10.5	11.3	13.8	27.8	38.5	23.7	20.4	23.5
Interpretive	60	52.6	45.3	55.2	72.2	61.5	15.8	57.1	39.7
On location	/	5.3	5.7	10.3	/	/	/	2	/
General intro/summary	/	31.6	37.7	20.7	/	/	59.2	20.4	36.8
N	5	19	53	58	18	13	76	49	68

(Adapted from Cushion, Lewis and Roger 2014)

and Huffman 2001 identified). Second, to supply the latest news. Third, to report from a location. Fourth, to interpret an issue or event. As Chapter 1 conceptualized (in Figure 1.2), greater interventionism can relate to an enhanced level of mediatization of news, with media actors increasingly interpreting rather than describing events or relying on external sources to shape coverage. Correspondingly, then, updating a story or offering interpretation live generates a greater degree of interventionism, since instant judgements are delivered during a bulletin as opposed to simply introducing/summarizing an edited package. The analysis is based on the central purpose of live news, such as being at the scene of flood damage (where the background scenery is pivotal) or providing a judgement about political events outside 10 Downing Street (where interpretation supersedes the location).

The findings were clear-cut. As Table 2.8 indicates, interpretation was the central purpose for going live during television news bulletins, with the exception of ITV in 2004 (which ran many shorter items introducing edited packages in this year, typically lasting 10–15 seconds each).

While what is known within the industry as the donut technique – a reporter introducing a package and wrapping it up – continued to be used in 2012, the primary rationale for live news was interpreting the significance of a news story. As previously acknowledged, post-millennium bulletins relied increasingly on two-ways to convey news, where anchors openly encourage reporters to interpret everyday events. On 19 February 2004, for example, in a story about the anniversary of the Iraq War the anchor began the two-way with John Simpson – the BBC's long-standing world affairs editor – by simply saying: "So, John, what's your judgement?" Although an edited package preceded John Simpson's response, the live two-way was used to supplement the story. In other words, the live two-way convention creates the space for journalists to analyse and update viewers about the latest event or issue. Since the amount of time spent on live news in 1991/2 and 1999 was relatively low, the analysis prior to the millennium was based on relatively few items (which did reveal, incidentally, that most live news was also interpretive). The finding that all live news has become interpretive thus needs to be viewed cautiously.

However, post-2000 – when more live news was evident – clear trends can be identified. When compared to other topics – health, crime, business, for instance – political news stands out as being the most interpretive. So, for example, all live BBC political news in 2004 was interpretive, as was over three-quarters of coverage in 2012. Whilst ITV's proportion of political news was less interpretive in 2004 (29.4 per cent) and 2012 (58.8 per cent), in both years it remained the most interpretive live topic covered. Likewise, close to two-thirds of Channel 5's political coverage was interpretive in 2012 (64 per cent). As a proportion of airtime, interpretive reporting was also the longest in length – occupying, for example, 88.9 per cent of live BBC political news in 2012, 83.3 per cent on ITV and 75 per cent on Channel 5. Overall, political news has become more interpretive over time. But as live news was relatively scarce in the 1990s, it could be that political news has become more interpretive simply because it is conveyed more often in a live format. In other words, the medium not the message could be the driving editorial force because – as this chapter has shown – live two-ways encourage reporters to be interpretive.

Interpreting mediatization and the logic of rolling news

The aim of this chapter was to explore whether the character of television news bulletins had changed over time to increasingly resemble rolling or instant news formats. It drew on the concept of mediatization to systematically ask if the values of the 24-hour news cycle had influenced routine reporting on fixed time bulletins. In doing so, news conventions were reinterpreted as journalistic interventions. After all, they can help convey the degree to which a journalist shapes a story (Semetko *et al.* 1991), such as relying on a reporter to deliver a live interpretive two-way as opposed to a less interventionist edited package, which typically draws on a number of external sources. A number of striking longitudinal trends were identified. First, television news bulletins had become shorter over time, notably due to two factors. Anchors became a more prominent feature in 2012, delivering brief 20–30 second packages. And live news steadily increased, although the average length of story items declined. The convention sacrificed was edited reporter packages, which typically lasted much longer (in most years over two minutes). In almost every year, political news was the most reported live topic and over time – notably from 1999 to 2012 – it became more interpretive. As a consequence the voices of politicians were downsized (although still appearing in edited reporter packages), with live two-ways reliant to a large degree on the interpretation of journalists. Despite many of these mediatized trends being associated with commercial forces, the comparative study found both ITV and BBC evening bulletins followed a similar editorial pattern over recent decades.

Overall, the chapter demonstrated the underlying media logic of fixed time television news bulletins had shifted into the new millennium. Of course, an evening bulletin has traditionally been associated with delivering 'the day's news' – gathering, editing and presenting the main stories over the course of a day. As a former head of BBC television news put it, "the Six O'Clock News on BBC one … provides a comprehensive digest of the day's news in an accessible and friendly manner."[2] However, over recent decades arguably the conventions used to convey the main stories on evening bulletins have more closely resembled the editorial priorities of 24-hour news channels, bringing 'news as it happens'. So, for example, the chapter established live news had increased on both BBC and ITV bulletins, with correspondingly less time granted to reporter packages drawing on a range of sources to inform the story. Instead, journalists appeared to act as the key sources, increasingly used in live two-way formats or in studio discussions to interpret and pass judgement about the latest news issue or event.

In making sense of the different conventions and roles adopted by journalists in evening bulletins, the chapter identified a mediatization of television news. For the values familiar to the world of rolling news channels or online instant formats appear to have rubbed off on routine television news conventions. However, this interpretation of competing media logics shaping fixed time bulletins challenges the dominant analytical framework in debates about the mediatization of politics. As Chapter 1 explained, it has been argued only a singular, overarching media logic is necessary to make sense of the relationship between media and political actors. The framework used in this and subsequent chapters interpreted the comparative degree of mediatization in different UK evening bulletins by developing specific content measures related to edited and live news television conventions aimed at distinguishing between competing media logics.

However, the reasons for the greater media logic identified in evening television news bulletins in this chapter both conform to and depart from conventional academic wisdom about the underlying causes of mediatization. So, for example, Esser's (2013a) interpretation of news media logic in political reporting is based on three factors. First, professionalization, which relates to the increasing independence and autonomy of journalists. Second, technological advancements, which shapes how news is produced and presented. Third, commercialization, where the profit and market imperatives override public service interests. While the chapter found evidence of the first and second constituents of Esser's news media logic, the third – commercialization – was not considered a precursor to greater mediatization.

In respect of changing technology, the ability to broadcast live significantly improved into the new millennium and – as the findings in this chapter suggested – broadcasters relied to a much greater extent on two-ways in UK television news bulletins. In 1991/2 and 1999, by contrast, live news was used much less, with the production values of two-ways appearing to be constrained. So, for example, rather than seeing live reporters on screen, they either appeared on a small television sat on the studio desk or a still picture was used. As Chapter 1 explained, as more sophisticated satellite equipment developed journalists could report with greater ease and mobility around the world. However, the location was not that often pivotal to a live convention and was instead used to signify their proximity to the action (outside No.10 Downing Street). Perhaps due to the novelty factor, in 2004 the purpose of many live two-ways was to introduce/conclude an edited package. But by 2012 this novelty had arguably worn off, since live two-ways were increasingly used by journalists to interpret a story, including within a studio format. In other words, the reason for going live a decade into the twenty-first century was driven less by technology and more by a changing editorial judgement about using journalists to interpret the significance of a story and to discuss it 'on-air'.

Moreover, fixed time bulletins appeared to have embraced the delivery of broadcasting in live news formats, reorienting their professional standards – a second factor of news media logic (Esser 2013a). The reporting of politics, in particular, was singled out for pursuing a live angle to convey news, with more space dedicated to journalists using the convention of two-ways and less time for politicians to voice their opinions about an issue or event. In 2012 television anchors were also given considerably more airtime to present news, supplying a steady stream of short packages. As a consequence, less time was spent on edited reporter packages – the longest type of news convention – meaning over time more news items were covered within a bulletin but in a relatively brief format and without the reliance on external sources. The reduction of reporter packages – a long-standing convention of bulletins – represents a significant shift in television news. As already argued, this changing cultural or professional reporting of news reflects a logic more consistent with the immediacy of rolling news formats, rather than fixed time bulletins.

But beyond the changing technology informing the production of bulletins or the professional willingness to depart from long-standing conventions, what were the reasons for and consequences of this editorial shift in television news? According to Esser (2013a), the third factor promoting news media logic over political logic is due to commercial influences and pressures. The evidence in this chapter, however, challenges this perspective, since the more commercial broadcaster – ITV – was broadly mediatized to the same extent over time as the BBC, the main public service broadcaster. But it would be hard to interpret the live two-way – the most interventionist convention – as being editorially consistent with a cynical market-led strategy. Indeed, politics – a hard, rather than soft crime/entertainment news story – was the main benefactor of enhanced mediatization. This suggests the greater mediatization of television news bulletins over time might be driven by wider public service objectives rather than commercial self-interest, with the aim of informing and enhancing viewers' understanding by supplying a greater interpretation of politics.

Since political reporting was identified as being the main driver of mediatized content, the next chapter takes a closer examination of how politics was reported compared to news generally. But first it provides a wider context to the mediatization of politics, drawing on the latest scholarship informing empirical research and theoretical debates. In doing so, the chapter tests well-established mediatized measures in UK news bulletins from 1991 to 2013 before then interpreting how far edited and live news conventions shape how politics is reported on television over time.

Notes

1 For Channel 4 broadcast licence, see http://licensing.ofcom.org.uk/binaries/tv/c4/c4drl.pdf. For Channel 5 broadcast licence, see http://licensing.ofcom.org.uk/binaries/tv/c5/c5drl.pdf; and for ITV, http://licensing.ofcom.org.uk/tv-broadcast-licences/current-licensees/channel-3/ (accessed 15 July 2014).

2 Quote taken from a former head of BBC Television News, Roger Mosey, explaining the value of evening bulletins: available online at http://news.bbc.co.uk/aboutbbc-news/hi/this_is_bbc_news/newsid_3280000/3280277.stm (accessed 20 July 2014).

Chapter 3

The media logic of immediacy

The mediatization of politics in UK news bulletins

Introduction

In most Western democracies, the way in which politics is portrayed in the media attracts considerable attention. After all, the decisions made by political actors impact on most people's everyday life, making it essential for citizens to be informed about contemporary politics and public affairs. Since television is the primary source of information for understanding the world, how politics is reported on national evening bulletins is most assiduously picked over. Not least by politicians, who meticulously monitor what is included and excluded from coverage, or in how issues are framed and interpreted by different broadcasters. During elections, for example, despite campaigning having radically changed over recent decades – with blogs, social media platforms and dedicated news channels operating around the clock – spin doctors continue to spend a great deal of time carefully orchestrating the images they would like to appear in evening television news bulletins. When Gordon Brown famously called a voter a "bigot" after a staged walkabout chat during the UK's 2010 General Election campaign, prior to realizing he still had a microphone on he can be heard muttering "they'll go with that one" – a reference to the pictures most likely to be edited for that evening's TV bulletins. Unfortunately – for the then prime minster – the pictures selected carried far graver consequences than he could have ever imagined.

Television news coverage of politics in most advanced democracies, then, appears more heavily scrutinized than most other media, whether newspapers or more recently online and social media platforms. Of course, newspapers and, in particular, new media are often celebrated for offering a myriad of views and opinions in blogs, say, or Twitter feeds, appealing to niche audiences. By contrast, national television news bulletins address huge swathes of viewers, meaning they could wield considerably more influence and sway when reporting daily political events. Consequently, in most advanced democracies – with the exception of the US – television news is tightly regulated to ensure broadcasters remain impartial and balanced in their presentation of politics (Cushion 2012a).

However, over the last decade or so – as television news has operated alongside digital platforms not subject to the same statutory obligations – regulators have faced considerable pressure to relax impartiality guidelines. So, for example, the UK's regulator of largely commercial broadcasting – Ofcom – noted in a 2007 report that "the expansion of digital channels and the internet mean there are now very many more sources of news than ever before. In future, when multiple sources – some regulated for impartiality, and others not – are all available through the same reception equipment, issues may be more complicated" (Ofcom 2007). A great deal of attention has been paid to evaluating how far objectivity, impartiality, bias and partisanship – terms that convey journalistic balance (Sambrook 2012) – influence contemporary media coverage of politics. But while most Western regulators and legislators have so far rejected attempts to lighten impartiality requirements, in an increasingly converged media environment there have arguably been more systemic and subtle changes to the editorial content of political news. Since political journalists on evening bulletins also report between different mediums – on 24-hour news channels, online blogs or social media platforms – and operate in competition with these instant news formats, the wider journalistic culture could have influenced how political news is produced, packaged and conveyed to viewers.

This chapter offers a longitudinal analysis of political coverage on UK television news evening bulletins from 1991 to 2013. In doing so, it can assess whether television bulletins have, over this time period, adapted their conventions according to the values embraced on 24-hour news channels, online news and social media platforms. Building on the findings of Chapter 2, all political news – including a broader definition that includes all UK domestic as well as international political news (wars and diplomatic events) – will be systematically compared with non-political news. This will allow political news to be isolated and more carefully analysed. In developing a comparative analysis, the chapter enters into debates about the mediatization of politics (Strömbäck 2008), since one of the major observations about how political news has changed over recent decades is that politics is being driven by a media as opposed to a political agenda. The media, in other words, have become an increasingly autonomous force, shaped by their own needs as opposed to the inherent value of reporting news about politics, diplomatic relations or international affairs. Drawing on the analytical framework introduced in Chapter 1, the concept of journalistic interventionism will be applied to the different types of conventions used in UK evening news bulletins to convey routine politics. As the wider culture of journalism has increasingly delivered news with greater immediacy (see Chapter 2), to what extent have television bulletins produced live or edited news about politics? Moreover, to what extent has this impacted on the role political actors have in television coverage compared to journalists?

Since scholarly attention about the mediatization of politics has intensified over very recent years, the chapter will begin by contextualizing these key studies and debates in journalism studies and political communication. It will then explain the sample and methodological scope of the chapter, including the way political news has been operationalized for this study. The findings of the study will then be discussed in the context of relevant debates about the changing nature of political news and the broader developments in journalism over recent decades.

Mediatization of politics debates: context and method

According to Djerf-Pierre *et al.* (2014: 322), "Research on mediatization has been booming since the late 1990s and there is currently ample evidence for mediatization as a pervasive and transformative force in politics". In very recent years, arguably scholarly attention on the mediatization of politics has been brought into even sharper focus, moving beyond mediatization debates more generally and gaining greater traction within the disciplines of journalism studies and political communication. As Blumler (2014: 31) observed, "the concept of 'mediatization' is doing heavy duty these days at several levels of communication analysis ... a burgeoning literature of 'mediatization-in-politics' has produced well-defined, well-analyzed and research-serviceable versions of the concept". So, for example, an edited collection – *The Mediatization of Politics* – was recently published by Esser and Strömbäck (2014a) and developed a sustained analysis of the key debates, established research traditions and democratic implications of debates about the mediatization of politics. The same authors also acted as guest editors for the journal *Journalism Studies* in a special edition about the mediatization of politics. The call for papers generated 84 submitted abstracts, which led to the editor of the journal expanding the special edition so its sister journal, *Journalism Practice*, could also publish a greater range of contributions. A total of 14 articles were published in both journals – an acceptance rate of 14 per cent overall – exploring the mediatization of politics from both theoretical and empirical perspectives (Strömbäck and Esser 2014b).

Strömbäck and Esser have defined the mediatization of politics as a "*long-term process through which the importance of the media and their spill-over effects on political processes, institutions, organizations and actors have increased*" (2014a: 6; their emphasis). Many studies draw on Strömbäck's (2008) analytical framework of four phases – introduced in Chapter 1 – to interpret how far politics is mediatized. To recap, phase one asks if the media are the most important source of information in a democracy and phase two asks how far the media can operate independently of political institutions. Since both these phases – notably the first – are typically met to different degrees in most advanced Western democracies, it is phases three and four where scholarly focus is most concerned, testing the relative strength of mediatization empirically between media systems and political cultures cross-nationally. Phase three asks how far media independence shapes how journalists select, shape and structure the political content of news. Or, put in the language of mediatization debates, how far does a media logic – the news values driving contemporary media culture – shape how politics is routinely reported? The fourth phase, by contrast, explores how political actors – politicians, political parties etc. – adapt and refine their own actions and behaviour in order to appeal to the different values underlying media logic.

As Chapter 1 explained, the focus in this book is on phase two and in particular phase three, since the empirical aim is to explore whether different television news bulletins have changed their practice and conventions, more closely resembling the format and style of 24-hour news media in how they report politics. Put differently, it asks how far television news bulletins have subscribed to a media logic – adopting journalistic values prevalent in the wider culture of news, such as producing live and instant news coverage – or how far they reflect a political logic, where the actions and voices of political actors remain central to coverage. As previously acknowledged, both media and political logics have been subject to recent scholarly debate about how each can be defined and theorized. As discussed in Chapter 1, they can be sometimes conceptualized in a uniform way, rather than conveying different logics (Landerer 2013). The focus in this chapter is on testing how a media logic can be empirically operationalized in television news bulletins over time. As Strömbäck and Esser (2014a: 20) explain:

> when studying the extent to which the media coverage is guided by political logic or news media logic – the third dimension of mediatization – there is a need to specify which elements of the news media coverage follow from political logic and news media logic respectively. The basic question should be whether a particular feature of news media coverage – for example, the length of soundbites, or the framing of politics – follows from the news media's interests or from the interests and logic of political actors or institutions.

Over the last decade or so, empirical studies exploring the mediatization of political content have experimented with different measures to help characterize whether a political or media logic is displayed. These have primarily related to exploring election coverage using content analysis in cross-sectional or longitudinal studies in order to explore either national or cross-national differences in how media report politics.

So, for example, Takens *et al.* (2013) examined television news coverage of Dutch national elections between 1998 and 2010, using three mediatized indicators – personalized, contest and negative frames – to explore whether they have become more or less pronounced over time. All three, of course, represent well-established characteristics of media logic: personalizing news (focusing on individual politicians, namely the leaders rather than parties); prioritizing the contest of politics (on campaigning rather than on issues); and concentrating on negative stories (reporting conflicts between political actors above other substantive issues). Contrary to the prevailing trends, their findings revealed that political news "has simultaneously become decreasingly personalized, less focused on the contest and less negative" (Takens *et al.* 2013: 277). However, they did identify a different media logic shaping election news on television news and newspapers.

Meanwhile, Zeh and Hopmann (2013) carried out a content analysis of Danish and German television news coverage of elections from 1990 to 2009, testing whether five content indicators – horse race coverage, shrinking soundbites, personalization, visualization and negativity – had increased over time. Taken together these characteristics again reflect trends that represent a mediatization of political content. On the face of it, they found evidence to support a greater degree of mediatized campaign coverage in both countries. However, they discovered coverage of mediatization was not enhanced into the 2000s, suggesting – in their words – "the described changes took place in the 1990s. Subsequently, the process seems to have stalled. This finding raises the question of whether mediatization peaked in the 1990s – at least with respect to effects on election news coverage" (Zeh and Hopmann 2013: 236).

Both longitudinal studies, then, suggest the process of mediatization should not be assumed to be increasing uniformly between different media systems or cross-nationally. However, the *Journalism Studies* and *Journalism Practice* (2014) special editions featured studies that demonstrated strong evidence of an enhancement in media logic over recent decades in news media. So, for example, Seethaler and Melischek (2014) examined how far Austrian political parties set the agenda of election coverage on the main bulletins, along with two quality and tabloid newspapers over five campaigns in 1970, 1983, 1990, 1999, and 2008. They discovered the strength of news media independence had increased, since they gradually became more selective in the press releases they responded to from political parties. Moreover, political parties had to adopt their campaign approach thus responding to the more assertive agenda set by the media. Seethaler and Melischek (2014: 273) concluded by arguing the Austrian political parties in the 1990s became

> the driving forces behind the overall agenda dynamics by adapting to the rules and norms of journalism. However, in recent times, a more competitive media system has led to a more powerful role for the media during election campaigns ... While in former times the party-media relationship was a one-way street, in the last Austrian election campaign the adoption of media logic by political parties has begun to turn this relationship into a reciprocal one (as typical for the most recent manifestation of the mediatization process).

Sampert *et al.* (2014), by contrast, focused on how two elite Canadian newspapers reported party leadership contests between 1975 and 2012 – a decisive moment in time, they argued, when the long-term policy direction is established in the selection process. They characterized whether a mediatization of coverage was displayed by exploring whether opinion writing had become more polarized, if more visual photos accompanied reporting, if news was more personalized – focusing on individuals rather than parties – and if the game frame had increased. Evidence was found to support all their hypotheses. Overall they identified the reporting of leadership contests had decreased over several decades and that coverage had become more mediated, "that is, filtered, interpreted, framed and assessed by the editorial writer, columnist or photographer" (Sampert *et al.* 2014: 290). All of which, they argued, demonstrated that political journalism had become interpretive, game-orientated, personalized and negative in its headline framing of leadership contests. Drawing on a metaphor of "jumping the shark" – a term critics use to demonstrate moments in popular culture that cynically strive to raise media publicity – they concluded that post 2000 both newspapers had become far more market-driven, dispensing with much of the political logic that had previously shaped the reporting of leadership contests.

As explored so far in the chapter, there are a number of different content indicators scholars have used to empirically explore whether political news has become mediatized over time. Strömbäck and Dimitrova's (2011) election study of US and Swedish television coverage – introduced in Chapter 1 – is particularly significant for the approach taken in this book because they draw on the concept of media interventionism in order to explore the comparative differences between each nation. This, in their words, is a term that can help test "the degree to which the content of political news is shaped by journalistic interventions" (Strömbäck and Dimitrova 2011: 35). Their content measures were similar to those already cited – such as the length of soundbites or the framing of politics – as well as some more original variables, including the type of on screen journalistic performance.

Whilst this chapter will draw upon some of the variables already tested in previous mediatization of politics studies, as outlined in the opening chapters the analytical framework adapted throughout this book empirically operationalizes journalistic interventionism from a fresh perspective. It does so by focusing on the routine practices and conventions – beyond election time – of television news bulletins to explore if coverage has become more interventionist in how politics is reported over recent decades. In doing so, it will compare political news specifically with all news generally to test the proposition – as Chapter 2 suggested – that political reporting is communicated in a distinctive way. A longitudinal content analysis of early evening BBC and ITV news bulletins over three weeks in 1991/2, 1999, 2004 and 2013 will be drawn upon to compare coverage over time.[1] As previously explained, each broadcaster has different levels of public service obligations, although both are legally bound to produce news impartially. While the BBC is a wholesale public service broadcaster, ITV is a commercial public service broadcaster with less regulatory responsibilities. Since mediatization is a process commonly identified with commercial rather than public service broadcasters – adopting a market-led approach to political reporting – comparing BBC and ITV coverage will confirm or challenge this prevailing wisdom.

As Chapter 1 explained, the conventions of television news will be reinterpreted according to four types of journalistic interventions: 1) edited packages, 2) anchors presenting an item, 3) a studio discussion and 4) a live reporter two-way. Whilst the first two types of intervention represent a more tightly scripted and edited format, the latter two are more free-flowing and spontaneous. Or, put differently, whereas the first two reflect a logic more accustomed to a fixed time bulletin – editing news over the course of a day – the latter two deliver news more instantaneously – 'as it happens' – more closely resembling rolling news channels or live online blogging. Taken together, the level of journalistic interventionism can be seen to be enhanced the higher up the scale (1–4), since reporters more actively shape the output of news.

A total of 1,484 journalistic interventions were examined over the sample period (1991–2013). The total N was divided into two subsamples of non-political items (N = 1117) and political items (N = 367). The definition of "political" news coverage went beyond sampling only news about institutional politics, such as the UK Parliament (as Chapter 2 focused on). Instead, politics was interpreted in a broader sense, including wider diplomatic affairs and international events, such as when political actors were involved in wars or conflicts. "Non-political" throughout the chapter refers to all news not included in the "political" category. Whilst political and non-political news will be compared throughout the chapter, the subsample of political news will be brought into sharper focus. In doing so, specific mediatized indicators will be used to interpret television news over time to assess whether the reporting of politics has changed and, if so, what aspects of journalism have modified the way television news operates. Is political news, for example, mediatized to a greater extent in edited or live journalistic interventions?

The mediatized variables this chapter will draw upon – many of which have already been introduced – include examining how far a political or media logic shapes coverage. In terms of a political logic, the analysis examines the volume and length of soundbites as well as offscreen sources (e.g. when journalists refer to an external source) and imagebites – when a politician visually appears on screen. To assess the degree of media logic shaping political coverage, the analysis will record when a journalist appeared on screen – thus illustrating their presence/importance – and assess the value of a reporter's role in supplying either descriptive or interpretive coverage. More specifically, the principle value of live political news – as previously explained in Chapter 1 – will be assessed according to whether the aim was to bring 1) interpretation to a story, 2) the latest developments, 3) the background locale or 4) to introduce an edited package – often referred to as a donut shot (Tuggle and Huffman 2001).

Overall, the chapter asks to what extent political – and non-political – news is mediatized in edited and live coverage between 1991 and 2013 across different media systems. It begins by first discussing journalistic interventions related to edited news. As Chapter 2 demonstrated, this was the dominant mode of communication in television news prior to the new millennium. It then focuses on live news, which correspondingly rose over the last decade or so, and considers the nature of political coverage when reported in more fluid and improvised formats.

The mediatization of politics in edited news conventions: from soundbites and imagebites to journalistic visibility

Mediatization of politics debates are fundamentally about the power struggle between political and media actors. To what extent – considering Strömbäck's (2008) third phase of mediatization more specifically – have journalistic voices replaced politicians and political parties? Of course, this is a long-standing debate in political communication, with politicians regularly complaining about the relative degree of time they are afforded in media coverage or in what issues are debated. But over recent decades scholars have evidenced a trend in many advanced democracies – especially in the US and during election time – where journalists themselves have increasingly shaped and informed media coverage of politics. Understood within the mediatization framework, this refers to a media logic superseding a political logic, with politicians' voices and actions subservient to journalists. Before examining how far and in what ways media actors shape politics in television news reporting, first the chapter will explain how scholars have researched the role of politicians in media coverage.

When a politician appears in an edited television news package – typically juxtaposed with other actors and journalistic dialogue – it is commonly referred to today as a soundbite, an on screen source featuring their views for a relatively short period of time (e.g. seconds). According to Rosenbaum (1997: 91), a soundbite reflects "a brief, self-contained, vivid phrase or sentence, which summarises or encapsulates a key point". The term found widespread purchase in the US during the 1980s, against the background of more sophisticated edited newsgathering and the growing influence of PR techniques in election campaigns. Michael Dukakis, a Democratic presidential candidate in the 1980s, claimed for example that soundbites had reshaped television news access for politicians. He famously said: "If you couldn't say it in less than 10 seconds, it wasn't heard because it wasn't aired". Of course, politicians of that generation had grown up with television news in the 1960s when politicians were given substantially more time to air their views with minimal editing or journalist interruption. But since the relationship between PR and politics has grown closer in subsequent decades – with the emergence of dedicated spin doctors – journalists were also faced with not just covering political news but uncovering the substance from the spin.

Table 3.1 The average length of political soundbites and the proportion of a bulletin made up of soundbites on US network television 1968–1988 (in seconds)

	Average length of soundbites	Proportion of bulletin made up of soundbites
1968	43.1	17.6
1972	25.2	11.9
1976	18.2	11.4
1980	12.2	7.4
1984	9.9	6.3
1988	8.9	5.7

(Adapted from Hallin 1992a)

These observations – that the length of politicians talking on television had reduced – were supported by longitudinal studies exploring US news from the 1960s to the 1980s. So, for example, Adotto (1990) compared soundbites in the 1968 and 1988 campaign and empirically measured a shift from 42.3 to 9.8 seconds. Further still, the study found in 1968 that "almost half of all soundbites were 40 seconds or more, compared to less than one percent in 1988. In fact, it was not uncommon in 1968 for candidates to speak, uninterrupted, for over a minute on the evening news (21 percent of soundbites); in 1988 it never happened" (Adotto 1990: 4). Meanwhile, Hallin (1992a) examined television network news coverage of every presidential election campaigns over twenty years and discovered the average political soundbite had shifted from 42.8 seconds in 1968 to just 8.9 seconds in 1988 (see Table 3.1). Whilst there may be more soundbites within an edited news package, Table 3.1 also shows the proportion of time devoted to political soundbites had declined steadily from the 1960s to the 1980s.

In the UK, by contrast, there is evidence of a similar if somewhat less significant reduction in soundbites on television news coverage in election campaigns over a similar timeframe. Rosenbaum (1997: 94), for example, cites one observational study that suggested soundbites were "under ninety seconds" during the 1964 UK General Election. A decade later, the BBC's *Nine O'Clock News* median soundbite length was measured at 45 seconds and ITV's *News at Ten* 25 seconds during the 1979 General Election, compared to 22 and 16 seconds respectively in the 1992 campaign (Rosenbaum 1997: 94). Making sense of the evolving US broadcast environment over twenty years – much of it, as Chapter 1 explained, the UK and many other advanced Western democracies have also embraced – Hallin concluded:

> Today's television journalist displays a much different attitude toward the words of candidates and other newsmakers from that of his predecessor. Now such words, rather than being reproduced and transmitted to the audience, are treated as raw material to be taken apart, combined with other sounds and images, and woven into a narrative (Hallin 1992b: 34).

Table 3.2 Average length of politician soundbites in national television news bulletins during US, UK, German and French elections in the 2000s (in seconds)

	United States 2000		UK 2001		Germany 2002		France 2000
	ABC	NBC	BBC1	ITV	ARD	RTL	Not coded
Average length of soundbite for political candidates (secs)	8.8	12.7	12.3	10.3	15.3	9.3	/

	United States 2004		UK 2005		Germany 2005		France 2007	
	ABC	NBC	BBC1	ITV	ARD	RTL	TF1	F2
Average length of soundbite for political candidates (secs)	9.5	7.9	16.8	17	10.8	11.9	10.9	12.6

(Adapted from Esser 2008)

A cross-national study examining television news coverage of elections into the 2000s suggested the length of soundbites had remained relatively short in the US (see Table 3.2).

However, many of the European bulletins granted politicians longer soundbites than on US network television. With the exception of NBC in 2000, all the soundbites on US network bulletins were under 10 seconds, whereas the average was as high as 17 seconds in the UK and over 15 seconds on ARD, the German public service broadcaster. Indeed, one study of US network news coverage of the presidential elections found soundbites lasted just 7.7 seconds in 2004 – a decline from 9.2 seconds in 1992. In other words, in countries where television is shaped by an overarching public service broadcast ecology – on both wholesale and commercial public broadcasting systems – soundbites were generally longer than the US's free-market model (other studies have shown US soundbites to be relatively low: see Farnsworth and Lichter 2007; Patterson 1993, 2000).

As scholars have begun to make sense of the changing format of television bulletins, their more sophisticated editing techniques and the increasing speed of news delivery (as Chapter 2 established), the visual representation of political actors has begun to be taken more seriously. Grabe and Bucy's *Image Bite Politics: News and the Visual Framing of Elections* (2009) is one of the most sustained attempts to consider how images of politicians should be analysed in television news as well as their verbal contributions. They argued that "visual stimuli serve an informational purpose. When the stimulus happens to be an image of a major party nominee during a presidential election, visuals convey information on multiple levels" (Grabe and Bucy 2009: 272). To methodologically operationalize the visual representation of politicians, the term "imagebites" was coined to measure the length and nature of how political actors appeared on screen in television news, irrespective of their verbal contribution. For they identified that imagebites steadily increased in coverage of US network television coverage of presidential elections between 1992 and 2004, whilst soundbites actually decreased. Or, put differently, viewers saw politicians more on screen into the new millennium during television coverage of US presidential elections but heard them less.

Esser's cross-national election study of soundbites also extended to imagebites. It found the use of imagebites just as prevalent among European broadcasters, but their length was greater on commercial rather than public service broadcast bulletins. As Table 3.3 demonstrates, the commercial stations – with the exception of France – such as ABC and NBC in the US, ITV in the UK and RTL in Germany, featured longer imagebites than their public service counterparts. As Esser (2008: 419) observed, "the heavy reliance on visual-driven reporting constitutes a transnational trend in Western election news coverage, but it is more pronounced on commercial than public stations" (Esser 2008: 419).

Overall, then, over the last 20 to 30 years academic research exploring soundbites and imagebites systematically and longitudinally have generally shown that while politicians appear more on screen, they tend to be heard less in television news.

Table 3.3 Average percentage story length of imagebites in national television news bulletins during US, UK, German and French elections in the 2000s

	United States 2000		UK 2001		Germany 2002		France 2000	
	ABC	NBC	BBC1	ITV	ARD	RTL	Not coded	
Candidates seen but not heard as percentage of average story length	16	19	10	16	7	17	/	

	United States 2004		UK 2005		Germany 2005		France 2007	
	ABC	NBC	BBC1	ITV	ARD	RTL	TF1	F2
Candidates seen but not heard as percentage of average story length	13	15	10	12	9	16	11	12

(Adapted from Esser 2008)

However, most of the research informing these empirical observations has been made during election campaigns, an important but atypical period of time. For cross-national studies examining media coverage of politics during elections have long shown the campaigns are framed by a game or strategy focus, trends in political coverage that follow more of a media than a political logic. When political news is reported during more 'routine' periods of time it could be the sourcing of political actors might differ, with politicians informing television news coverage to a greater degree. A longitudinal study of UK television news bulletins from 1991 to 2013 *outside of election time* could, in other words, shed considerable empirical light on the changing way in which politicians visually and verbally inform routine television coverage of politics. The study drawn upon in this book, however, not only examined soundbites produced by politicians, but included all on screen sources (such as citizens or business leaders). After all, external actors play an important role in shaping how politics is reported. Nevertheless, over the 22 years of analysis the overwhelming majority of sources drawn upon were political actors. The consequence of relying primarily on politicians as sources in coverage of politics is considered at greater length in Chapter 5.

Table 3.4 suggests that while soundbites have shrunk in size during recent decades at election time, they have not steadily reduced in routine reporting of politics. Of course, the classic soundbite studies illustrate trends from the 1960s to the 1980s which are beyond the scope of this study (e.g. Adotto 1990; Hallin 1992a). Although there are fluctuations over time in more recent decades (on ITV soundbites shrunk to just 9 seconds in 2004), the mean average length from 1991 to 2013 actually increased by a second on the BBC and ITV (from 15 to 16 seconds and 13 to 14 seconds respectively).

With the exception of the BBC in 2013, the length of soundbites was relatively consistent (as indicated by the standard deviations) between broadcasters. The reason for the greater variation in the length of soundbites on the BBC in 2013 was primarily due to one long speech by David Cameron about the death

Table 3.4 Mean average length (M) and Standard Deviation (SD) of soundbites and imagebites in political news in BBC and ITV evening television news bulletins 1991–2013 (in seconds)

	1991/2	*1999*	*2004*	*2013*
BBC soundbites	M = 15 secs, SD = 7	M = 12 secs, SD = 7	M = 16 secs, SD = 10	M = 16 secs, SD = 18
ITV soundbites	M = 13 secs, SD = 8	M = 11 secs, SD = 4	M = 9 secs, SD = 6	M = 14 secs, SD = 8
BBC imagebites	M= 15 secs, SD = 9	M = 10 secs, SD = 8	M = 17 secs, SD = 9	M = 16 secs, SD = 9
ITV imagebites	M = 13 secs, SD = 9	M = 13 secs, SD = 7	M = 9 secs, SD = 4	M = 13 secs, SD = 9

(Adapted from Cushion 2014a)

Table 3.5 Ratio of sources (on screen) in political news per average news item in BBC and ITV evening television bulletins 1991–2013

	1991/2	1999	2004	2013
BBC	2.4	1.8	1.7	1.9
ITV	1.9	2.1	1.2	1.9

(Adapted from Cushion 2014a)

of Margaret Thatcher, which was somewhat unusually broadcast live on the 6pm bulletin. The soundbite lasted more than three minutes – a long and uninterrupted appearance by a politician reminiscent of the 1960s. But what arguably increased the news value of the speech – and thus bucked the prevailing trend in soundbite research – was the fact the BBC could broadcast it exclusively live on its bulletin. It was not, in other words, an edited soundbite.

While research has also suggested the trend of shrinking soundbites is most pronounced on more commercially produced bulletins, the comparative differences (apart from 2004) between broadcasters was not staggering (2 seconds in 1991/2 and 2013 and just 1 second in 1999). Nevertheless, the BBC did consistently allow politicians greater time to speak on screen compared to its commercial counterpart. Another subtle comparative difference between broadcasters emerges when the number of sources are isolated per news item. Table 3.5 indicates the BBC, on average, had comfortably more than 2 sources informing its news reporting in 1991/2, but this gradually declined over subsequent decades. ITV, meanwhile, relied on slightly fewer sources per item than the BBC, most notably in 2004 when little more than one shaped a typical news report.

However, in 2013 both broadcasters averaged precisely the same source ratio – perhaps an indication of the relative consistency/standardization in how political news is edited on UK television news bulletins. Of course, a subtle reduction in the use of soundbites by broadcasters might correspondingly mean more space can be dedicated to imagebites, since images of politicians could be visually juxtaposed into an edited package. But the study – as Table 3.4 showed – did not follow a clear unidirectional pattern. Excluding ITV in 2004 – when the average length dropped to under 10 seconds – imagebites remained exactly the same for ITV in 1991/2 and 2013, with only a second increase on the BBC. However – and challenging the prevailing trends – the use of imagebites did not actually increase over time. In 1991/2 and 2013 half of all ITV's political news featured an imagebite (50 per cent and 48.3 per cent respectively), but in 1999 and 2004 this reduced to a third (32.4 per cent and 32.7 per cent respectively). The BBC's use of imagebites more steadily declined over recent decades: one appeared in close to three-quarters of all political news in 1991/2 (71.2 per cent), approximately a quarter in 1999 (26.8 per cent) and just above a third in 2004 and 2013 (38.1 per cent and 35.6 per cent respectively).

Overall, then, the longitudinal study of UK television news bulletins would appear to challenge previous trends into soundbites and imagebites. For the length of soundbites has not markedly changed over recent years (although the volume of them informing a news item have slightly reduced) nor has the use or length of imagebites increased over time. Or, put another way, it would be difficult to argue there has been a mediatization of political news on television over recent decades because political actors appeared visually and verbally to the same extent between 1991 and 2013.

According to previous mediatization of politics studies, another indicator of media logic is whether a journalist appears in an edited news report or not (Esser 2008; Grabe and Bucy 2009; Strömbäck and Dimitrova 2011). This demonstrates a measure of journalistic interventionism, conveying a visual presence and asserting personal authority and involvement in the production and presentation of news. An indicator of this change is journalists' prominence in today's news. This is a long-standing observation made most vociferously in the US, as Patterson (1997: 451) identified in the 1990s: "An indicator of this change is journalists' prominence in today's news. Whereas they were once the relatively passive voice behind the news, they are now at times as active and visible as the newsmakers they cover". Subsequent research exploring television news coverage of politics empirically reinforces this trend. Grabe and Bucy's (2009: 62–63) study of presidential election coverage between 1992 and 2004, for example, found "reporters and anchors were seen speaking at an average of 34.22 seconds per election story. By contrast, candidates were seen speaking for an average of 18.59 seconds per story – a little more than half the time allocated to journalists". While they pointed out the images of politicians outweighed that of journalists, overall they argued television news coverage of elections operates in an "increasingly visual and journalist-centred news environment" (Grabe and Bucy 2009: 78).

Indeed, Barnhurst and Steele's (1997) analysis of presidential campaigns from 1968 to 1988 emphasized the changing visual contexts and pace in which journalists appeared on screen. While their detailed content analysis discovered the overall duration of journalists on screen reduced over time, reporters appeared more frequently in new and different types of edited formats. This not only, in their view, reflected a faster pace of news delivery, it turned television journalists into visual actors in the storytelling process. Overall, they observed that "[j]ournalists showed themselves in a greater mix of shots, more often from various locations. They used video clips showing a wide variety of scenes. Besides these images, they inserted a range of other visuals, from simple captions to highly designed logos and complex information graphics" (Barnhurst and Steele 1997: 9).

Esser's (2008) more recent cross-national election study also discovered the role of journalists – with the exception of France – featured journalists prominently on screen. He concluded, "there is an almost universal transnational rule across Britain, Germany and the United States, that reporters' narration

Table 3.6 Percentage of stories in which a journalist is visible in Danish television news
bulletins 1994–2007

	1994	1998	2001	2005	2007
Public service bulletin (DR1)	25	21	10	19	87
Commercial bulletin (TV2)	17	18	17	34	29

(Adapted from Hopmann and Strömbäck 2010)

outweighs that of candidates by three to one. Journalists set the tone in the verbal stream of election news" (Esser 2008: 413). Hopmann and Strömbäck (2010) examined the visibility of journalists in election news on the main Danish public service broadcaster and the commercial evening bulletins from 1994 to 2007.

As Table 3.6 indicates, the study revealed a steady increase of journalists on both broadcasters, most strikingly so on the public service broadcaster – DR1 – which in 2007 featured a reporter present in 87 per cent of all election stories. Hopmann and Strömbäck (2010: 951) suggested the enhanced visibility of journalists related to editorial changes by the public service broadcaster, which "decided to let individual journalists play a far more emphasized and involved role in news reporting". Once again, while there is a clear trend established by scholarly research towards a more visible presence of journalists in political reporting, the focus of attention is overwhelmingly on television coverage of election campaigns. How far journalists appear in routine television coverage of politics, however, remains an open question. Table 3.7 indicates the on screen visibility of journalists on the BBC and ITV from 1991/2 to 2013 in all political news stories.

Journalists appeared on screen to a lesser extent on the BBC in 1991/2 and 1999 (55.9 per cent and 40 per cent respectively) than ITV (65 per cent and 72.7 per cent). Into the 2000s the visibility of journalists increased on both bulletins, particularly so on the main public service broadcaster, which appeared to follow a similar trend to its Danish counterpart. In 2013, however, journalists' on screen presence on the BBC declined (85 per cent to 76.1 per cent), whereas on ITV it rose to its highest peak (82.5 per cent). It can thus be concluded that journalists played a greater visual role in UK television news bulletins into the new millennium, albeit a slightly reduced one on the BBC in

Table 3.7 Percentage of items in which a journalist is visible in BBC and ITV early evening
television news bulletins 1991–2013 (by time)

	1991/2	1999	2004	2013
BBC	55.9%	40%	85%	76.1%
ITV	65%	72.7%	75.5%	82.5%

(Adapted from Cushion 2014a)

2013. Unlike in Denmark, the on screen visibility of journalists was broadly similar between the commercial and public service broadcasters.

So far the evidence presented from the longitudinal study of UK television news has offered relatively lukewarm support for a mediatization of political news. For the length and use of soundbites has not been radically reduced nor have imagebites increased – contrary to many cross-national studies. The only indication has been the increase of journalistic visibility, which was relatively high in the 1990s – on average, they appeared in 58 per cent of news items – but was enhanced to over 80 per cent into the new millennium.

In order to explore the nature of political coverage over recent decades the chapter will now move beyond standardized mediatization of politics measures. It does so by building on the findings of Chapter 2 and examining the changing nature of television news conventions and practices. It systematically explores the type of journalistic interventions used in political and non-political news reporting over time, focusing on the key differences between edited and live conventions. Of course, edited news includes many aspects already considered – soundbites, imagebites and journalistic visibility, for example – whereas the rise of live reporting practices (established in Chapter 2) has not been scrutinized as closely. In doing so, the aim is to explore whether a media logic of editing news has been superseded by an editorial logic of delivering live news. Or, put differently, by treating routine edited and live conventions as journalistic interventions, the next section will explore whether a mediatization of political news has taken place over recent decades.

Interpreting the mediatization of news: enhancing the speed and liveness of political reporting?

As previous chapters have already explored, it has widely been claimed the pace of news delivery has accelerated over recent decades. Since the 1990s the media landscape has rapidly expanded, with dedicated 24-hour news channels, online and social media platforms supplying a rolling menu of instantly available news. It has been argued that in this changing environment speed has become an important news value to contemporary political journalism, prompting politicians to develop far more sophisticated media rebuttal systems to respond to fast-moving events. As a fresh-faced President Obama claimed back in 2008:

> Too many in Washington put off hard decisions for some other time on some other day ... an impatience that characterizes this town – an attention span that has only grown shorter with the twenty-four hour news cycle ... When a crisis hits, there's all too often a lurch from shock to trance, with everyone responding to the tempest of the moment until the furore has died away and the media coverage has moved on, instead of

confronting the major challenges that will shape our future in a sustained and focused way.

(President Obama cited in Frisch 2010)

This strive to 'go live' and deliver the latest breaking news or update to a story has been discussed from a variety of perspectives, including the implications for journalistic practice and the broader impact on society (Cohen 2008; Seib 2001). And yet – as Chapter 2 pointed out – there is little empirical long-itudinal or systematic research that has examined the extent to which edited news generally or political news specifically has been replaced by live reporting. For while the speed of news delivery might have increased, has this corre-spondingly resulted in shorter television news conventions? The aim of the study drawn upon in this section is to explore whether political news has become distinctive from other reported news over recent decades by comparing the types of journalistic interventions routinely shaping evening television bul-letins. Is political news, in other words, more interventionist than news more generally, relying to a greater extent on live and more improvised conventions? Tables 3.8 and 3.9 indicate the proportion of time spent on different journalistic interventions when reporting political news specifically and news generally from 1991/2 to 2013 on BBC and ITV early evening bulletins.

Before the turn of the century, both political and non-political news were conveyed largely by edited journalistic interventions – in particular reporter packages – on both broadcasters. This was especially the case on the BBC: in 1991/2 97.9 per cent of all political news and 93.4 per cent of non-political was reporter packages. In 1999, however, political news conveyed by reporter packages fell by over 10 per cent to 85.7 per cent, whereas in non-political news the use of this convention dropped by less than 5 per cent to 89.9 per cent. The differences were less significant on ITV over the same time period. Political and non-political news was made up of reporter packages by 89–91.1 per cent in 1991/2 and 1999. ITV anchors played almost no role in reporting political news prior to the millennium. BBC anchors likewise had a relatively small role in political reporting (0.6–1.9 per cent), but this was enhanced in non-political news (3.9–4 per cent). Television journalism changed gear into the twenty-first century, however, with a major shift from edited to live jour-nalistic interventions in news generally but most strikingly so in political reporting. Live BBC news in 1991/2 constituted a tiny fraction of political news (1.5 per cent) and non-political news (2.6 per cent). However, by 1999 live non-political coverage rose to 6.2 per cent and increased substantially in political reporting to 12.4 per cent. Live reporting on ITV, by contrast, was a more common practice in 1991/2 in non-political news and political news (8.6 per cent and 11 per cent respectively). However, non-political approximately halved in 1999 (4.2 per cent) and marginally declined in political news on ITV (8.9 per cent). The most substantial shift on ITV occurred in 2004 when live reporting in non-political and political news increased to almost 30 per cent and 24.3 per cent

Table 3.8 Percentage of time spent on journalistic interventions, average mean length (M) and Standard Deviation (SD) in BBC television news bulletins in political and non-political news items 1991–2013

	1991/92	1999	2004	2013
Pre-edited				
Reporter package (politics)	**97.9%, M = 2 minutes, 29 seconds, SD = 49 seconds**	**85.7%, M = 2 minutes, 7 seconds, SD = 32 seconds**	**71.2%, M = 2 minutes, 48 seconds, SD = 1 minute, 2 seconds**	**74.2%, M = 2 minutes, 54 seconds, SD = 1 minute, 10 seconds**
Reporter package (non-politics)	93.4%, M = 2 minutes, 9 seconds, SD = 23 seconds	89.9%, M = 1 minute, 57 seconds, SD = 35 seconds	80.5%, M = 2 minutes, 15 seconds, SD = 38 seconds	83.2%, M = 2 minutes, 28 seconds, SD = 34 seconds
Combined anchor only, image and package (politics)	**0.6%, M = 25 seconds, SD = 7 seconds**	**1.9%, M = 16 seconds, SD = 4 seconds**	**0.5%, M = 12 seconds**	**1.4%, M = 26 seconds, SD = 15 seconds**
Combined anchor only, image and package (non-politics)	4%, M = 27 seconds, SD = 23 seconds	3.9%, M = 23 seconds, SD = 14 seconds	7.8%, M = 25 seconds, SD = 27 seconds	5.8%, M = 22 seconds, SD = 7 seconds
Live news				
Combined reporter/ anchor two-way and reporter live (politics)	**1.5%, M = 2 minutes, 7 seconds**	**12.4%, M = 1 minute, 16 seconds, SD = 31 seconds**	**28.3%, M = 1 minute, 22 seconds, SD = 22 seconds**	**19.6%, M = 1 minute, 13 seconds, SD = 49 seconds**
Combined reporter/ anchor two-way and reporter live (non-politics)	2.6%, M = 1 minute, 40 seconds, SD = 43 seconds	5.8%, M = 1 minute, 14 seconds, SD = 26 seconds	11.7%, M = 49 seconds, SD = 28 seconds	9.3%, M = 47 seconds, SD = 27 seconds
Anchor reporter discussion/ studio discussion (politics)	/	/	/	**4.2%, M = 1 minute, 45 seconds, SD = 17 seconds**
Anchor reporter discussion/ studio discussion (non-politics)	/	**0.4%, M = 1 minute, 4 seconds**	/	1.6%, M = 61 seconds, SD = 32 seconds
Total politics N	59	41	21	59
Total non-politics N	140	182	212	118

(Adapted from Cushion 2014a)

Table 3.9 Percentage of time spent on journalistic interventions, average mean length (M) and Standard Deviation (SD) in ITV television news bulletins in political and non-political news items 1991–2013

	1991/92	1999	2004	2013
Pre-edited				
Reporter package (politics)	89%, M = 1 minute, 48 seconds, SD = 36 seconds	90.1%, M = 2 minutes, 9 seconds, SD = 31 seconds	69.8%, M = 2 minutes, 30 seconds, SD = 41 seconds	80.6%, M = 2 minutes, 32 seconds, SD = 40 seconds
Reporter package (non-politics)	89.5%, M = 1 minute, 39 seconds, SD = 32 seconds	89.7%, M = 1 minute, 57 seconds, SD = 40 seconds	75%, M = 2 minutes, 8 seconds, SD = 44 seconds	75.8%, M = 2 minutes, 17 seconds, SD = 51 seconds
Combined anchor only, image and package (politics)	/	**0.4%, M = 19 seconds**	**0.3%, M = 14 seconds**	/
Combined anchor only, image and package (non-politics)	1.9%, M = 23 seconds, SD = 16 seconds	5.3%, M = 24 seconds, SD = 22 seconds	0.7%, M = 32 seconds, SD = 9 seconds	1.5%, M = 19 seconds, SD = 6 seconds
Live news				
Combined reporter/ anchor two-way and reporter live (politics)	11%, M = 1 minute, 3 seconds, SD = 14 seconds	8.9%, M = 1 minute, 3 seconds, SD = 15 seconds	27.7%, M = 47 seconds, SD = 25 seconds	15.1%, M = 1 minute, 9 seconds, SD = 22 seconds
Combined reporter/ anchor two-way and reporter live (non-politics)	8.6%, M = 1 minute, 7 seconds, SD = 20 seconds	4.2%, M = 1 minute, 11 seconds, SD = 23 seconds	14.4%, M = 1 minute, 43 seconds, SD = 22 seconds	10%, M = 1 minute, 54 seconds, SD = 19 seconds
Anchor reporter discussion/ studio discussion (politics)	/	/	**2.2%, M = 1 minute, 43 seconds**	**4.4%, M = 1 minute, 47 seconds, SD = 8 seconds**
Anchor reporter discussion/ studio discussion (non-politics)	/	0.8%, M = 1 minute, 35 seconds	9.9%, M = 1 minute, 19 seconds, SD = 49 seconds	6.9%, M = 1 minute, 28 seconds, SD = 26 seconds
Total politics N	40	37	52	58
Total non-politics N	96	125	153	91

(Adapted from Cushion 2014a)

respectively – although this dropped to 19.5 per cent and 16.9 per cent by 2013. The BBC also enhanced its proportion of time dedicated to live political reporting in 2004 (28.3 per cent) – and to much a lesser extent than other news (11.7 per cent). In 2013, there was a marginal decline in live political BBC news (23.8 per cent) and non-political news (10.9 per cent). Despite the reduction of live news in more recent years, over several decades live reporting has become a routine practice in fixed time early evening bulletins. Political news, in particular, can be singled out as being distinctive because it appears to be shaped by live journalistic interventions to a greater extent compared to other topics – as Chapter 2 also evidenced. Less strikingly clear were the differences between broadcasters, since both the commercial and public service broadcasters reported live with relatively equal vigour over successive decades. To compare and contrast the character of political news with news generally, the comparative length of news items from 1991 to 2013 can be broken down. This needs to be interpreted in the context of the overall length of BBC and ITV bulletins. For the latter's were just 15 minutes long in 1991/2, increasing to about 20–25 minutes in 1999, which remains slightly shorter than the BBC's evening bulletin today (largely due to advertising requirements).

Table 3.10 shows political news was consistently longer than non-political news items, apart from ITV in 2004 (with a difference of just 3 seconds). Moreover, the average length of political news items remained relatively unchanged – when ITV is excluded in 1991/2, since the bulletin only aired for 15 minutes – increasing by 10 seconds on ITV and decreasing by 16 seconds on the BBC. In short, at first glance little has changed over successive decades. However, a closer inspection of the length of journalistic interventions in news generally and political news specifically – illustrated in Tables 3.8 and 3.9 – showed the structure of television news has changed over time. For the selection of different edited or live conventions – from reporter packages to live two-ways – can radically change the time afforded to a journalist to convey a story or in how they can communicate. Television news anchors, for instance, did not dominate the bulletin to the same degree as they do in the US (see Chapter 4). They presented relatively short items generally and less frequently in political news. As Chapter 2 established, the most widely used journalistic intervention was the reporter package on both channels – although gradually less

Table 3.10 Average length of political and non-political news items in BBC and ITV early evening television news bulletins 1991–2013 (minutes and seconds)

	BBC non-political items	BBC political items	ITV non-political items	ITV political items
1991/2	1m, 51 secs	2m, 23 secs	1m, 29 secs	1m, 41 secs
1999	1m, 38 secs	1m, 45 secs	1m, 35 secs	1m, 55 secs
2004	1m, 28 secs	2m, 2 secs	1m, 34 secs	1m, 31 secs
2013	1m, 35 secs	2m, 7 secs	1m, 25 secs	2m, 5 secs

time was spent on this convention into the new millennium – but the length of them remained roughly the same. On the BBC, reporter packages lasted between 2.07 and 2.54 minutes in political news from 1991 to 2013, with greater variation in length – as Table 3.8 revealed – into the 2000s. Non-political news, by contrast, was typically shorter than political news (between 1.57 and 2.28 minutes). Excluding ITV in 1991/2 – when the bulletin was shorter – the length of political news was again relatively similar (between 2.09 and 2.32 minutes) and on average longer than non-political news (1.57–2.17 minutes). In short, reporter packages about political news specifically on both broadcasters were typically longer than news generally. Interpreting the changing form and structure of live political reporting thus needs to be understood in the context of the overall increase in live news. The average length of live BBC political news was relatively consistent in the 1990s, for example, when there was much less of it compared to the 2000s. However, from 1999 to 2013 live reporting increased and political items became shorter in length (1.13–1.22 minutes), although they were typically longer than non-political news (47 seconds to 1.40 minutes). ITV's live political news was shorter than the BBC's – falling to 47 seconds in 2004 – and averaging just over a minute in every other year (1.03–1.09 minutes long). Apart from 1999, live political reporting was longer than non-political news on ITV. Overall, then, it can be concluded that live political reporting was generally longer in length than in non-political news. Indeed, by 2013 live two-ways were under a minute long on both broadcasters in non-political news items. But the length of political news items – live or edited – had not changed dramatically (with the exception of ITV in 2004) from 1991 to 2013. Nevertheless, because live reporting has generally increased over recent decades – and tends to be shorter in length than edited news – the overall character of political news has changed. Or, put differently, political news items have become shorter in length on the UK's evening bulletins post millennium due to journalists reporting to a greater degree in live formats.

The chapter has established journalists have become more central actors in television news bulletins over recent decades due to the rise of live reporting. For not only have journalists increasingly relied on their own views rather than those of politicians, they have become more visible in news-making by appearing on screen to visually illustrate their role in reporting a story. This is a trend evident in political journalism internationally as scholars have identified journalists taking on a more active role in coverage, not just describing issues or events but interpreting them. US scholar Thomas Patterson (1993, 2000) has written extensively and, for the most part, critically about the rise of interpretive political journalism. He suggests that traditionally – notably in the 1950 and 1960s, before US network television was extended to 30 minutes – "[a] standard formula for a news story was a descriptive account of what politicians said and to whom they said it. News accounts did not ordinarily delve into why they said it, for that would venture into the realm of subjectivity" (Patterson 1996: 101). However, Patterson (1996: 101) continues by arguing:

Today, facts and interpretation are freely intermixed in news reporting. Interpretation provides the theme, and the facts illuminate it. The theme is primary; the facts are illustrative. As a result, events are compressed and joined together within a common theme. Reporters question politicians' actions and commonly attribute strategic intentions to them, giving politicians less of a chance to speak for themselves.

At election time, in particular, longitudinal research appears to support Patterson's observations spanning several decades. So, for example, Steele and Barnhurst (1996) examined US network reporting of the presidential campaigns between 1968 and 1988 and discovered that "when journalists spoke at the end of a report, they gave factual information much less often, by a factor of ten (from 24.6 to 2.4 percent). Making judgements about the election events grew to almost 90 percent of these final remarks. Journalists made their opinions the last word, the final say". In more recent decades, scholars beyond the US have identified that journalists have also become more interpretive and adversarial in how they report the actions and behaviour of political actors (de Vreese 2001; Semetko et al. 1991; McNair 2000).

Esser and Umbricht (2014) carried out a comprehensive cross-national longitudinal content analysis study in order to examine how far and in what ways journalism had become more interpretive. Examining regional and national newspapers in the US, UK, Germany and Switzerland during the 1960s and 2000s, one aspect of their wide-ranging study empirically measured the degree to which news was shaped by straight news reporting, opinion, interpretation or commentary. While they identified some revealing comparative differences in coverage between nations and linked them to competing media systems, overall they established a general trend towards stories containing some interpretive or opinionated characteristics informing a routine news story. As a consequence, the traditional informational hard news format – devoid of any explicit journalistic interpretation or opinion – had in their view gradually reduced in newspaper coverage. Considering the nature of political coverage in more detail, their judgement about the rise of interpretive news was less critical than the prevailing literature (e.g. Patterson 2000). For they argued that "a more interpretive news style is not bad per se and may even contribute to an enriched public sphere *as long* as it is applied more to covering 'policy' than 'process' – and we have identified only one press system (Italy) where this was not the case" (Esser and Umbricht 2014: 244; their emphasis). While they further observed that process driven reporting had increased in each country – a trend identified elsewhere as coverage of policy is pushed to the sidelines – the study raised important questions about assessing the normative value of the rise of interpretive news.

Indeed, Salgado and Strömbäck (2012) conducted a review of studies exploring interpretive news and similarly found strong evidence that this journalistic approach to news reporting had increased in many Western countries. However, they further concluded there were many different and conflicting ways 'interpretive news' had been defined and understood by scholars. Moreover, many studies were not always clear in explaining the competing formats under analysis – such as live reporting compared to opinion pieces in broadsheet newspapers – which might shape the type and nature of journalism pursued.

To make sense of the rise of live political reporting established in the chapter, and greater visibility of journalists and reliance on their views (rather than external sources), the final focus in this chapter will be on understanding why news was reported live. Following the approach outlined in Chapter 2, the value of every live political item was put under the spotlight. To recap, the primary purpose of live news was classified in four ways. First, to introduce or wrap up an edited reporter package. Second, to bring the latest news or update. Third, to report from a specific location which informs the story rather than acting as background scenery (e.g. standing outside 10 Downing Street on a Sunday night). Fourth, to provide some interpretation or analysis about politics. The focus here is on the degree to which live political was interpretive or more descriptive. While interpretive journalism can be difficult to operationalize (Salgado and Strömbäck 2012), in most instances it was relatively easy to draw a distinction between interpretive or descriptive live news. After the chancellor of the exchequer's 2004 annual budget, for example, the BBC's television news anchor explicitly invited the then political editor, Andrew Marr, to pass judgement about the posturing of political parties: "Now, Andrew, do you think this budget sharpens the dividing line between Labour and the Conservatives?" In this context, it would be difficult to avoid being anything other than interpretive.

The study identified a mixed level of interpretive political journalism over time but by 2013 a clearer pattern emerged. In 1991/2 all political news was interpretive, but very few live political items were reported. A more comprehensive picture can be interpreted post 1999 when live reporting increased. In 1999, for example, 60 per cent of live political news on ITV was interpretive. This was higher than the BBC (42.9 per cent), which used live news to the same degree to introduce/conclude an edited reporter package. The roles were reversed in 2004, with the BBC using live news to interpret politics to a much greater extent (88.9 per cent) and ITV using two-ways to introduce/conclude a political item (55.2 per cent). Approximately a third (34.5 per cent) of live ITV political coverage was interpretive in 2004. In 2013 the majority of live political news was interpretive on the BBC (52.2 per cent) and ITV (63.2 per cent). In addition, over a fifth of live political reporting – 21–22 per cent – was primarily used to bring new information to light or update a story. Apart from ITV in 2004, then, the overall value of delivering live political news was to interpret the politics behind a story, rather than in a more descriptive way. In Chapter 5 the role of interpretive political news in live two-ways will be examined more systematically over time. For now, the conclusion of this chapter will reflect on its key findings – namely the rise of live political reporting, the increasing centrality of journalists in news-making along with the reduction of edited political news.

Understanding the mediatization of politics: towards a live and interpretive media logic

The longitudinal trends of how UK bulletins reported politics from 1991 to 2013 outlined in this chapter run counter to many of the prevailing trends in academic research about the mediatization of politics (Esser 2008; Strömbäck and Dimitrova 2011). So, for example, whereas many studies – predominantly during election campaigns – have established that soundbites have shrunk over recent decades, on UK television news they have remained broadly the same. With politicians heard less, some scholars have suggested they appear more as imagebites. But neither the length nor use of imagebites had been enhanced on UK television coverage of politics. The only measure of mediatization identified was in the increasing visibility of journalists over time. However, whilst these measures of mediatization have been well-established in relevant journalism studies and political communication literature, they predominantly related to politics being reported in an edited rather than live format. Imagebites, for instance, refer specifically to editing the visual appearance of politicians – in Parliament delivering a speech or meeting foreign dignitaries – as part of a reporter package. Likewise, soundbites in almost all cases appeared in edited reporter packages. In one instance where a politician was sourced at length (over 3 minutes) – a David Cameron speech about Margaret Thatcher's death – it was broadcast live. Finally, while the visibility of journalists increased over time – supporting a mediatization indicator – this was largely due to the rise of live two-way reporting, which requires the on screen presence of a reporter. If live news was excluded, journalists were 10–20 per cent less visible in 2004 and 2013 – appearing in about two-thirds of coverage, which indicates a less clear-cut pattern of mediatization. In other words, in edited political news there appears to be little evidence of a mediatization of political content on UK television news bulletins from 1991 to 2013. The evidence instead suggested the driving force behind mediatization was in live reporting, which – as Chapter 2 also established – was most evident in how broadcasters chose to cover politics. For as live reporting became a more stable part of UK bulletins post 2000, the level of journalistic interventionism was enhanced in the reporting of politics. The two-way was the most widely used live convention, relying much less on external sources – including politicians – than edited reporter packages, whilst privileging the views of journalists who supplied a greater level of interpretation (with the exception of ITV in 2004) from 1999 to 2013.

Interpreted in this context, mediatization of politics debates arguably need to place a greater focus on the changing nature of media logics shaping journalism, rather than focusing so much attention on the role of political actors (in, say, soundbites or imagebites). As this chapter has demonstrated, the more interventionist conventions used in live news – of increasingly interpretive two-ways – have influenced the way in which political news is routinely made sense of in UK evening television bulletins. Put differently, the values of rolling and more instant news formats appear to have impacted on fixed time bulletins, injecting greater immediacy into the media logic of political reporting. Whilst this was most apparent in live interpretive reporting, by 2013 a greater immediacy of political coverage was also evident in bringing the latest update to a story. Routine updates could, in other words, become a more familiar part of political reporting in evening bulletins.

As Chapter 6 explores in more detail, this suggests future mediatization of politics studies should consider theorizing new media logics – rather than relying on a singular one – and testing them empirically in a range of different news media formats. Of course, as Blumler and Kavanagh (1999) have argued, it is understandable why journalists have become more interpretive, since they are responding to political actors' greater use of PR in communicating their decisions and policies, more skilfully evading difficult questions and remaining 'on-message'. In this respect, the enhanced use of the live two-way convention – as Chapter 5 explores – could be interpreted as an attempt by broadcasters to counter the new professionalized class of politicians and slick PR tactics of political parties. Indeed, political news was most consistently covered live compared to other topics, an editorial sign of the more interventionist way journalists chose to report politics. Moreover, journalists reporting news about politics were given greater time live 'on-air' than in news generally, reinforcing the more interpretive role they are asked to play in television news. Needless to say, from 1991 to 2013 live broadcasting has become far more easy to report beyond the studio. ITV's live two-ways in April 1991, for example, would appear almost comical for viewers today. For the news anchor was pictured talking to a tiny television sat on the edge of a desk, where the then political editor – Michael Brunson – appeared on screen from a Westminster studio. In 2004 – when live news was perhaps at its most rampant (see also Chapter 2) – arguably the novelty and technological ease of 'going live' explains its widespread usage. By 2013, however, journalists increasingly interpreted political news within the studio alongside the news anchor. In other words, whilst technology could facilitate journalists live reporting from far-flung locations today, an emerging convention appears to ask journalists to act as expert sources, inviting them to react and respond to the political day's news as opposed to acting as a roving reporter.

As political news has become an increasingly live topic over recent decades, UK evening bulletins appear to be relying less on what politicians say and more on the views of journalists. The centrality of journalists in news-making thus means their power and influence has grown over time, since their judgement and interpretation can potentially shape how viewers understand routine political events and issues. Chapters 5 and 6 examine more closely the interpretive nature of political reporters and consider the evidence about the impact different television news formats – edited or live – have on viewers. But whether – as the prevailing literature about the effect of mediatization implies – a rise of live and interpretive news equates to a commercialization of political content is open to considerable debate. There was little difference, in this respect, between the level of journalism interventionism in political reporting over time on BBC or ITV evening bulletins. If anything, in very recent years the BBC has become the more interventionist broadcaster, delivering live two-way political reporting to a greater degree. Whilst it could be argued an editorial shift towards greater two-ways is part of the BBC's commercial strategy, it could also be motivated by well-intentioned public service values of better informing viewers. This challenges the notion that greater mediatization is a precursor to market logic – a conclusion reached in Chapter 2 also. The lack of major differences in the level of mediatization in political reporting between BBC and ITV television bulletins could also be shaped by the UK's unique broadcast ecology. For while the BBC is a wholesale public service broadcaster, ITV is a commercial public service broadcaster with long-standing regulatory obligations safeguarding the quality of its journalism. In other words, compared to "commercial" channels operating in other parts of the world – in the US, for example – the overarching public service framework of UK television news could prevent excessive commercial logic.

The next chapter develops a more international perspective about the relative degree of mediatization in television news and political reporting. It begins by charting the growth and importance of cross-national studies in journalism studies and political communication before drawing on recent comparative studies examining the journalistic interventions shaping US, UK and Norwegian television news bulletins.

Chapter 4

Comparing news cultures and media systems

Developing a comparative study of
television news bulletins in the
UK, US and Norway

Introduction

Over recent decades, comparative research between the media and political
systems of different nations has grown steadily. Most academic studies today
rarely exhibit the kind of "naïve universalism" Blumler and Gurevitch (1995: 75)
once described of scholarly inquiries limited to discussing media systems
within *just* a national focus. For the significance of theoretical interventions or
empirical conclusions in journalism, media and communication research is
increasingly understood in the context of broader international debates and
trends. Academics have increasingly sought to collaborate on cross-national
research projects, sharing their knowledge and understanding at international
conferences, in scholarly journals and books (Esser and Hanitzsch 2012). Of course,
the level of scholarly activity remains shaped by the economic influences of the
richest nations – the US, in particular – but in order for debates to gain traction and credibility within scholarship new empirical observations or theoretical
insights are expected to be tested cross-nationally. Moreover, as scholarship has
become more globalized, developments in the most advanced democracies –
again, most notably the US – have generally been understood as potentially
shaping the future direction of other countries.

According to Esser (2013b: 113), "Virtually no other approach has potential
to bring communication studies further forward in the age of transnationali-
zation than the comparative approach". As the world has become increasingly
connected – or globalized – there remain unique national characteristics that
shape why communication is different cross-nationally. Comparative research,
in this context, allows communication scholars to empirically investigate and
theoretically explain the reasons behind these differences whereas single country
studies could only postulate about them. Of course, comparative research has
become more sophisticated over time – or matured, as Gurevitch and Blumler
(2004) have put it. Siebert *et al.*'s (1956) *Four Theories of the Press*, for example,
ambitiously interpreted the nature of media systems according to the political
identity of just three countries – Russia, the US and England. While pioneering
comparative media research, it has since been criticized for its generalizability

in a global environment (Curran and Park 2000; McQuail 1987). More recently, Hallin and Mancini's (2004) *Comparing Media Systems: Three Models of Media and Politics* has become the most influential comparative study. It explored 18 nations in different Western European/North American contexts with similar histories and mature democracies. The study developed 3 models – liberal, democratic corporatist and polarized pluralist – and classified the 18 different countries based on their political and journalistic identities. Hallin and Mancini have since expanded upon their 2004 study in an edited volume called *Comparing Media Systems beyond the Western World* (2012). This was intended, according to the authors, to encourage scholars to develop an understanding of media systems by studying the media and political environments they inhabit, rather than applying models empirically grounded within Western Europe or North American contexts.

The advancement of comparative research into media systems has brought wider political and cultural influences into sharper focus, encouraging scholars to consider how different environments shape communication processes and outcomes. So, for example, Semetko *et al.*'s (1991) *The Formation of Campaign Agendas* identified a number of systemic reasons explaining the comparative differences between US and UK election reporting and political campaigning. They concluded the more professionalized environment of US political actors, for instance, shaped a more sophisticated approach to campaign strategy than in the UK, with spin doctors closely managing the media agenda. In the UK, by contrast, the election was more prominently reported, which – they argued – related to the overarching public service framework shaping the broadcast ecology compared to the US's more market-driven system. Their conclusions were wider reaching, of course, and went beyond system influences to include micro-level factors (see Semetko *et al.* 1991: 8–9). But the broader point is their comparative design enabled them to reach conclusions based on the wider cultural and political environments shaping election campaigns. Needless to say, if the authors were to revisit their comparative study today they might draw different conclusions because of the changing media and political landscape over recent decades.

The aim of this chapter is to offer a comparative cross-national dimension to understanding the contemporary form, structure and style of television news bulletins. While previous chapters in this book have interpreted the changing character of UK television news generally and political news specifically in light of cross-national studies, the focus now turns to developing a more systematic comparative assessment. Television news bulletins in the UK, US and Norway will be compared using the same analytical framework as previous chapters, considering the level of journalistic interventionism displayed in routine television news coverage. Or, put another way, the chapter will examine the extent to which television news is mediatized on UK, US and Norwegian evening bulletins. Whereas rolling news has been a long-standing influence in the US – after CNN began broadcasting in 1980 – in Norway the first dedicated 24-hour news is less than a decade old. In the UK, by comparison, Sky News launched a news channel in 1989, with the BBC establishing one eight years later. The sample selection thus allows the contrasting cultures of news to be compared along with other influences such as the greater public service regulation shaping television bulletins in the UK and Norway compared to the US.

The chapter will then focus on the media and political environment in the UK and US, interpreting the degree to which political news is mediatized in early evening bulletins using a range of measures to understand the comparative differences between nations. Over recent decades, the US has largely been understood as the most mediatized nation, which operates in a largely free-market environment of broadcasting that has historically championed an interventionist approach to journalism (Schudson 2001). Since the US's more interventionist and commercialized model of broadcasting are considered system level influences that enhance the mediatization of politics, the UK's less interventionist and more public service regulated broadcasters could offer some revealing comparative differences.

When interpreting the mediatization of news or politics, of course, overall the typical aim is to empirically investigate whether a media logic has increasingly shaped reporting. After all, mediatization of politics refers to a process, where political reporting over time subscribes to the values of news media (Lundby 2009a; Strömbäck and Esser 2014a). This was the research design of Chapters 2 and 3, where UK national television news bulletins generally and political news specifically were longitudinally examined. But while it would have been illuminating to interpret the changing nature of bulletins in the UK, US and Norway from the 1990s into the 2000s – particularly since the development of dedicated 24-hour news differed between each nation – it was not possible to archive television coverage cross-nationally.

Developing comparative research: interpreting television news cross-nationally

The intention in the first part of the chapter is to systematically explore television news bulletins – in the UK, US and Norway – during a 'routine' period of time. The aim of the analysis is to make sense of the conventions used to interpret everyday events as well as to ask whether the wider culture of news and television journalism more generally plays a role – as a mediatizing agent – in the making and shaping of television news bulletins. Although the US, UK and Norway are all countries that represent advanced democracies, they have different media systems and political cultures – which will be discussed further – that could potentially influence the degree to which news is mediatized. This chapter is designed to empirically explore the characteristics of news bulletins and assess if they remain distinctive from the culture of rolling or instant news. For the very presence of live news in fixed time news bulletins cross-nationally could be seen to represent the wider influence of 24-hour news values. Or, put another way, journalistic interventions displaying immediacy and pace in routine coverage could reflect a mediatization of television news bulletins. The media systems of the three countries examined thus need to be discussed along with the methodological details of the studies informing this chapter.

As already acknowledged, Hallin and Mancini's (2004) three models of media and politics (democratic corporatist, polarized pluralist and a liberal model) among 18 Western nations is widely considered an important study that characterized media systems according to various criteria. Evident in Britain, Ireland and the US, they classified the liberal model "by a relative dominance of market mechanisms and of commercial media"; the democratic corporatist model, representing northern Europe, "by a historical co-existence of commercial media and media tied to organized social and political groups, and by a relatively active but legally limited role of the state"; and the polarized pluralist model, reflecting southern European countries, by "the integration of the media into party politics, weaker historical development of commercial media and a strong role of the state" (Hallin and Mancini 2004: 11). According to these definitions, the countries examined in this chapter fall into the corporatist (Norway) and liberal (UK and US) models.

However, while Hallin and Mancini's (2004) study has become an important resource in cross-national communication research, it has also been used to dispute the *generality* of grouping certain countries together and for broadly interpreting mass media. If US broadcast news is compared to the UK, for example, there are striking differences in the media structures and regulatory cultures that shape television news. For the UK has a long established public service media infrastructure (compared to the US's minimal provision) and robust broadcast regulation (compared to the US's light-touch system). The UK's broadcast news culture arguably has greater symmetry with Norway than the US. While US network television channels operate with minimal obligations in the provision of news and current affairs, both the UK and Norway have commercial public service broadcasters which are legally obliged to air certain news programming and in peak time hours (Aalberg *et al.* 2010). At the same time, longitudinal evidence suggests television news has become more down-market, embracing a more tabloid agenda over recent decades (Barnett *et al.* 2012). In other words, the sample represents bulletins operating under a strong corporatist (Norway) and liberal (US) model. The UK arguably sits between these models, primarily due to its overarching public service broadcast ecology which makes it distinctive from the US.

Irrespective of the media and political culture shaping journalism in each country, in all three nations television news is the most watched (The Pew Research Center's Project for Excellence in Journalism 2012; Ofcom 2013; Medienorge/TNS Gallup 2012). The chapter will examine the 6.30pm bulletins broadcast on ABC and NBC in the US; the BBC's 6pm and ITV's 6.30pm in the UK; and the 7pm NRK and 9pm TV2 in Norway. To develop the comparative analysis in the chapter, the differences between the wholesale market-driven bulletins (ABC and NBC in the US) will be compared to the wholesale public service broadcasters (BBC and NRK) and commercial public service broadcasters (ITV and TV2) in the UK and Norway respectively. In other words, the journalism shaping evening bulletins can be compared according to the relative degree of their public service broadcast obligations or market pressures.

In the first part of the chapter, the same two weeks of coverage in the US, UK and Norway in April and May 2012 were examined (weekdays only). This study generated 1,417 items overall, with researchers from the UK and Norway regularly discussing how television news was coded and analysed according to specific criteria. In the second part of the chapter, a follow-up study focused in on three weeks of coverage in the US and UK in April and May 2013 (weekdays only). Overall, 946 items were examined with the comparative differences in political reporting – as explained further below – subject to closer scrutiny.

In both sample years no major events or issues dominated the news agenda in each country. But as previous chapters have explained, the analytical framework for the study is primarily concerned with the types of conventions used to report routine television news rather than comparing news agendas (crime, health, politics, etc.). As with previous chapters, routine television conventions will be reinterpreted into four journalistic interventions in order to assess how far evening bulletins resemble the broader culture of rolling news. In short, to what degree are television news bulletins mediatized cross-nationally and between media systems?

Interpreting the mediatization of television news cross-nationally: the use of journalistic interventions

Consistent with the longitudinal findings established in UK television news in previous chapters, reporter packages were the most used convention in each country's evening bulletins (see Table 4.1). But there were some major differences in the degree to which television news was edited and live between nations. So, for example, reporter packages occupied just 56 per cent of NBC airtime in the US compared to 81 per cent on TV2 in Norway. In the UK, by contrast, both broadcasters spent approximately two-thirds of their bulletins using edited reporter packages. The most consistent difference between nations was in the use of television news anchors. Norwegian news anchors, for example, appeared on screen the least amount of time (15 per cent on NRK and 17 per cent on TV2) compared to approximately a fifth of airtime on UK evening bulletins (19 per cent on ITV and 20 per cent on the BBC). US news anchors, by contrast, occupied between a quarter (25 per cent on ABC) and a third of time (32 per cent on NBC) presenting stories in evening bulletins. Of course,

Table 4.1 Percentage use of journalistic interventions in US, UK and Norwegian television news bulletins in 2012 (by time)

	US		UK		Norway	
	NBC	*ABC*	*BBC*	*ITV*	*NRK*	*TV2*
Pre-edited news						
Reporter pack	56	64	66	65	63	81
Anchor	32	25	20	19	15	17
Live news						
Anchor/reporter two-way live reporter location	7	2	11	14	8	2
Anchor/reporter studio discussion	5	9	3	2	14	/
Total N	222	216	325	285	372	201

(Adapted from Cushion, Aalberg and Thomas 2014)

the significance of anchors in the US is represented in the title of bulletins, where the presenters are name-checked. So, for example, the titles of the US evening bulletins included NBC *Nightly News with Brian Williams* and *ABC World News with Diane Sawyer.* In the UK and Norway, by contrast, the titles reflected the more serious public service face of each broadcaster with generic titles such as the *BBC Six O'Clock News* (known from 2008 as *BBC News at Six*).

The contrasting use of reporter packages and anchors in television bulletins meant edited news was conveyed differently cross-nationally. Likewise, the conventions used in live reporting were also different between nations and, in the case of Norway, between the public and commercial public broadcaster. In the UK most live news was devoted to either live reporters or two-ways between anchor and reporter (11 per cent on BBC and 14 per cent on ITV). In the US and on NRK – the Norwegian public service broadcaster – live news was conveyed to a greater degree within the studio by either reporters or guests discussing a story with the anchor. TV2, by comparison, stood out as the most distinctive because reporting was overwhelmingly dominated by reporter packages (81 per cent) with little time dedicated to live two-ways and no studio discussions. In short, live reporting informed evening television news bulletins to different degrees cross-nationally.

But the prominence of live reporting was perhaps strikingly on display in headline stories, typically reserved for the most important items of the day. As Table 4.2 indicates, although reporter packages and anchor only conventions remained the most used types of journalistic interventions to report headline stories by most broadcasters – notably in Norway – live coverage played a significant role in the UK and US especially.

Live reporting on NBC and the BBC, for example, represented close to half (47 per cent) and precisely a third of all headline items respectively. This was all the more striking on NBC because it dedicated relatively little time overall to

Table 4.2 Percentage use of journalistic interventions in headline news items in US, UK and Norwegian television news bulletins in 2012 (by frequency)

	US		UK		Norway	
	NBC	ABC	BBC	ITV	NRK	TV2
Pre-edited news						
Reporter package	24	28	29	33	33	56
Combined anchor only, image and package	29	31	38	46	54	41
Live news						
Combined reporter/anchor two-way,reporter live	26	13	24	18	7	4
Anchor/reporter discussion, studio discussion	21	28	9	3	6	/
Total N	42	32	63	55	46	27

(Adapted from Cushion, Aalberg and Thomas 2014)

live news – just 6 per cent on two-ways compared to 26 per cent of live headline items, a greater prominence granted to reporter packages. It could thus be concluded that, with the exception of Norwegian bulletins, live news was used in particular to punctuate the opening story of evening bulletins. That live conventions were used to convey the most significant story of the day in the UK and US arguably represents the editorial importance of immediacy in fixed time evening bulletins.

While the prominence of live news has been established so far, attention now turns to assessing the value of these types of conventions. The same four categories used to interpret the value of live news interventions in previous chapters is drawn upon to compare evening bulletins cross-nationally. To recap, these include whether the primary aim was to introduce an edited package, to deliver a live update, to be out on location or to interpret the significance of a news story. Because TV2 reported relatively few live items it was excluded from this part of the analysis.

Table 4.3 clearly shows that, apart from the BBC to some degree, on location reporting was not the principle reason for 'going live' in evening bulletins

Table 4.3 Percentage of the primary purpose of journalistic interventions in live reporting in UK, US and Norwegian television news bulletins in 2012 (by frequency)

	US		UK		Norway
	NBC	ABC	BBC	ITV	NRK
Interpretive	49	26	56	69	43
Latest news	18	28	12	17	35
General introduction / Summary to reporter package	33	46	25	14	22
On location	/	/	7		/
Total N	40	46	59	49	40

(Adapted from Cushion, Aalberg and Thomas 2014)

cross-nationally. It was only the BBC which stressed the locale of a live journalist, such as a reporter being sent to Derby after a house fire had killed five children. Of course, a reporter live on location not only generates a semiotic display of immediacy, it can help journalists in the field investigate or contextualize the latest twist to a story or issue. While over half the time journalists in the UK reported from the capital, most of the nations and the regions had a live reporter over the two weeks examined. There were also five international live two-ways. Like the UK, half of the US's live reporters on location were based in the capital, but only a handful of states were represented and three international stories covered. Norway, by contrast, had less than a quarter of its stories reported live from the capital, but contained 10 international two-way exchanges (all but one on NRK). In short, the use of live on location reporters appears to vary cross-nationally rather than between media systems.

Beyond the lack of location reporting, however, there were some distinct differences between nations and broadcasters in the use of live news. In the US, for example, live news was used to the largest extent to introduce or conclude a reporter package (representing close to a third of items on NBC compared to almost a half on ABC). Another role journalists occupied during live television news was bringing the 'latest news' to a bulletin. This would typically be in the form of an update to an event or issue, focusing on any new developments that might have occurred since an edited package had been filed or when a bulletin began broadcasting. The study found over a third of live news sought to bring an update to a story on NRK (35 per cent) and just over a quarter (28 per cent) on NBC. But the most prominent purpose of live news was to provide some degree of interpretation to a story, most notably in the world of politics or business. With the exception of ABC news in the US, being interpretive was the dominant purpose of live reporting, in particular in the UK (56 per cent on the BBC and 69 per cent on ITV). Overall, then, live news contained a high degree of interpretation – strikingly so in the UK – but it also included a steady stream of live updates. In the US most distinctively, live news reporting was used to introduce or summarize a news story.

Since it has already been established that different interventions cast journalists in a variety of roles – whether introducing or reporting an issue or event, updating a story or interpreting the day's action – it is important to establish the credentials of a journalist operating in these different contexts. As journalists might have to deliver immediate judgements about a particular story or event, it could be anticipated that in live reporting they might be assigned an editorial title that demonstrates their relative expertise. After all, in lengthy two-way exchanges reporters not only need to sound knowledgeable, they need to appear authoritative whilst reacting to live news 'on-air'.

While journalists were not always given a title in a news item, when a *reporter* was named they were categorized according to how they were introduced. This created three categories: whether they were named as a 1) reporter generally, without any apparent expertise, 2) by area, where the reporter's title was determined by some geographical reference such as "our Scotland corre-spondent" or "Middle Eastern correspondent" and 3) by topic, where the reporter's title referenced a specialism such as "Home Affairs Correspondent" or "Foreign Correspondent".

In reporter packages, US journalists were always introduced by a topic spe-cialism, rather than by any geographical attachment. This was nearly always the case in the UK too (in over 9 in 10 items). By contrast, Norway over-whelmingly labelled journalists filing edited packages as a "reporter" and only occasionally as area specialists but seldom by any topic reference. In live reporting no US journalist had any apparent geographic expertise, but in a handful of UK items they were identified as being an area specialist. Instead, in live news in the UK and US – where reporters were often used to interpret the news (see Table 4.3) – journalists were more often cast as holding specialist knowledge in a wide range of topics (see Table 4.4).

By specifically identifying journalists with an expertise – whether a crime correspondent or a political editor – during television news bulletins in the UK

Table 4.4 The reporter titles used in live US, UK and Norwegian television news bulletins

US (NBC and ABC)	UK (BBC and ITV)	Norway (NRK and TV2)
Political Correspondent	Political Editor	Political editor
Senior Political Correspondent	Crime Correspondent	Political Correspondent
Medical Editor	UK Editor	Senior Political Correspondent
Chief Investigative Correspondent	Political Correspondent	Sports reporter
Senior White House Correspondent	Senior Political Correspondent	Our correspondent
Senior National Correspondent	Sports reporter	News Correspondent
Chief White House Correspondent	Business Editor	Senior News Correspondent
Chief Medical Editor	"Our" correspondent	
National Security Analyst	News Correspondent	
Senior Foreign Correspondent	Senior News Correspondent	
Chief Foreign Affairs Correspondent	Security Correspondent	
Justice Correspondent	Social Affairs Editor	
Chief Science Correspondent	Scotland Correspondent	
Chief Political Correspondent	Business Correspondent	
White House Correspondent	Sports Correspondent	
Chief Foreign Correspondent	Medical Correspondent	
	Sports Editor	
	Europe Editor	
	Wales Correspondent	
	Arts Editor	
	Social Affairs Correspondent	

Table 4.5 Percentage use of titled reporters in all news and live news conventions in US and UK television news bulletins (by frequency and time)

	US		UK	
	NBC	ABC	BBC	ITV
Time spent by titled reporter as percentage of all news	21	20	51	55
N (number of titled reporter contributions in all news)	39	37	72	61
Time spent by titled reporter as percentage of live news	60	40	80	79
N (number of titled reporter contributions in live news)	23	20	31	22

and US, the aim could be to highlight the significant role they played not only in reporting the news but reacting to it whilst live 'on-air'.

This is not to suggest Norwegian journalists held less expertise than those of the other countries, but that UK and US news bulletins decided to signify some degree of knowledge in a reporter's title, most prominently during live television news reporting. While it might be expected that expert reporters would play a prominent role in reacting to news on-air, perhaps not to the degree identified in live news compared to all news output (see Table 4.5).[1]

The next section takes a closer look at evening bulletins in the US and UK, considering in more detail the form, structure and style of different journalistic interventions. It will then more specifically examine political reporting. In doing so, the aim is to explore the degree to which politics is mediatized between both nations and broadcasters operating with different market pressures and public service obligations. But it also moves beyond examining types of journalistic interventions used to routinely shape bulletins in order to explore the mediatization of politics in more detail. In particular, the focus will be on exploring the extent to which journalists intervene and interpret routine reporting of politics compared with how far politicians appear and shape coverage. A comparative content analysis of US and UK evening bulletins will examine mediatization measures well established in the literature, including the degree of soundbites and imagebites informing coverage, along with how far journalists use "lip flaps" or "wrap up" political stories (Grabe and Bucy 2009; Esser 2008; Strömbäck and Dimitrova 2011).

Comparing levels of mediatization in television journalism: political reporting in US and UK evening news bulletins

The contrasting media and political environments in the UK and US offer an interesting perspective from which to explore how far this shapes the degree of mediatization in evening television news bulletins. Freed from the same degree of regulatory oversight many European journalists have grown up with, historically US reporters have been associated with being more independent and interventionist in their approach to journalism. Schudson (2001) has argued the US adopted a distinctive professionalized approach to journalism in the nineteenth and twentieth centuries, developing an objectivity norm that, for example, was shaped by different economic, social and political forces compared to much of Europe.

At the same time, Schudson (2001: 167) identified the UK as a "kind of halfway house between American professionalism and continental traditions of party-governed journalism". Indeed, several scholars have observed an Anglo-American tradition of journalism, notably in developing a more adversarial relationship with political parties compared to other European countries, such as France (Chalaby 1996; Hallin and Mancini 2004). Hence, for example, Hallin and Mancini's (2004) three models of Western media systems classified the US and UK together, since both countries have a robust private media culture operating independently from political interference. UK broadcasters, nonetheless, have also been influenced by government intervention, operating with specific public service obligations and long-held impartiality requirements. The US, by contrast, withdrew its impartiality requirements for broadcasters in 1987 and, decades on, many cable news channels have become increasingly partisan in their approach to journalism. Arguably, however, it is the US where journalists have increasingly displayed their independence by moving from a factual to more interpretive approach to news reporting. Longitudinal studies have shown US journalism in particular has become increasingly interpretive over successive decades (Esser and Umbricht 2014; Fink and Schudson 2013; Steele and Barnhurst 1996).

As a consequence, the US is often considered one of the most mediatized nations, comparatively displaying the most interventionist approach to political reporting. This is reflected in recent comparative studies examining news coverage of elections. So, for example (as Chapter 3 acknowledged) Esser's 2008 content analysis study of election reporting on television bulletins with a mixture of public service broadcasting obligations and commercial pressures in the US, UK, Germany and France drew on a range of mediatized measures – including soundbites and imagebites as well as the visibility of journalists – to evaluate how far politicians informed campaign coverage as opposed to reporters talking over them. Bulletins with the strongest public service broadcasting influence granted politicians the most time to air their views, with the longest average soundbites whereas the most market-driven bulletins – in the US – recorded the least. Conversely, imagebites – where political actors appear but are not necessarily heard – were the most prevalent on the commercial US television bulletins. This, Esser argued, reflected journalists intervening in political coverage more forcefully, rather than letting politicians talk for themselves. He concluded that overall the findings represented "a strongly interventionist U.S. American approach" to political journalism compared to "a moderately interventionist Anglo-German approach, and a noninterventionist French approach" (Esser 2008: 401).

The specific sample of television news drawn upon in this section includes ABC's and CBS's 6.30pm bulletins in the US and Channel 5's 5pm, BBC's 6pm and ITV's 6.30pm bulletins in the UK during three weeks in April and May 2013 (weekdays only). As acknowledged at the beginning of this chapter, the research design aimed to build on the greater emphasis on comparative communication research in recent years (Esser and Hanitzsch 2012). But this section not only develops a comparative dimension between the US and UK but also within the UK's sample due to the hybrid public-commercial broadcast ecology. As the chapter began by explaining, while all UK broadcasters have to abide by due impartiality requirements, the three bulletins examined – the BBC, ITV and Channel 5 – have different levels of public service broadcasting responsibilities. The BBC is a wholesale public service broadcaster and has substantial regulatory obligations overseen by the BBC Trust. In the US, ABC and CBS do not have any public service broadcasting duties. ITV and Channel 5 in the UK, however, are commercial public service broadcasters subject to regulatory conditions policed by Ofcom. Within the specific licence agreements of both broadcasters, there are some subtle but significant differences in respect of delivering news programming. While ITV has held long-standing public service obligations in the supply of local and national news at peak time, Channel 5 is a relatively new broadcaster (launched in 1997) and does not attract as many viewers. It could therefore be argued that Channel 5 has fewer public service broadcasting expectations than ITV, with regulators more relaxed about its programming style and influence over viewers. Over successive decades the channel has experimented with its style of journalism, adopting a tabloid format and softer news agenda compared to other terrestrial broadcasters (Barnett et al. 2012). In other words, Channel 5 is perhaps most similar to the US network bulletins, whereas ITV is more closely scrutinized as a public service broadcast provider. The section can thus explore whether – as previous studies have suggested – the most commercially driven bulletins supply the most mediatized coverage of politics.

Analysing news by the different types of journalistic interventions introduced throughout the book, this final part of the chapter draws on a study examining 946 US and UK news items (Cushion, Roger and Lewis 2014). However, if an intervention related to a political news item – which included local, national and international news stories – it was examined more closely and according to a number of mediatized measures. The length of soundbites and imagebites was recorded, for example, to assess how far politicians shaped coverage. The role of journalists was also examined, quantifying how visible they were in political items, whether they spoke over a politician – what is called a "lip flap" (Grabe and Bucy 2009) – if they concluded a story (known as a 'wrap up') and if they interpreted politics rather than conveyed a more fact-based approach. As previously acknowledged in Chapter 3, these have become well-established measures in empirical studies exploring the mediatization of politics because they indicate the degree to which a journalist intervenes in coverage. Put differently, these measures help compare how far a media or a political logic shapes UK and US television news operating under different levels of regulatory oversight.

Comparing the structure, form and style of television news bulletins in the US and UK

Edited reporter packages were clearly the most dominant television news convention in both the UK and US evening bulletins (see Table 4.6) – consistent with the pattern of findings earlier in the chapter and in the longitudinal data (in Chapters 2 and 3). The most striking differences between countries was in the time dedicated to live reporting. All UK bulletins reported live to a greater degree than the US networks. In the US greater emphasis was placed on television news anchors, with presenters on screen longer. As previously acknowledged, the personality-led bulletins in the US contrasted with the traditionally more neutral role adopted by anchors on UK television. Channel 5 – the channel with the least public service obligations – was the most similar to the commercially driven US bulletins, since news anchors had a greater role than on the BBC and ITV bulletins and marginally less time was granted to reporter packages.

The differences between US and UK bulletins become more apparent when the form and structure of conventions are more closely compared. So, for

Table 4.6 Percentage use of journalistic interventions and mean length (M) in US and UK television news bulletins in 2013 (by time)

	US		UK		
	ABC	CBS	BBC	ITV	Ch. 5
Edited					
Anchor	14.1%	8.9%	4%	3.7%	6.2%
	M = 31 secs	M = 27 secs	M = 22 secs	M = 19 secs	M = 24 secs
Reporter package	74.9%	75%	79.8%	78.2%	77.1%
	M = 1 m, 10 secs	M = 1 m, 14 secs	M = 2 m, 36 secs	M = 2 m, 25 secs	M = 1 m, 27 secs
Live					
Anchor/reporter two-way	7.2%	11.9%	11.7%	10%	14%
	M = 37 secs	M = 31 secs	M = 59 secs	M = 1 m, 15 secs	M = 50 secs
Live location	0.4%	0.1%	1.8%	2.4%	1.7%
	M = 28 secs	M = 9 secs	M = 1 m, 7 secs	M = 37 secs	M = 53 secs
Anchor/reporter studio	3.5%	3.9%	2.7%	5.7%	1%
	M = 26 secs	M = 54 secs	M = 1 m, 23 secs	M = 1 m, 34 secs	M = 55 secs
Total N	215	223	177	149	182

(Adapted from Cushion, Roger and Lewis 2014)

example, whilst the average mean length of a journalistic intervention is 1 minute and 12 seconds, in the UK it is 1 minute and 38 seconds. Conventions on the most commercially driven bulletins have shorter mean averages (ABC = 1 minute and 10 seconds, CBS = 1 minute and 15 seconds and Channel 5 = 1 minute and 29 seconds) than the more public service orientated broadcasters (ITV = 1 minute and 41 seconds and BBC = 1 minute and 45 seconds). Needless to say, the average length of conventions helps shape the form and structure of different journalistic interventions. As Table 4.6 indicates, the length of reporter packages was far longer on bulletins with the most public service obligations (BBC = 2 minutes and 36 seconds, ITV = 2 minutes and 25 seconds) compared to less than 90 seconds on the more commercially driven channels (ABC, CBS and Channel 5). Similarly, live two-ways lasted considerably longer on UK bulletins (BBC = 59 seconds, ITV 1 minute and 15 seconds and Channel 5 = 50 seconds) than their US counterparts (ABC = 37 seconds and CBS = 31 seconds).

While the form and structure of US and UK television of *all news* was different, the focus now turns specifically to political news. Figures 4.1–5 show the types of journalistic interventions used in political items in comparison to non-political reporting.

In the UK the average length of political reporting was longer than in non-political items (lasting 1 minute and 55 seconds compared to 1 minute and 25 seconds). Journalistic interventions in Channel 5's political reporting, however, were less than the UK average (1 minute and 35 seconds) compared to ITV (2 minutes and 7 seconds) and BBC news (2 minutes and 6 seconds). US political news was exactly the same as the length of news generally (1 minute and 15 seconds). Channel 5, in short, appears to most resemble the length of US political news reporting. A trend shared across both countries, however, was in live reporting (see Figures 4.1–4.5), which increased substantially in political reporting. All bulletins aired more live reporting in political stories than in non-politics items. Indeed, three bulletins – ABC, BBC and Channel 5 – routinely featured live news in their headline items. Live political reporting, in other words, regularly played a prominent role in communicating the top stories of the day on both US and UK bulletins.

The chapter now moves beyond journalistic interventions to explore alternative ways of interpreting the degree of mediatization in political reporting in different countries and between media systems. In doing so, it examines how far news featured the views and images of politicians as opposed to journalists. This analysis relates to edited news only – principally reporter packages – since live bulletins rarely contain on screen sources. UK bulletins (1.7–1.8 per item), on average, had a higher ratio of on screen sources than their US counterparts (1.2–1.4 per item). They were also much more likely to feature a source (ITV = 65.5 per cent, BBC = 57.6 per cent and Channel 5 = 50 per cent of items), compared to the US networks (ABC = 43.1 per cent and CBS = 42.7 per cent of items). Overall, then, the views of politicians were heard to a greater extent on the UK's most public service orientated bulletins.

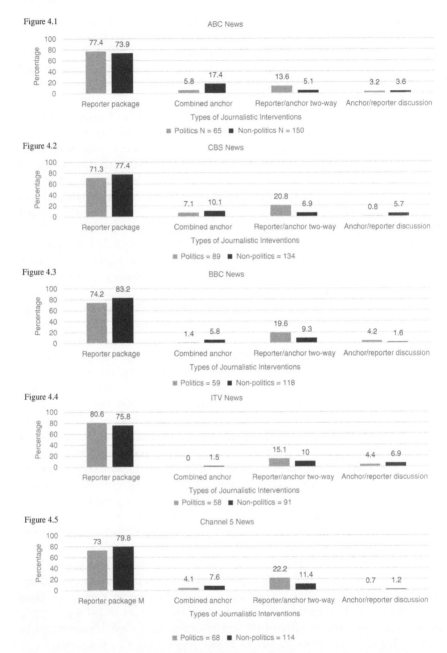

Figure 4.1 — ABC News

Figure 4.2 — CBS News

Figure 4.3 — BBC News

Figure 4.4 — ITV News

Figure 4.5 — Channel 5 News

Figures 4.1 to 4.5 Percentage use of journalistic interventions in US and UK television
bulletins in political and non-political news items in 2013 (by time)
(Adapted from Cushion, Roger and Lewis 2014)

As Chapter 3 explored, the average length of soundbites in political coverage has also become a familiar measure used in mediatization of politics studies. For this indicator empirically reveals the relative time granted to politicians when politics is reported. Rather than just include the views of politicians, however, all sources were examined. Political actors, nonetheless, were overwhelmingly the dominant source drawn upon in routine reporting (as Chapter 5 explores in detail). The mean average length of soundbites was the shortest on US bulletins (just 7 seconds on ABC and 10 seconds on CBS) whereas they were slightly longer on the UK's commercial public service broadcasters (14 seconds on both ITV and Channel 5). The wholesale public service broadcaster – the BBC – had the longest soundbite at 16 seconds.

The comparative study further examined the visual representation of politicians appearing in coverage but not necessarily speaking on camera. This, as already acknowledged, has become known as an imagebite (Grabe and Bucy 2009), a measure used to convey the mediatization of political news because journalists speak over political actors rather than allowing them to speak for themselves. Again, this analysis extends to reporter packages rather than live reporting, since imagebites represent clips of politicians integrated into edited news packages. Contrary to expectations, it was the bulletins with the most public service obligations – BBC and ITV – that had the longest mean imagebite in the UK (13 and 11 seconds respectively), with Channel 5 the shortest (9 seconds). However, imagebites in the US were on average even shorter at just 6 seconds on both ABC and CBS. Overall, imagebites were used far less than soundbites – in about a third or less for most broadcasters (30.3 per cent of CBS items, 30.9 per cent of Channel 5 items, 32.2 per cent of BBC items, 33.8 per cent of ABC items) while ITV featured one in 44.8 per cent of its items.

Moving from political to media actors, how far journalists appeared and shaped coverage of politics in US and UK evening bulletins was also examined. As Chapter 3 explained, this measure can indicate how journalist-centred routine coverage of politics is between broadcasters and different countries. So, for example, the use of "lip flaps" was quantified – when journalists talk over a politician, such as during a speech to the UN – which is seen as an interventionist approach to reporting politics (Grabe and Bucy 2009). Journalists, in other words, interpret rather than source political actors directly. Lip flaps occurred in less than a third of political news items – ABC (32.3 per cent), BBC (32.3 per cent), CBS (31.5 per cent) and Channel 5 (29.4 per cent) – with the exception of ITV (36.2 per cent). While a UK broadcaster lip-flapped to a greater extent than either US channel, the difference between bulletins was marginal. However, the visibility of journalists – when they appeared on camera presenting a news story – was different between broadcasters. In the US journalists were visible in over half of political items on ABC (53.7 per cent) and close to a third on CBS (37.3 per cent). Channel 5, meanwhile, had the least visual presence of journalists (31.7 per cent). It was bulletins with the strongest public service broadcasting obligations – BBC and ITV – that featured journalists the most (66.7 per cent and 69.8 per cent respectively). Moreover, UK journalists on average appeared on screen (BBC = 18 seconds, ITV = 16 seconds and Channel 5 = 21 seconds) to a greater extent than in the US (CBS = 13 seconds and ABC = 11 seconds). It can thus be concluded that US journalists – widely considered the most interventionist cross-nationally – were the least visible in routine political reporting. As previously acknowledged, this could partly be a consequence of the much shorter length of political items in the US by comparison with the UK. However, the paucity of time is not a factor in how reporters sign off a political news story. This is known as a "wrap up" – another measure of mediatization (Strömbäck and Dimitrova 2011) – asking whether a journalist or a politician has the final say at the end of a package. Rather than US journalists intervening in routine political stories – as previous studies have suggested – UK reporters wrapped up news more often. So, for example, 86.1 per cent of political news items were wrapped up on the BBC, 92.7 per cent on Channel 5 and, on ITV, every story was. In the US journalists wrapped up less news overall, 73.2 per cent of items on ABC compared to 68.6 per cent on CBS.

The mediatization of politics measures so far have focused primarily on edited news. But there were also differences in the degree of journalistic interventionism in live reporting. The same framework for analysing the purpose of live news – as explored earlier in the chapter – was drawn upon to ascertain the comparative extent of interpretive reporting. The findings reinforced previous trends, such as the insignificance of the location/backdrop of live television news reporting. Overall, political news was interpreted to a greater degree on the most public service broadcast orientated bulletins (see Table 4.7).

A striking difference in the reporting of live political news between broadcasters was the length of items when journalists were interpretive. For US reporters were given, on average, just 38 seconds (ABC) or 31 seconds (CBS) to interpret a political story. By contrast, the broadcasters with the strongest public service obligations were given greater time to offer their interpretation to a story (BBC = 1 minute and 24 seconds, ITV = 1 minute and 22 seconds and Channel 5 = 45 seconds). The next chapter puts live reporting – in particular

Table 4.7 Percentage of the primary purpose of journalistic interventions in live political reporting in UK and US television news bulletins in 2013 (by frequency)

	US		UK		
	ABC	CBS	BBC	ITV	Ch. 5
Interpretation	41.7	38.9	47.6	52.9	30.8
Latest news	16.7	22.2	23.8	23.5	23.1
General intro. / Summary	41.7	38.9	28.6	23.5	42.3
On location	/	/	/	/	3.8

(Adapted from Cushion, Roger and Lewis 2014)

two-ways – into a sharper focus, providing a close textual exploration of how politics is reported using this convention compared to edited news.

The influence of 24-hour news culture: towards a rolling news logic in evening bulletins

The aim at the beginning of this chapter was to explore how far the practices and conventions of rolling news had influenced the type of journalism on display in evening bulletins between different nations, cultures and media systems. Consistent with previous chapters examining UK television news, reporter packages remained the dominant convention of television evening bulletins. However, live news was used not only to different degrees between nations, its very purpose was somewhat distinctive.

Needless to say, financial resources play a significant role in the type of journalistic interventions employed by different broadcasters. After all, interventions that involve journalists out in the field, in far-flung locations, with satellite equipment facilitating two-ways between anchor and reporter, are highly costly interventions. But even covering 'the nation' can be difficult, particularly for the US, which is far bigger geographically than either Norway or the UK. Beyond the confines of the studio, then, it is an expensive business to fund television journalists and journalism. This perhaps explains why US broadcasters, on average, were the least likely to invest resources in either pre-packaged reports or in two-ways internationally than either Norway or the UK. However, financial resources alone cannot interpret cross-national differences, since there was no fixed pattern among commercial broadcasters of avoiding either edited packages or live news.

Nonetheless, there were some distinct characteristics in television journalism between different nations. In the most market-driven media system, US network television relied most heavily on news anchors to present stand-alone items. This was not only represented in the titles of their respective bulletins – with the names of presenters – but also in the more informal mode of address that stamped the personality of the anchor on the programme. Unlike in the UK and Norway, the newsreader acted on occasions as both a newsreader and a reporter. This can perhaps be seen to reflect the liberal model of American journalism, representing the more commercialized and less regulated landscape than Norway's corporatist model (Hallin and Mancini 2004). Indeed, the US bulletins have the freedom to comment and interpret coverage, whereas both UK and Norway have strict broadcasting impartiality requirements. This perhaps also explains the level of interpretive journalism in live journalistic interventions on US television news bulletins.

However, it was UK television news bulletins – most strikingly in two-ways – that had the most interpretive live reporters. UK journalists, in other words, routinely interpreted news stories – most notably in the world of politics – in spite of the strict impartiality requirements policing broadcasters. In the US and UK especially, the emphasis of reporters interpreting news live was reflected in the wide range of job titles they occupied – from political, justice and crime correspondents to medical, business and sport editors. Norwegian television news, by contrast, stuck primarily with the title 'reporter' – not a symbol of inferior knowledge but perhaps an indication of the less interpretive role they are expected to fulfil in live coverage. Moreover, it arguably represents a broader reluctance to inject the same level of immediacy in news conventions or send journalists out to report live compared to US and UK news bulletins. For the significance of reporters acting in a live capacity out on location (except in Norway) increased in headline stories – emphasizing the importance placed on conveying immediacy at the beginning of a bulletin. Indeed, in assessing the value of live news conventions, delivering the 'latest news' was a key function of live reporters.

In order to understand the higher degree of journalistic interventionism in US and UK reporting – beyond the role of political journalists – the presence and influence of rolling news culture within each country needs to be considered. For whereas Norway did not have a dedicated 24-hour news channel operating until 2007, in both the US and UK – as acknowledged at the beginning of the chapter – rolling news channels have been operating since well before the new millennium. CNN, the world's first rolling news channel, was launched in 1980 and into the 1990s many other cable news channels began broadcasting (Cushion 2010). Sky News in the UK was the first European 24-hour news channel, launched in 1989, followed by the BBC's eight years later. Today there are many dedicated news channels operating in the UK. In other words, rolling news culture has been a feature of US and UK television journalism for several decades. In Norway just TV2 has a 24-hour news station, with NRK running a news and current affairs channel, rather than a continuous rolling news service.

Since 24-hour news culture is not as familiar to Norwegian television journalism as it is to the US and UK, this could explain why its evening bulletins were not shaped to the degree by the kind of conventions routinely displayed on rolling news channels. Of course, while international news channels are available – from CNNI to BBC World – this does not necessarily impact on the editorial routines of Norwegian journalists working on NRK and TV2. Although TV2 has recently launched a 24-hour news channel, an ethnographic study of its newsroom suggested there was a lack of convergence between the production of bulletins and the rolling news service (Lund 2012). As TV2's 24-hour news channel evolves it could be that journalists integrate more fluidly between bulletins and rolling news channels, impacting on the types of interventions produced. The BBC by comparison has – from March 2013, as Chapter 1 explained – converged the production of much of its output into a large newsroom based in London in order to integrate its services not just on the medium of television but in other media such as online.

The conclusions of this cross-national study thus suggest the wider culture of 24-hour news journalism could be having a systemic impact on the interventions made on fixed television bulletins. For it appears television news bulletins in the US and UK especially are beginning to structure and shape their journalistic interventions to keep pace with rival rolling news formats (in television but also online) by using more immediate forms of communication. In the UK and US, then, this enhanced use of live reporting arguably represents a greater degree of mediatization – fuelled by the domestic culture of rolling news journalism – compared to Norwegian news bulletins.

A closer examination of journalistic interventions generally and political news reporting particularly on UK and US evening bulletins revealed not only cross-national differences between media systems. The commercially driven stations had a different form, structure and style of television journalism compared to bulletins with the strongest public service broadcasting obligations. Of course, this is partly a consequence of advertisements that mean commercial bulletins were shorter in length. As a consequence, reporter packages in the UK were considerably longer than in the US, which meant a greater range of actors could be drawn upon (both in soundbites and imagebites). While the UK had more airtime to broadcast more stories, interestingly they did not cover many more stories than US bulletins. Instead they chose – in particular the BBC and ITV – to report stories for longer and arguably in greater depth (with sources informing coverage to a greater extent) than in the US. This perhaps suggests the commercial necessity to run advertisements does not necessarily mitigate the possibility of in-depth journalism. US bulletins, in other words, could have aired fewer stories and covered them for longer with more sources shaping coverage.

The comparative study also established UK journalists acted as sources to a greater extent in political reporting than in US bulletins. In doing so, the more interventionist characterization of US journalists compared to other developed countries in previous academic studies (Esser 2008; Schudson 2001) has arguably been challenged. For the UK exhibited – according to a range of mediatized measures – a more interventionist approach to routine reporting of politics than US bulletins. Moreover, contrary to commercialization enhancing the mediatization of politics it was the bulletins with the strongest public service broadcasting responsibilities that displayed a more interventionist approach to journalism. UK political journalists "wrapped up" stories to a greater degree than in the US – where they have the final say in a package, rather than a politician – were more visible on screen, and relied to a greater extent on "lip flaps" and imagebites. Of course, the more general study of bulletins in Norway, the UK and US identified the interpretive nature of journalism in the latter two countries. But the final part of the chapter's closer examination of political reporting highlighted that the UK's public service broadcasters were the most interpretive in spite of operating under strict impartiality requirements.

This chapter's overall findings have important consequences for debates about the mediatization of politics cross-nationally and between media systems.

As previous chapters have discussed, academic theorizing about the likely cause of mediatization in political news has generally been associated with the pressures of commercialization. However, this chapter's cross-national study reinforced the findings of Chapters 2 and 3 and discovered it was bulletins on the UK's public service broadcasters – not the market-driven US stations – that supplied the most mediatized political content. Moreover, the evidence suggested political reporting was mediatized to a greater degree by bulletins with the strongest public service obligations. For it was Channel 5 – the station with the fewest public service responsibilities – that was the least mediatized in the UK, according to range of measures. Indeed, the form, structure and style of Channel 5 was most similar to US network bulletins. This chapter's findings thus strike a chord with Strömbäck and Dimitrova's (2011: 42) comparative study of US and Swedish election television news, which concluded that "media commercialism may be moderated by national journalism cultures and national political news or political communication cultures". As the cross-national study drawn upon in the first part of the chapter discovered, the national culture of rolling news has arguably had a systemic impact on US and UK evening bulletins. But more specifically about political reporting, the moderation of national journalism in the UK arguably relates to the broader culture of fulfilling public service broadcasting objectives. For the BBC and ITV especially chose to cover politics in live formats with journalists supplying the most interpretive style of reporting.

The next chapter examines more closely the role of live two-ways generally and in political news especially in television news bulletins. As the longitudinal studies identified in Chapters 2 and 3 revealed, live news has risen steadily into the new millennium on evening bulletins and plays a prominent part in reporting routine political coverage. It is thus necessary to examine the value of live two-ways more closely, considering how this form and style of journalism interprets the world of politics in television news bulletins.

Note

1 Since the figures were so low for Norway, NRK and TV2 have been excluded from Table 4.5.

Chapter 5

The rise of live news and the two-way convention

Evaluating the value of journalistic interventionism

Introduction

When television began all broadcasting was live (Marriott 2007). Without the ability to record a programme in advance or pre-edit material, when audiences turned on the TV set they were sharing the experience of watching television in 'real time' (Crisell 2012). As technology improved, gradually television schedules began to be filled by pre-filmed programming, such as soap operas or game shows. Into the 21st century, live broadcasting continues to be a prominent part of television culture. But in popular programming it tends to be reserved for particular types of television programming, including breakfast shows, sporting events and weather bulletins. Or, on special occasions – to mark an anniversary, say, or celebrate a season finale – programmes are broadcast in 'real time', using the novelty of liveness to deliver a tension and edginess. In the last season of *The West Wing*, for example, a live episode of a televised presidential debate was broadcast, a fictional attempt to recreate the 'real time' political pressure candidates face in reality.

News, however, is a distinctive television genre (Ellis 2000), driven by a long-standing editorial aim of delivering the latest news headlines. Indeed, Ofcom – the commercial regulator of UK television news – requires broadcasters to air news live and only in exceptional circumstances to pre-record bulletins.[1] Television news, in other words, is almost always presented in a live format so it has the *potential* to deliver the latest news or break news 'on air'. Famously, for example, news about the shooting of US President John F. Kennedy in 1962 interrupted the routine schedule of the US networks. Or, more recently, US networks captured the terrorist attacks in 2001 live when a second plane crashed into the Twin Towers.

But these atypical moments do not represent the routine day-to-day delivery of news in fixed time bulletins. As Chapter 1 explained, the evening bulletin – the object of study in this book – increasingly relied on pre-edited conventions as television news matured from the 1960s onwards. For technology allowed pre-filmed packages to be juxtaposed with the presentation of live news in a studio format. By the 1990s it was the norm for evening bulletins to dedicate most of its coverage to pre-edited material. This was empirically confirmed in Chapter 2, where approximately 90–95 per cent of BBC and ITV bulletins in 1991/2 were reliant on edited packages to convey the day's news. Into the new millennium, however, pre-packaged news reduced and live reporting was enhanced both in volume and prominence (see Chapter 2). This was not due to any major breaking stories – say, a terrorist attack – but an editorial shift in routinely conveying news live principally by way of the two-way convention. As Chapter 3 explored further, the most striking use of live two-way reporting was in the world of politics, with journalists spending more airtime interpreting the day's events. As a consequence, television bulletins were less informed by political actors and more dependent on journalists routinely acting as sources. The cross-national study of UK, US and Norwegian television news – in Chapter 4 – suggested that live and interpretive political reporting shaped bulletins to different degrees based not only on the characteristics of different media systems but the broader influence of 24-hour news culture.

In short, in over 60 years of television's history, liveness has moved from being a technological necessity to a broadcasting novelty, with more recent years witnessing a resurgence in live television news reporting. Post-millennium it appears the accepted norm for evening bulletins to convey news in live conventions and for journalists to adopt a more interventionist style of political journalism.

The aim of this chapter is to therefore put the rise of the live two-way convention under closer empirical scrutiny and to consider the more interventionist role journalists have adopted in the reporting of politics. As the previous three chapters have argued, recent decades have witnessed what can be characterized as a mediatization of news – strikingly so in political reporting – where journalists more actively shape news stories, speaking for and about political actors. But while previous chapters have painted a broad quantitative picture about the rise and value of live two-way conventions, it is now necessary to consider more qualitatively the different ways in which the use of this convention shapes routine political reporting. The chapter will first begin by engaging with debates focused on understanding broadcast talk, where scholars close textually interpret the discourses shaping television news conventions and practices.

Understanding broadcast talk: scholarly readings of the live two-way convention

Writing in the 1990s, the linguist Norman Fairclough (1994: 235) coined the phrase "conversationalization" to characterize a shift in popular discourse where a more informal mode of address and 'ordinary' style was increasingly being embraced in contemporary media culture. This trend has since been applied to broadcast news, where – it is argued – the presentational aspects of journalism have changed to convey a more conversational style and mode of address (Hutchby 2006; Montgomery 2007; Tolson 2006). Montgomery's (2007) forensic analysis of television news, for example, deconstructed this increasingly spontaneous approach to reporting, picking apart the changing language and everyday conventions of broadcasting. Where once political actors were treated with great deference, today senior broadcast journalists adopt a more combative role, challenging – sometimes even snarling at – elected representatives. Leaving aside the watchdog role of the political interview, for Montgomery (2007: 181) this represents "a shift from narration to dramatization, in which what is dramatized is in part the making of the news itself but also in which a society or community can be seen in conversation with itself about matters of the moment". In other words, the interviewer adopts the role of an aggrieved 'ordinary' member of the public to engage viewers and informalize the conversation about politics.

But of most relevance to this chapter – and indeed the book – is Montgomery's (2007: 117–43) understanding of the live two-way convention. A binary table of oppositional features compares the live two-way with the more traditional form of news presentation (see Table 5.1), such as an anchor only item or reporter package (see Chapter 1).

In his words, "Overall, if the discourse of the news-reader is shaped and delivered under the constraint of 'doing factuality' (sounding objective and unbiased), the discourse of the live two-way is about 'doing being interesting' (sounding lively and engaging) in relation to facticity already established" (Montgomery 2007: 128). From this perspective, the rise of the live two-way convention in evening bulletins empirically demonstrated throughout the book represents a broader shift from a stuffy and formal world of broadcasting towards a more informalized and conversational culture of television journalism. But while previous chapters reinforce the view that two-ways signal a departure from conveying 'facts' towards delivering more interpretation, Montgomery (2007) leaves open the consequences of conveying news live rather than in an edited format. Whilst the newsreader's pursuit of "factuality" appears more laudable than the two-way's "'doing being interesting'", this does not arguably encapsulate the different degrees of interventionism displayed by

Table 5.1 A comparative schema of the live two-way and an edited news item

Live two-way	Edited news item
Unscripted	Scripted
Informality	Formality
Marked modality	Unmarked modality
Statements of possibility	Statements of fact
Interpretative (reaction/comment)	Descriptive
Personal voice	Institutional voice

(Adapted from Montgomery 2007)

journalists when reporting in different formats or subject areas. As Chapter 3 showed, live two-ways about politics – when isolated – were more interpretive than other topics reported. Moreover, Chapter 4 suggested the purpose of live news was comparatively different in evening bulletins between the UK, US and Norway. In the US, for example, live news was used to a greater extent to punctuate an edited reporter package – the donut convention – not necessarily to reinforce the factuality of a report. In short, to better understand the role of live two-ways the broadcaster and topic being reported needs to be considered.

Higgins and Smith (2012) explored the role of live two-ways during the 1991 Iraq War, a specific moment in time when the convention was not routinely drawn upon – as Chapter 2 established. But with the opportunity to exploit, for the first time, new satellite technology, bulletins could link live to correspondents in the 'thick of the action'. They specifically examined the reporting of the BBC's Kate Adie, a much celebrated war journalist, who was embedded with UK forces and could thus deliver two-ways from the 'front line'. In this context, Higgins and Smith (2012) suggested the live two-way convention was primarily employed to offer an 'insider' perspective from a UK standpoint, emphasizing the journalist's own involvement and experience with British forces. In their words:

> Adie was able to sustain her recorded reporting strategy of providing generalized narratives of 'readiness', the troops keen to 'get on with the job'. She demonstrates an authoritative knowledge of the daily lives of the troops – what they listen to on the radio. There are also particular sorts of claims to authenticity to her narratives, where she mentions her own participation in the air raid drills, and of course she is visually aligned with the embodied commitment of the armed forces through her camouflage clothing.
>
> (Higgins and Smith 2012: 216)

They further suggested an emotionality was attached to Adie's reporting, a more personalized narrative and understanding of the military conflict than perhaps a more conventional pre-packaged report would convey. It would appear, from this perspective, the broader military or diplomatic context to the war was thereby marginalized, arguably depoliticizing the involvement of UK forces. In other words, embedded two-way reporting is not ideologically neutral – as will be explored later in the chapter – and can limit how a journalist communicates a story and the wider context of it.

Tuggle and Huffman's (2001) analysis offers perhaps the most critical interpretation of live two-ways in routine television news coverage. As Chapter 2 acknowledged, their study examined the role of live coverage in 24 US local television news stations, questioning the very purpose of two-ways or reporters speaking to camera outside the studio (Tuggle and Huffman 2001). They considered this amounted to little more than "black hole" shots, a mostly vacuous form of journalism devoid of substance or significance (Tuggle and Huffman 2001: 335). They concluded that much of live news was "gratuitous with no apparent journalistic justification" (Tuggle and Huffman 2001: 342). Further still, they argued:

> There was no compelling news value associated with the live portion of nearly all the donuts [where a reporter introduces or wraps up an edited package], as no new information or video resulted from the presence of the news crew beyond what had been gathered earlier ... Stations may be using live for its promotional and production value rather than for its ability to get late-breaking information and video into their newscasts.
>
> (Tuggle and Huffman 2001: 342)

Questioning the value or authority of live reporters has become a familiar criticism of television journalism, although it is typically voiced in respect of conventions used by 24-hour news channels (MacGregor 1997), rather than evening bulletins. Cottle and Rai (2008: 163), for example, have observed that "[t]he pursuit of 'breaking news' as well as 'live two-ways' and 'hotel stand-ups' are professionally lamented ... by many within the industry who argue that these have become a poor substitute for in-depth reportage delivered by knowledgeable correspondents based in the field". But as suggested later in this chapter, it would be hard to apply this critique to the evening bulletins examined throughout this book. For a considerable degree of live reporting was delivered in evening bulletins by highly experienced political editors.

A high-profile moment involving a BBC correspondent in the run-up to the 2003 Iraq War prompted considerable debate about the journalistic merit of the live two-way convention. Andrew Gilligan, a military correspondent, famously – in a 6.07am broadcast on the *Today* show, a leading Radio 4 news programme – accused the Government of exaggerating claims Iraq could deploy WMD within 45 minutes. While the BBC robustly defended the broad facts behind the story after the Government vehemently complained, an inquiry later castigated the broadcaster's editorial oversight of the live two-way. Although the BBC's internal review found a general script of the live two-way had been cleared (following protocol), the casual and somewhat imprecise way Gilligan had broadcast the claims in the 6.07am broadcast – which just an hour later was more carefully worded – left the BBC wide open for criticism. As the then head of BBC News, Richard Sambrook (2004: 12–13), has since conceded:

> *Today* set out to broadcast a report about genuine and, as we now know, well-founded reservations among parts of the intelligence community about the September 2002 Iraq dossier. That was the script which the programme approved. In a live interview Andrew Gilligan used a form of words which wrongly suggested bad faith on the part of the Government.

The BBC, concentrating on intending what it had intended to report, was slow to recognise the significance of this departure from the script.

The term "script" is loosely conceived here because – as Montgomery (2006) has argued – the two-way was also an interview, a more conversational form of news discourse that is distinctive from the more scripted conventions of edited packages. The inaccuracy of Gilligan's now notorious live two-way caused considerable commotion with the BBC – leading to its director general eventually resigning – and drawing critical attention to this convention in the reporting of politics.

Despite the many criticisms levelled at live two-ways, this book has shown so far that the convention – from the late 1990s into the new millennium – has become an increasingly prominent part of television evening news bulletins. Even Montgomery's (2006) suggestion that the BBC – post–Hutton Inquiry – might significantly downsize the reliance on two-ways has not materialized. As Chapters 2 and 3 evidenced, more than a decade into the 2000s the live two-way has not only become a routine part of bulletins but a prominent convention sometimes used to punctuate important headline stories. Far from being cowed from interpreting the world of politics, then, live two-ways continue to be selected by editors to convey and interpret everyday events and issues.

But the rise of interpretive journalism has been the subject of considerable criticism. It is argued that it pushes journalism away from the 'facts' towards more opinionated and instant forms of communication. This, as Chapter 3 acknowledged, has been voiced prominently by the political scientist Thomas Patterson. His critique is worth quoting at length:

> interpretive journalism thrusts the reporter into the role of analyst and judge. The journalist gives meaning to a news event by supplying the analytical context. The journalist is thus positioned to give shape to the news in a way that the descriptive style did not allow. The power of the journalist to construct the news is apparent from the extent to which journalistic voices now dominate the coverage. Whereas reporters were once the passive voice behind the news, they now get more time than the newsmakers they cover.
>
> (Patterson 2002)

In this context, Patterson's observations relate specifically to the reporting of presidential elections and not necessarily to all live news. But the evidence amassed in this book has suggested – to paraphrase Patterson – that the live two-way is a convention that thrusts a journalist into an interpretive position, where their own perspective (rather than external sources, such as a political actor) is central to the narrative. Moreover, it appears to promote a particular type of election news story, one – according to Patterson (2002) – that is negative and candidate-focused. For he suggests, "Interpretive reporting has unleashed the skepticism traditional in American journalism. The candidates' failings and disputes have been played up; their successes and overtures have been played down" (Patterson 2002). Seen from this perspective, the rise of interpretive news appears to be associated with a more commercialized turn in journalism where – echoing Tuggle and Huffman (2001) – reporters are used to inject excitement or drama into a story, commenting or speculating on the campaign itself rather than addressing more substantive issues. In other words, relying less on sources shaping political news and more on reporters interpreting it delivers – they argue – a less informative and more trivial form of journalism, primarily due to the focus on the process of politics, rather than addressing a more substantive policy or issue-based agenda.

However, while this might be the dominant critique of the rise of interpretive journalism (see Salgado *et al.* 2012), McNair (2000) offers a counterargument to this perspective, more positively understanding the shift from factual to a more opinionated and analytical culture of contemporary political news. According to McNair (2000: 61), this form of journalism represents the "*interpretive moment* in the news cycle" (his emphasis), "where evaluation of, and opinion about either the substance, the style, the policy content or the process of political affairs replaces the straight reportage of new information". Due to a new generation of politicians learning slick media-management skills over recent decades, employing specialized spin doctors, rapid rebuttal machinery and dealing with aggressive lines of questioning, McNair (2000) welcomes journalists responding to this professionalized turn in political communication (see also Blumler and Gurevitch 1995). Further still, he argues:

> We *need* the interpretive moment in journalism ... because the world is too complex, its information flows too rapid, for us to make sense of on our own. With the expansion of the public sphere ... interpretation has become an even more crucial element of the journalistic function, and nowhere more so than in coverage of political affairs.
>
> (McNair 2000: 82; his emphasis)

Whereas many commentators and scholars have argued the departure from fact-based journalism towards more opinionated forms journalism – such as the live two-way convention – represents a commercialized treatment of news and politics in particular, McNair (2000) suggests the opposite, since it offers a type of adversarialism consistent with traditional fourth estate goals. In other words, interpretive journalism challenges rather than accepts the views of the governing elite.

Needless to say, it is important not to over generalize how the rise of interpretive journalism is understood. It can, after all, represent many different types of journalism – from partisan opinions offered in tabloid newspapers to more impartial analysis of political affairs in broadsheet newspapers or by public service broadcasters. Understanding interpretive journalism, as Esser and Umbricht (2014) have argued, needs to be assessed by the specific format of news and, most importantly, its informational value, which can clearly differ between different media platforms and systems. Further still, interpretive news could also be more clearly defined – a sometimes difficult task when operationalized quantitatively – since the term can represent many subtle forms and styles of competing journalisms. As the analysis of previous studies offered by Salgado *et al.* (2012: 155) concluded, it is:

> important to acknowledge that there are different types of interpretive journalism. While in some cases, a public service orientation guides the jour-nalistic work, in others the journalist's personal style is more accentuated, or the news story is based on a more speculative approach … As the assess-ment of different kinds of interpretive journalism may vary, this is another argument why it is important that the concept per se is not normative.

The intention of this chapter is to make an evidence-based judgement about the normative value of interpretive journalism in political reporting by *focusing on this approach to news in the live two-way television convention*. It was, after all, the dominant function of 'going live' in both the longitudinal and cross-national content analysis studies drawn upon in the previous three chapters. But, as Salgado *et al.* (2012: 155) further noted, "it may be difficult to distinguish between different amounts of journalistic interpretation and explanation, and hence to achieve strong intercoder reliability". The aim therefore is to offer a more qualitative assessment of interpretive journalism – following, as previously acknowledged, recent studies analysing 'broadcast talk' (Hutchby 2006; Tolson 2011; Montgomery 2007) – unpacking how reporters routinely communicate politics and public affairs in live two-ways over recent decades.

Before focussing on interpretive journalism, however, the analysis begins by examining how live two-ways compare with edited packages, still the most widely used television news convention but one that has reduced over recent decades.

Comparing edited and live news: towards a better understanding of politics?

In considering the rise of live reporting and the value it brings to television news bulletins, it is important to consider what it replaced (edited news). While the growth of live news has often been pejoratively interpreted – repre-senting, in different ways, a commercial logic (Tuggle and Huffman 2001) – there is almost an assumption it brings less value than edited news. But this leap of faith has not been subject to much empirical scrutiny. Previous chapters have empirically confirmed UK evening bulletins have increasingly chosen to report politics in a live as opposed to edited format, thus raising questions about the way news is routinely interpreted and conveyed by journalists.

Table 5.2 Ratio of on screen and off screen sources in edited packages and two-way/reporter live conventions in BBC and ITV television news bulletins 1991–2013

	BBC		ITV	
	Edited package	*Two-way/reporter live*	*Edited package*	*Two-way/reporter live*
1991/2	4.1	2	3.7	1.4
1999	4.1	0.9	5.2	1
2004	4.3	0.3	5.3	1
2013	5.6	1.6	3.5	1.6

(Adapted from Cushion 2014a)

What, in other words, are the editorial consequences of reporting live over edited news?

One measure of exploring the changing nature of television journalism is to examine the sources used to inform routine political news. Table 5.2 compares the average ratio of both on screen and off screen sources (such as when a journalist refers to an actor – e.g. "the Prime Minster said today") used from 1991 to 2013 in reporter packages and live reporter/two-ways on BBC and ITV evening bulletins.

On both BBC and ITV edited reporter packages consistently drew on more sources – approximately 4 per item over recent decades – than in live reporting, where the average was roughly 1 per item. Typically, edited packages featured a representative of each of the main political parties – Labour, Conservative and the Liberal Democrats – as part of a political item to meet impartiality requirements. Live political reporting, by contrast, was focused more on journalistic interpretation with more limited references to political actors (1–2 typically). Indeed, in some years – notably on the BBC – many live political items contained no references to political actors and instead focused on a journalist's analysis and interpretation. In short, the overall pattern from 1991 to 2013 was relatively similar on both commercial and public service broadcasters – edited reporter packages were far more reliant on external sources in political news than during live reporting.

To further compare the value of news in an edited or live format, examples of political stories will be drawn upon from the sample periods of UK evening television news bulletins from 1991 to 2013 used throughout the book. After reviewing the relatively small number of live two-ways throughout the 1990s – which were primarily used to supplement an edited reported package – some distinctive structural and stylistic characteristics can be observed compared to how this convention was used in the 2000s.

Sourcing politicians outside Parliament in pseudo-interviews

As Chapters 2 and 3 confirmed, political news was conveyed more often in an edited rather than live format in the 1990s compared to the 2000s, particularly

Table 5.3 The location of stories (when identified) of actors sourced in Parliament in BBC
and ITV early evening television news bulletins 1991–2013 (by frequency)

	1991/2	1999	2004	2013
BBC	30	14	15	6
ITV	32	18	19	11

on the BBC. As such, pre-millennium political coverage was often confined to
the views of politicians, rather than journalists acting as sources, considering
their perspectives or questioning their positions (a point developed in a later
section). Moreover, the voices of politicians were often captured inside Parliament in edited clips taken from debates that day in the House of Commons.
Indeed, when the on screen location of a politician was apparent (in many
cases it was not), Table 5.3 shows that, both on the BBC and ITV, there has
been a reduction of actors sourced in Parliament from 1991 to 2013.

On the BBC this was most striking – from 30 to 6 actors sourced in Parliament – representing a steep and steady fall over the sample period. In a 1992
story about pensions – where citizens were seeking compensation after Robert
Maxwell's fraudulent business practices – a lively debate in the House of
Commons was captured by the BBC. Its evening bulletin featured a statement
from the social security and shadow secretaries, as well as a contribution from
a backbencher. Similarly, ITV reduced the number of sources taken from Parliament – from 32 in 1991/2 to 11 in 2013 – approximately a third less. In a
1992 story related to the Maastricht Treaty, for instance – a time when Conservative politicians were particularly incensed about their Party's European
commitments towards EU integration – ITV sourced three actors in the House
of Commons.

This is not to suggest Parliament has been airbrushed out of contemporary
political reporting. But it appears today to be reserved for special occasions,
such as Margaret Thatcher's death in 2013. In 2013, 4 of the 6 sources from
Parliament on the BBC and 6 of the 11 on ITV were edited tributes to
Thatcher from MPs in Parliament. Excluding Thatcher's death, there were
very few images of politicians in Parliament debating. However, the exception
is arguably Prime Minister's Questions (PMQs) – a lively parliamentary event
where the prime minster is quizzed by the opposition of the House and back-
benchers – which is typically covered on Wednesday evening bulletins. In the
1991 sample period both BBC and ITV early evening bulletins covered PMQs
as part of a debate about unemployment figures. Since PMQs moved to a
weekly rather than bi-weekly parliamentary event at 12pm in 1997, it could
be – although further systematic research is needed – that MPs debating in the
House of Commons appear less often on television news bulletins. The Hansard Society (2014) has recognized the significance of PMQs and, in a review of
its impact on viewers, suggested it should be moved to a prime-time evening
spot to appeal to a wider audience.

Of course, the general reduction of political sources in Parliament is partly a consequence of political news being reported in a less edited format in the 2000s. It could also be the novelty factor of using images and politicians in Parliament has gradually worn off, since – as Chapter 1 acknowledged – cameras were only allowed into the House of Commons in 1990. However, the ratio of politicians being sourced remained relatively stable over time (see Table 5.2). This means political actors continue to be sourced in relatively equal measure – contrary to many studies about shrinking soundbites during elections (Esser 2008) – but their appearances lie outside the chamber. Indeed, reviewing the 2004, 2012 and 2013 sample periods it can be observed that politicians increasingly appeared in filmed conversations with individual journalists (what might be labelled a pseudo-interview, since there were rarely on screen questions posed), rather than in raw edited clips in Parliament. While journalists were not always 'in shot', many politicians appeared as though they were responding to the voice of the narrator – the reporter – who filed the edited package.

Of course, it could be that the edited clip of a political actor is a soundbite shared among a pool of journalists, but the impression nonetheless is of a more personalized interaction with a journalist. On occasions – when a journalist was conducting the interviewing – this was brought into sharper focus by cut-aways of journalists talking to politicians which appeared as images whilst the journalist narrated over the package. In this sense, journalists today appear as more central actors in the construction of television news, with their presence – either on screen or implied from an interview with a politician – conveying a more interventionist style of reporting than a clip taken from a parliamentary debate might invoke. Indeed, as Chapter 3 explored, the visual presence of journalists in reporting is seen as a measure of mediatization (Strömbäck and Dimitrova 2011) – a media logic – conveying actuality and immediacy, stamping a journalist's own line of questioning/interpretation on a news item. While it was argued this logic was most displayed in live two-ways – when journalists were on screen talking at length – the changing role of reporters in edited packages (which was more difficult to quantify over time) also suggests a more interventionist role. In particular, more sustained analysis about the changing nature of piece to cameras – where reporters typically wrap up their edited package – could reveal a more interpretive trend in edited television news coverage.

Another possible indicator of media logic apparent in edited reporter packages post-millennium was the sourcing of political actors from other news outlets. So, for example, on 1 April 2013 a story involving Iain Duncan Smith – the pensions secretary – featured him sourced in a pseudo-interview but also on *Today* (a leading BBC Radio 4 programme) claiming – after being asked by a journalist – he could live on £53 a week. The quote led to an on-line petition of 90,000 people challenging the pensions secretary to "prove his claim". There were also increasing instances in the 2000s when edited packages referred to prominent newspaper stories or used images of their headlines to graphically convey the significance of an issue or the pressure surrounding the topic. In other words, a media agenda – even if reliant on other journalistic sources – will often help set the scene to a story or more directly inform it.

Overall, then, while the evidence suggests the views of politicians on evening bulletins are as regular as they were over 20 years (in edited packages), the contexts in which they appear have changed. Viewers no longer watch politicians debating at Parliament to the same degree, but instead in pre-edited pseudo-interviews, talking to a journalist posing questions rather than debating fellow MPs. This appears part of a broader shift where journalists – not necessarily political actors – set the agenda, even if this means evening bulletins drawing on other media to help shape a story.

The live two-way and the promotion of the game frame?

Previous chapters have concluded that interpretation has been the primary function of live two-ways both in news generally and political reporting specifically. However, less attention has been placed on the type of political news journalists have made sense of, such as the policies of political parties or the personalities, infighting or tactics – the processes surrounding politics – which has been labelled the strategic game frame (Aalberg et al. 2012). The prevailing trends in political communication research suggest in many advanced Western democracies politics is increasingly shaped by game or strategy reporting, superseding concerns about the policies of competing parties. From a normative perspective, many critics suggest this divorces viewers from policy deliberations which should be more central to political reporting. Aalberg et al. offer a definition of the strategic game frame informed by a review of existing studies:

> 1. The *game frame* refers to news stories that portray politics as a game and are centered around: who is winning or losing elections, in the battle for public opinion, in legislative debates, or in politics in general; expressions of public opinion (polls, vox pops); approval or disapproval from interest groups or particular constituencies or publics; or that speculate about electoral or policy outcomes or potential coalitions.
>
> 2. The *strategy frame* refers to news stories that are centered around interpretations of candidates' or parties' motives for actions and positions; their strategies and tactics for achieving political or policy goals; how they campaign; and choices regarding leadership and integrity, including news coverage of press behavior.
>
> (Aalberg et al. 2012: 172; their emphasis)

However, the empirical studies informing this definition relate primarily to media coverage during elections, an atypical moment in time when campaigning comes to the fore and the strategy of parties and politicians is put under the microscope. Working with this definition in routine political reporting over time, the researchers on the various studies drawn upon throughout this book found it difficult to reliably and consistently categorize either game or strategy stories using this criterion.

Moreover, not only did aspects of the game or strategy overlap within political stories, there were moments when both blurred with matters of party policy or other substantive issues. Since the focus of the studies throughout the book was on interpreting different conventions used to portray news and politics specifically, more discursive categories measuring the degree of policy or game-type reporting were not developed further (see Coleman 2010). In this sense, it could be concluded that there was no manifest evidence to confirm whether particular television news conventions – notably two-ways – promoted the game or strategy of political news to a greater extent.

However, after inspecting over 400 live two-ways in previous decades and across different media systems examined throughout the book, when journalists responded live to anchors during evening bulletins there were moments when the characteristics associated with the game or strategy frame were explicitly exhibited. When the then US President, Bill Clinton, was facing the prospect of impeachment in 1999, for example, both BBC and ITV evening bulletins on occasions covered this story without any reporter package. Instead, both used a Washington correspondent in live two-ways to consider the possible implications for the President's own future career. The following exchange between a BBC anchor and reporter illustrates the speculative licence granted to the journalist in the live two-way convention:

ANCHOR: Philippa [Washington correspondent], the dying hours of the impeachment process, how's it all going to be wrapped up?
REPORTER: Well we've just heard the result of the vote that senators have been taking. They are going to conduct their deliberations behind closed doors, which may well speed it up if they're not speaking for the cameras and for their constituents out there across the country. So it may be up to 25 hours of deliberations over three days but the key point is that they want to vote on the articles on the impeachment by Thursday or Friday at the latest.
ANCHOR: And Clinton likely to survive if he does – what have the Republicans gained through this whole process?
REPORTER: A good question, and the answer could be very little in fact. Because the way it's worked out is that President Clinton is almost certain to survive – everybody's been expecting an acquittal. And what the Democrats have been saying throughout is that it is a Republican trial, it's a partisan trial, little short of a witch hunt, the public hasn't wanted the trial to go on and have been very weary of it and so in fact the Republicans have come out of it rather badly.

The two-way, in this context, allows 'the latest' news to be delivered live but also for the reporter to forecast the political fortunes of Clinton based on her assessment of 'public opinion' and the party political mood within the 'Washington village'. A latter section deals with the judgements made by political reporters and the informative value in live two-ways. But in the reporting on Clinton's impeachment, the example reveals how the live two-way convention was used to convey the political temperature of a political story, with the journalist in the 'thick of the action' and close to the actors involved. Indeed, this was even apparent in two-ways broadcast in the early 1990s. Reporting on a speech the Queen was due to make to the European Parliament in May 1992, for example, ITV's anchor asked the political correspondent in a live two-way studio link up:

ANCHOR: Tomorrow the Queen makes an important speech to the European Parliament. While we've been on air word has emerged from Westminster that the speech will be a ringing endorsement for Europe. Peter Allen at Westminster what more can you tell us?

POLITICAL CORRESPONDENT: We're just getting the first indication of what's in this speech as you said … It does sound that it is very enthusiastic indeed about the European Parliament.

While the correspondent enters into the kind of speculative and fast-paced journalism characteristic of the strategy frame (Aalberg *et al.* 2012), at the same time the central tenor of the two-way is to inform viewers about the substance of a highly political speech related to the relationship the UK enjoys with Europe. After all, this was a crucial point in time when the Conservative Government (controversially within its own Party) agreed to closer political union with the EU. To interpret – or dismiss – this two-way as a game- or strategy-only story, in other words, would overlook the inherent policy tension at the heart of the story – how is European integration, at this critical democratic moment, being understood by the British establishment?

Unlike the reporting of some stories about Bill Clinton's possible impeachment, the majority of the hundreds of two-ways examined from 1991 to 2013 in this book were used to supplement rather than act as a stand-alone news convention. In doing so, it can be observed that they (typically) followed an edited reporter package, a chance to update viewers on the latest action but mostly to deliver further interpretation of a political story. In practice, this meant journalists could touch on aspects of their edited package without the need for lengthy explanation or context in the live two-way but also to consider and ruminate on some of the implications of the report. This suggests that live two-ways can still deliver informative value despite – as Chapter 2 established – the increasingly limited time granted to this convention post-millennium. In the week of February 2004, for example, the BBC's then political editor, Andrew Marr, used live two-ways to not just bring viewers the latest developments in Washington and London about the setting up of a review into the intelligence that led to the Iraq War, but to wax lyrical about the consequences for the Labour Government and then prime minster, Tony Blair. This was displayed in various exchanges between the television news anchor and Marr – following edited reporter packages – over the course of the week:

ANCHOR: How difficult is all this [pressure about the setting up of an independent inquiry about the intelligence that led to the war] going to be for the prime minister?
REPORTER: Well, I think it will be difficult but frankly I think it's now unavoidable. With President Bush announcing that there's going to be the inquiry in Washington there's absolutely no way they can avoid having one in London as well.

(BBC 6pm bulletin, 2 February 2004)

ANCHOR: And how high are the stakes going to be for Tony Blair in all this?
REPORTER: Pretty high, I mean it puts the arguments off obviously for a few more months. And some people … will be suspicious of the fact that it's a secret and establishment type inquiry. Nevertheless, it will look in essence at the WMD and therefore the legal justification for war. And that's a very very tricky important subject for Tony Blair. In the end, however, the political verdict won't be for the politicians, won't be for committees like this, it will be for the voters in this country sometime next year.

(BBC 6pm bulletin, 3 February 2004)

In both examples, then, while the immediate and long-term strategic aims of the Government were considered by the live two-way reporter, the strength of intelligence – the basis of foreign policy – was also evaluated and the possible inquiry that would be set up to review it. In other words, the live two-way acted as a useful follow-up convention – moving beyond the party political sources informing the edited package – by adding further context and speculation about what will follow.

Of course, crucial to the delivery of greater context and explanation in live two-ways is the informative quality of it. The next two sections consider both the degree to which journalists' interpret everyday politics and the broader ideological consequences of reporting politics in live two-ways.

The role of political editors and interpretation in political news: a post-millennium turn of interventionism?

The focus now turns to the journalists delivering the live two-ways, considering who they are and whether their style, tone or level of interpretation has remained the same or changed over time. Chapter 4's comparative cross-national analysis of evening bulletins revealed US and UK reporters especially held specific journalistic titles – spanning many areas, from health, crime and business to world affairs, security and social affairs – but particularly in the world of politics. This, it was argued, reflected the more interventionist role political journalists were cast in, asked not just to report the news but to interpret and make sense of it. Or, put differently, a mediatization of political reporting was evident, with increasing time spent on journalists interpreting coverage in live two-ways rather than depending on political actors in reporter packages (as Table 5.2 testified to earlier in the chapter).

As previously acknowledged, relying on journalists to convey news live 'on air' has been a long-standing criticism of 24-hour news channels and the type of journalism they promote. In the early years of CNN, for example, the acronym of the organization was parodied as the Chaotic News Network to reflect the amateurish mix of live and edited conventions (Cushion 2010). The views of journalists narrating over live pictures or waxing lyrical into cameras for extended periods of time attracted criticism not just within the industry but by scholars reflecting on the rise of 24-hour news culture (Cottle and Rai 2008; Tuggle *et al.* 2010; MacGregor 1997). Nonetheless, longitudinal research has shown rolling news channels have enhanced – rather than reduced – their reliance on liveness, turning repeatedly to journalists live 'at the scene' for regular updates even when little has changed or if a story has not developed (Cushion and Lewis 2009; Lewis and Cushion 2009; Tuggle *et al.* 2010).

Most recently, Sambrook and McGuire (2014) launched a wide-ranging attack on the 24-hour news medium, considering it a dated form of communication in the age of social media. They take particular issue with the (over) use of live reporters punctuating the 24-hour news cycle. They argue this turns 24-hour news into

> a sausage machine, dedicated to filling airtime. Hours a day are spent on live feeds waiting for something, anything, to happen. "Vamping" it's called in the business. A correspondent talking to fill empty airtime until the press conference or event begins. The editor can't risk broadcasting a different report or going live somewhere else in case he misses the start and a rival channel can claim to be "first".

In doing so, they suggest further that this "need to fill airtime – and particularly the need to be seen to be live – means that in the heat of the moment questionable editorial judgments can be made". They used the derogatory label "Dish Monkeys" to characterize the role of live reporters, robotically delivering live updates on hotel roofs to satisfy the demands of satellite televisions without drawing on their own journalistic capabilities or curiosity to understand the background or context to the stories they repeatedly recycle.

As previous chapters have suggested, fixed time news bulletins increasingly resemble the format, style and speed of dedicated 24-hour news channels. But to what extent could this critique of 'on air' reporting extend to the rise of the live two-way convention in today's evening bulletins and, in particular, to how politics is routinely covered? In a 2012 UK study the role of specialist reporters was examined closely (Cushion and Thomas 2013). It found the title 'political' was most used in coverage overall, typically involving a deputy editor, senior correspondent or just correspondent. This was most striking on Channel 5 news (73 per cent of all live airtime) and to a lesser extent on ITV (39.5 per cent) and the BBC (19.2 per cent). As chapter two suggested, the prominence of political journalists can be partly explained by the the propensity to report politics in live two-way conventions.

With titled political reporters a regular and routine fixture of UK evening bulletins, the study further examined which journalist was the most dominant actor (Cushion and Thomas 2013). In all three bulletins examined – the BBC, ITV and Channel 5 – it was the political editors that stood out, representing not just a significant amount of airtime reporting everyday politics, but taking up a considerable portion of the bulletin overall (see Table 5.4). The BBC and ITV political editors – Nick Robinson and Tom Bradby – occupied approximately 10 per cent of all news and between a quarter and fifth of all live news. But it was Andy Bell, Channel 5's political editor, who appeared most on screen, taking up a fifth of all news and over 40 per cent of all live news. In short, UK evening bulletins rely on the most senior political television journalists to convey – and interpret – a sizeable portion of all news and in particular live two-way reporting. For when all live news was isolated in 2012 and compared to live political news (see Table 5.5), the degree of interpretation was far higher in the world of politics compared to other topics, such as business or crime.

All broadcasters enhanced the level of interpretation in political news compared to other subject-matter reported but the BBC stood out with close to 9 in 10 two-ways acting as a vehicle to interpret the world of politics. Not surprisingly, the power and influence of political editors has been recognized by past governments of the day and their associated spin doctors. A former press secretary, for instance, has suggested the main political editors are important "contextualizing voices" (cited in McNair 2000: 73), drawing attention to and making sense of the big Westminster stories.

Table 5.4 Percentage of all news and live news involving the political editor in BBC, ITV and Channel 5 evening news bulletins in 2012 (by time)

	BBC Nick Robinson	ITV Tom Bradby	Channel 5 Andy Bell
Appearance as a percentage of all news	9.2	10.4	19
Two-way appearance as percentage of live news	23.9	19.7	41.4

(Adapted from Cushion and Thomas 2013)

Table 5.5 Percentage of journalistic interventions in live and live political reporting in BBC, ITV and Channel 5 television news bulletins in 2012 (by frequency)

	All live BBC N = 58	Political Live BBC	All live ITV N = 49	Political Live ITV	All live Ch. 5 N = 68	Political Live Ch. 5
Latest news	13.8	11.1	20.4	/	23.5	6.3
Interpretation	55.2	88.9	57.1	83.3	39.7	75
On location	/	/	2.0	/	/	/
General intro / Summary	12.9	/	20.4	16.7	36.8	18.8

(Adapted from Cushion and Thomas 2013)

While the presence and power of political editors has been recognized in recent years, has the degree to which they interpret everyday politics changed over time? Both Chapters 2 and 3 showed – with the exception of ITV in 2004 – interpretation was consistently the dominant function of live two-ways in political reporting. However, a closer comparative inspection of live political coverage in the 1990s and 2000s suggests post-millennium the tone and tenor of political reporters was more *explicitly* interpretive, reaching more decisive conclusions and delivering more judgemental verdicts on everyday political stories. So, for example, in an April 1991 story about the Government's proposal for a new poll tax – one that was controversially removed in later years – ITV political editor, Michael Brunson, was asked to comment upon the new policy and how it would work in practice:

ANCHOR: Well Michael how exactly is this new tax going to work?
REPORTER: Well, the details are beginning to emerge and what is going to happen is this – they're basically going to be probably four types of house, say a cottage or a flat, a semi-detached house, a detached house, and then a mansion. And your house will fall into one of those categories. And then the local council will set a local tax figure, say of £500 for the sake of argument. And if you live in a cottage you'll say probably pay only £300 of that and if you live in a mansion you'd pay £700. You do it like, that, that's how you link it to the ability to pay. And those proportions will be decided by central Government. And the other element is that if there's only one person living in the house you will get a reduction. Figure on that probably still to be decided.
ANCHOR: Michael, why do you think they decided to do it this way?
REPORTER: Well, one of the advantages of this system is if you simply relate the size of your house to your local tax bill you don't have to worry about the variations up and down the country between the values of property. So the idea is, you see, if you, say, have a cottage in Kent and a cottage in Cumbria those will be vastly different in value but you'll still actually be

paying the same proportion to your local authority in Kent and your local authority in Cumbria. And so it's thought to be a far fairer system.

ANCHOR: Michael Brunson at Westminster, thank you very much indeed.

As the example demonstrated, the live two-way reporter – in the follow-up question – focused on explaining the substance of the policy without interpreting or evaluating the strategy or politics behind the poll tax. The interpretation, in other words, was free from any explicit political judgements.

Similarly, a BBC live two-way in October 1999 about the possible banning of French meat in the UK and the diplomatic tension between the countries could potentially have been interpreted in a dramatic and sensationalist way, since it inflamed public anger and was the subject of some heated tabloid headlines. However, the then chief political correspondent, John Sergeant, interpreted coverage dryly, coolly explaining the latest news about the response from the Government's science expert and considering the longer term political impact of the dispute.

ANCHOR: The Government scientists, the statement they put out this evening, are they saying the French meat is totally safe?

REPORTER: Well, it's interesting. What the ministry is saying when asked about this, it's saying 'safe' in the normal use of the word 'safe'. They're not saying 100 per cent in the same way as they're not saying it's a 100 per cent to cross a road. It's a matter of risk assessment. What they're really saying is in terms of public health practice, this product, these products from France are safe and they're as safe from that point of view as British meat is. But it's not saying this is a 100 per cent guarantee, no one will ever be hurt from French because they can't give that guarantee.

ANCHOR: John, on the question of a trade war, which people have been talking about in the last couple of days. Both governments clearly want to avoid this. But do you think we're heading towards some kind of unofficial trade war?

REPORTER: Well, we certainly are in terms of the action taken by the supermarkets and the coverage that it's got in the French press. So there's no doubt now that the French Government fully understands British anger. And although that's not been fuelled by the Government, they're simply pointing to the anger consumers and farmers feel, there's no doubt this could help to put pressure on the French Government when the big decision comes about lifting the ban on British meat going into France.

Once again, the example illustrates how the reporter's words were delivered calmly, with clear and straightforward commentary. Post-millennium, however, this more dispassionate mode of address was less evident and – as live reporting increased – two-way reporters appeared more strident and confident. So, for example, when the then leader of the Conservative Party, Michael Howard, delivered a speech about the UK's relationship with Europe in February 2004, Andrew Marr was invited by the anchor to interpret the speech and the politics behind it, he duly obliged by offering an explicit critique of Tory Party policy:

ANCHOR: So how much of a change in the thinking is this for the Tories?
REPORTER: A change in words, not a change in thinking. Very friendly in tone, very relaxed in tone compared to some of the earlier speeches on Europe from previous Conservative leaders. Less angst, if you like. But look at the detail; there is not any substantial change here. This is not some kind of U-turn or for that matter L-turn in Conservative policy. And this would work very very well so long as the major Continental European countries are perfectly happy to get rid of their idea of everyone pulling together in a single ever more united European Union. But I have to say fat chance of that.
ANCHOR: And, as you said, Michael Howard is nearing his 100th day as leader, what's the verdict on his leadership?
REPORTER: Well, within about half a mile of where I'm standing in Westminster most people think he's done very well indeed. He's been very effective in the House of Commons chamber. He's cheered the Conservative Party up when it badly needed cheering up. And he's started to move policy in a large range of issues. He's brought in some of the people like Ken Clarke, who'd been left outside in the cold before. However, the real question is whether that's yet making any impact in the country. And if you look at the polling the answer is at the moment relatively little impact. Everyone will be watching for a substantive and sustained change in the polls, then we'll be able to judge.

By 2012 it can be observed that the political editors of the BBC, ITV and Channel 5 – who as previously established occupied a significant proportion of live reporting – *routinely* supply evaluative judgements about the burning issues of the day and deliver verdicts about the day's political machinations at Westminster. An example from each political editor in different contexts reveals the more emphatic and self-assured style of live political two-ways post-millennium.

This was the day that things got really serious for David Cameron … at issue, at stake, the Government's reputation for competence and integrity. Now I've no doubt at all that for most people the economic news is what matters more. Squeezed like never before, many voters will now ask themselves "Was it really worth it?" … There's an old saying when things are bad in politics things can only get better. It's wrong [George]. Things just got a whole lot worse.

(BBC's political editor, Nick Robinson, discussing the Government's economic performance, 25 April 2012)

Well, I think that's an open question [how much trouble Government minister Jeremy Hunt is in]. The reality of this is very simple. Vince Cable clearly didn't want this bid [News Corporation's proposed wholesale takeover of BSKYB] to go ahead and was clearly somewhat pushing the envelope in terms of quasi-judicial position to stop it ... Jeremy Hunt I think probably did want it to go ahead ... and I think the question is, how hard was he pushing the envelope the other way? ... but I think we know, those of us who have been here a while remember, how close the old Labour Party was to the Murdochs, and that was very, very close ... to be honest, I don't think too many of them [the Conservatives] can throw too many stones.

> (ITV's political editor, Tom Bradby, at the
> Leveson Inquiry, 24 April 2012)

The Coalition needs better economic news to get back on the front foot ... but others have doubts about proposed measures. It didn't feel like a dramatic, agenda-setting Queen's Speech [the Government's legislative agenda for the year ahead], but I think where this could get very interesting is concerning the topic of House of Lord's reform. There's a danger of division (within the Coalition).

> (Channel 5's political editor, Andy Bell, analysing
> the Queen's Speech, 9 May 2012)

Since these political editors, between them, clock up a considerable amount of airtime, how they regularly interpret politics clearly matters to how everyday issues and events are understood by viewers. While Chapter 6 considers the possible impact the rise of the live two-ways – and a more journalist-centred style of political reporting – may have on viewers, an assessment can be made about the agenda adopted by political editors. After all, while audiences might construct different meanings from media content (Lewis 2001), this is limited somewhat by the range of views and perspectives offered by journalists. The final section therefore considers the ideological role of two-ways, examining *the range of views* supplied in political coverage generally but most especially in live reporting.

Interpreting impartiality: the ideological limits of live two-ways in political reporting

All UK broadcasters are legally required to adhere to strict impartiality requirements. Unlike in the US – where the requirements of impartiality were lifted in 1987 – the regulation safeguarding balance has remained intact. Lobbying to 'Foxify' UK television bulletins – to make them more opinionated like Fox News in the US – have so far been resisted. Of course, interpreting impartiality can be difficult to operationalize and measure (Cushion 2014c), but at its core is the aim to understand the range of views and opinions which regularly appear – or do not – in broadcasting. The primary intention of this section is to explore this question in respect of understanding the interpretive framework of reporters during coverage of politics by way of the live two-way convention. In short, do live two-way reporters largely stick to reflecting the views of mainstream party politics or is politics interpreted more broadly, beyond Westminster politicians?

Before exploring this question, research confirming the dominance of party politics in broadcasting more generally – in all news (live or edited) – needs to be acknowledged, including in the studies informing this book. So, for example, the BBC Trust carried out a comprehensive and systematic assessment of impartiality in BBC news reporting (Wahl-Jorgensen et al. 2013). Drawing on a content analysis of a wide range of BBC outlets in 2007 and 2012, the study showed BBC news reported politics through a relatively narrow party prism, relying heavily on mainstream politicians (Conservative, Labour and Liberal Democrats) as sources to inform everyday coverage. In doing so, the authors argued that "a striking dominance of party political voices in the output and topics" was established over successive years (Wahl-Jorgensen et al. 2013: 5). Reviewing coverage over a longer period, the studies drawn upon throughout this book similarly revealed political actors – sourced overwhelmingly in edited news – were also the dominant players in news reporting generally (Table 5.6).

As Chapter 1 explained, the variation of sources in each year needs to be interpreted in the context of the overall supply of political news. But despite varying levels of political news, the broad picture shows – with the exception of members of the public on ITV in 2004 – politicians were the dominant actors in coverage generally. When political reporting was further isolated, this dominance grew even stronger, limiting the space for other potential actors – from NGOs to academics – to inform routine coverage. Moreover, it is primarily the leaders of the main three political parties and cabinet and shadow secretaries that make up the vast majority of sources. As already acknowledged, this reinforces long-standing findings about the dominance of party political actors in UK television news (Eldridge 1993) as well as the most recent BBC Trust study about the breadth of opinion in broadcast coverage (Wahl-Jorgensen et al. 2013).

Table 5.6 Percentage of political sources in BBC and ITV early evening television news bulletins 1991–2012 (by frequency)

	1991/2	1999	2004	2012
BBC	67.9	57.1	53	81.6
ITV	83.3	70.8	56.8	76.8

However, the BBC Trust study also revealed – without much fanfare – that BBC reporters were regularly drawn upon to shape political coverage. In their words, "our research has demonstrated that media sources – usually correspondents asked to give their professional judgement on a story or issue – are prominent across 2007 and 2012, making up a greater presence than any profession outside of politics" (Wahl-Jorgensen *et al*. 2013: 64). It can thus be concluded from the study that the BBC's breadth of opinion was confined to the usual suspects – Westminster politicians and journalists – in routine coverage. Of course, the opinions of politicians are relatively easy to decipher – since most today remain 'on message' and toe the party line – but the role of reporters being impartial when delivering "professional judgements" was not subject to interrogation in the study or wider discussion. And yet, political reporters – as the previous section showed – not only occupy a significant proportion of airtime, it was suggested they have increasingly delivered more decisive judgements and verdicts about political events and issues. To explore how politics is interpreted more closely, the reporting of two-ways from an ideological perspective needs to be considered, making a judgement about whether reporters deliver balance and impartiality in live political news.

Following the familiar cast of politicians that regularly inform the vast majority of edited television news – as Table 5.6 revealed – a consistent feature of live two-way reporting over previous decades was from within or just outside the Westminster chamber. Reporters were repeatedly asked to supply an inside scoop by interpreting the immediate reaction from mainstream parties and politicians. So, for example, an ITV anchor simply asked a reporter in May 1992 – after Margaret Thatcher had just delivered a speech to the European Parliament – "How's this gone down at Westminster?" Politics was thus interpreted by the Conservative Party's internal conflict about the relationship the UK should have with Europe, rather than a broader consideration about the consequences of being more closely entwined with or distant from European political institutions. Indeed, interpreting party splits was also a recurrent feature of live two-ways, with reporters – informed by the key actors involved in the drama on the ground – able to speculate about how votes will be cast and any immediate ramifications. In a May 1999 vote about potentially cutting benefits, for instance, an ITV television anchor first asked Michael Brunson for his inside knowledge about the imminent vote and the scale of the party political fall-out.

ANCHOR: And, Michael, when can we expect the vote and the size of the revolt tonight?
REPORTER: It may actually not be until 8 or 9 o'clock tomorrow morning. There's a big debate going on about tactics: Is it better to talk through the night and therefore focusing attention on this? Or is it better to be done quickly? But it will be a very very late vote on this, perhaps even tomorrow morning.

Being on hand ready to update evening bulletins about the latest Westminster showdown thus appears to be central to the role of a political reporter and the purpose of a live two-way.

Post millennium it was not just the presence of live two-way reporters at Westminster that was emphasized, but – as the previous section suggested – their impressions and interpretation of the day's action were brought into sharper focus. A minute into the BBC's 6pm bulletin coverage of the 2004 budget, for example, a live two-way was used to make sense of the politics behind it, with a short but pointed introduction: "Our political editor watched the chancellor's speech, Andrew". In other words, it was left to the political editor to convey the day's machinations. Indeed, after the political editor introduced his lengthy reporter package – where the (albeit brief) soundbites of the mainstream political parties were surveyed – the anchor invited Marr to interpret the budget within the framework of the two main parties.

ANCHOR: Now, Andrew, do you think this budget sharpens the dividing line between Labour and the Conservatives?
REPORTER: Well, I certainly think that's what Gordon Brown wants it to do.

Just to further elevate the status and authority of the political editor, at the end of the bulletin another live two-way featured Andrew Marr, who was asked to offer a final thought of the day's budget. In so doing, the political editor returned to the struggle between the two main parties – and the election battleground the following year.

ANCHOR: Now, let's get a final thought on the budget from our political editor, Andrew Marr. Andrew, do you think there's one big theme we can take away from this budget?
REPORTER: Well, I'm sorry to have to say this, but I think the big theme is that the election isn't quite as far away as many people might have hoped it was. It was a very very political day. If you talk to all the kind of pointy headed, shiny clever people, who understand the numbers, the economists and people like that, they think it's been a bit boring because not a great deal has changed, and most taxes have stayed the same and so on. But if you look at the politics, this is really about the Labour Party still being con-vinced that the voters, when push comes to shove, are still up for more investment in schools and hospitals on the front line and are less worried about the fear that taxes might have to go up in the longer term. Now that is a gamble. And the other thing that has been clear today is that the Labour Party in Government has been concerned and worried by the Tory Party, above all, that they may be spending your money and my money but they may not be spending it very well and waste and bureaucracy are really politically important now.

While a vague reference is made to economists – "and people like that" – the primary actors involved in the debate were the two mainstream parties. Thus, the economic – and political – lens through which the budget was largely understood was by the 'tax and spend' Labour Party or 'reduce the size of the state' Tory Party. While, on the face of it, this appears a relatively clear-cut distinction between the positions of both mainstream parties, the differences – when directly compared and wider debates considered – could be interpreted as relatively minor (Elliott and Atkinson 2012; Heffernan 2001). In other words, the reporter characterized the ostensible choice between the main Westminster parties, but the broader ideological picture – considering a greater divergence of views and perspectives – was not included within the live post-budget political two-way. It is a critique acknowledged more widely in economic reporting, such as during the financial crisis in 2008. In making sense of how the UK should respond, Berry's (2015) systematic review of the BBC's 10pm bulletin immediately after the crash found coverage centred on a small band of elite actors from the financial services or between cabinet or shadow Conservative and Labour politicians. In doing so, it was argued "BBC reports ... operated with a shared framework of understanding which endorsed the necessity of pre-emptive austerity to placate the financial markets" (Berry 2015).

The reliance on interpreting politics from a narrow Parliamentary framework was also on display in April 2013 when Margaret Thatcher passed away. Although references were made to the divisive way successive Thatcher governments operated throughout the 1980s in BBC, ITV and Channel 5 bulletins, days after her passing the focus turned to how Parliament responded. A lengthy BBC reporter package, for example, included the views of not just the leaders of the main political parties but also backbench MPs and Lords – taken from debates that day in Westminster chambers (a rare occurrence – as the chapter already established – in contemporary television news reporting). The follow-up live two-way then asked Nick Robinson, the BBC political editor, for his impressions about the influence of Thatcherism on today's party political generation. While Robinson momentarily acknowledges the broader impact of people generally living in the era of Thatcher rule, the focus was primarily on the three main party leaders at Westminster.

ANCHOR: Well, let's get the impressions of our political editor, Nick Robinson, who's at the Houses of Parliament for us now. Nick, you know, listening to those debates I couldn't help thinking that so many of those who spoke today grew up in the Thatcher era.
REPORTER: Well, not just them, but us George, let's be honest. All those of us who grew up in the Thatcher era – and remember the debate and the divisions and the drama so vividly – can all too easily forget that it was quite some time ago. After all, David Cameron, our current prime minister, was just 12 when Margaret Thatcher became prime minster. Ed Miliband the leader of the opposition was just eight years of age. And yet they were all,

I think, shaped in their political attitudes by what she did in the 11 years that followed her entry to No. 10. So today might look like a sort of nostalgia fest, looking from the outside, but I think it really has genuine significance looking forward as well. David Cameron today praised Margaret Thatcher as a politician who had saved the country. I think he has always believed that, but I think in part he will hope it convinces the wider Tory family that he really does want to be the heir to Thatcher – not merely the heir to Blair as he once allegedly said in private. Ed Miliband was careful to list areas where he agreed with Margaret Thatcher as well as those areas where he disagreed. I sense that perhaps he wants to signal to the country that he's not really 'red Ed' as the tabloid Tory press once claimed. It was Nick Clegg who looked the least comfortable today, forced as he's in a coalition to stand up next to a Tory prime minister to praise a Tory icon and he really didn't want to do it, not one little bit. The truth about all these politicians, the truth about half of MPs who were children when Margaret Thatcher was first elected prime minster, they are all, whether they like it or not, Thatcher's children, and they always will be.

This impressionistic account of Thatcher's legacy was thus conveyed through the personalities of Westminster's leading party figures and its immediate political impact. A reference was even made to the impact of Westminster journalists shaping the debate – in the form of tabloid headlines characterizing Miliband's brand of left-wing politics – further revealing the reporter's relatively narrow analytical framework. A tacit acknowledgement, incidentally, of the mediatization of politics.

Of course, routinely reporting politics through the prism of elected party politicians could be interpreted as fulfilling a broadcaster's 'due' impartiality requirements. After all, 'due' involves a journalist making a judgement about what is – and is not – relevant to a story. This is clearly explained in Ofcom's guidelines: "'Due' means adequate or appropriate to the subject and nature of the programme. So 'due impartiality' does not mean an equal division of time has to be given to every view, or that every argument and every facet of every argument has to be represented".[2] Informing a judgement about the appropriate sources to shape everyday politics, UK regulators typically refer to the amount of votes cast at the last general election or the parties currently riding high in the opinion polls (see Reynolds 2014). But, in doing so, the potentially vast world of politics arguably turns into a tiny village centred in Westminster and reliant on a highly select cast of characters. Moreover, ideologically speaking, these actors represent a political class not necessarily 'in touch' with the opinions of a huge swathe of the general public. Or, put differently, it is arguably not the most balanced or impartial way to understand the daily drama of politics. This is not to advance an argument for relaxing the impartiality requirements of UK broadcasters. Nor should this observation be interpreted as UK bulletins being in breach of their impartiality commitments. It is to suggest that live two-ways need not be as preoccupied with – or constrained by – reflecting the political voices they will have sourced (in most cases) *already* in an edited package.

The most explicit – and now infamous – example of the ideological limits of live two-ways examined throughout the book was on display in the year after the 2003 war in Iraq. For Andrew Marr, the BBC's political editor, tacitly conceded the obedient role he – and other journalists – adopted when accepting rather than challenging the Government's argument that WMD existed in Iraq. As a consequence, following the lead of the Labour Government – and the Conservative Party who, at the time, supported the war and the intelligence informing it – meant many journalists were largely duped, which in turn led to misinforming the public.

ANCHOR: … It must be well over a year since this 45-minute claim [in the Government's intelligence document] was made and still the argument goes on.

REPORTER: Well, that's right. If you go back to basics, does it matter? I think it does. That original dossier had three things within about two inches of the page. That Iraq had long-range missiles that for instance could hit Cyprus. That it had chemical and biological warheads. That weapons could be launched in 45 minutes. Now all of those claims, you know, about the size of my thumb, I guess, that they made together, the overall effect was extremely alarming. *And that's the effect that people like me and journal-ists across Westminster conveyed to the public.* Now if that is entirely wrong or largely wrong it's a big question and worth politicians arguing about. But I have to say the mood in Government is pretty robust about this. They feel all this is done with perfect 20/20 hindsight and that in the end it wasn't simply the 45-minute claim that triggered the war it was all sorts of other issues, including the breaching of the UN motions.

(BBC, 5 February 2004; emphasis added)

The BBC was not alone in replicating the perspectives of Western govern-ments' – namely the US and UK – portrayal of Iraq's WMD capabilities. Many mainstream outlets accepted their version of events (Cushion 2012a). *The New York Times* even apologized for not fulfilling its fourth estate duties and more robustly challenging the intelligence supplied by the US Government (*New York Times* 2004). Of course, this is a well-rehearsed and long-standing critique – echoing Becker's (1967) hierarchy of credibility or Bennett's (1990) elite indexing – about the reliance on institutional actors in coverage of politics more generally rather than anything specific about how coverage is interpreted in live two-way formats. But the rise of the live two-way arguably offers a distinctive format from the reporter package, which – as the beginning of this chapter established – typically relies on several sources to inform it. Having already

delivered a balance of elected mainstream parties, this perhaps represents a missed opportunity for the follow-up live two-way to not *only* reflect on the ruling party political viewpoints. For live two-way reporters could interpret politics within a broader framework, considering the views of a larger pool of experts outside of the Westminster bubble, or even listen to the policy preferences and concerns of voters when setting the day's political agenda (Lewis *et al.* 2005). In short, live two-ways appear to reinforce rather than potentially extend the routine ideological perspectives of politics in everyday bulletins.

Assessing the value and purpose of live two-ways in political reporting

Although the live two-way is open to ideological critique it does not necessarily mean the rise of live two-ways should be viewed as an adverse development in evening television bulletins. For while political editors do not appear to regularly move beyond the ideological dialogue of party politics, there is ample research to suggest routine reporter packages do not either. In the various studies drawn upon in this book, political actors of the main political parties – the Conservative and Labour Party in the UK and the Republicans and Democrats in the US – largely defined the ideological territory of political content in relatively short and snappy soundbites. So, for example, in the reporting of the 2004 budget almost all sources in Andrew Marr's package were MPs from competing parties offering their immediate (and brief) reaction. It was the two-way where the budget was made sense of for viewers, moving beyond the carefully choreographed soundbites and interpreting the differences between parties (admittedly, largely from a Westminster-only perspective). Indeed, Marr (2006: 286) – in his book *My Trade* – agrees, "two-ways can have a huge impact ... it does put the reporter into a different role than simply telling ... its joy is for once you can forget about what filmed pictures you do or don't have and can simply give verbal information". In other words, the live two-way – rather than edited news – privileges a reporter's opinion and analysis. Moreover, the aim of live two-way political reporting, Marr (2006: 286) continues, "should be to cut through the spin. Politicians do get a lot of coverage, but they tend to speak in the code of their trade. The job of the two-way is to tell the viewers and listeners, so far as one is able, what is actually going on". Montgomery (2007) – and other scholars analysing broadcast talk (e.g. Hutchby 2006; Montgomery 2007; Tolson 2006) – have rightly identified that two-way reporters have sought to communicate politics in a more informal and personal way. I "think", "sense" or "feel", for example, are the modes of address that today's two-way reporters – as exampled throughout this chapter – adopt to convey their impressions, opinions, analysis and judgements about everyday political stories.

But beyond the changing lexicon of emotionality and personalization in broadcasting, this more enhanced interpretive repertoire of two–way reporting has important democratic consequences in television news bulletins, a departure from just gathering facts and conveying them to routinely delivering verdicts about political events and issues. For the evidence in this chapter – and the book more generally – has suggested over time two-way reporters have more become more strident and interpretive, de-spinning the soundbites of politicians and questioning their tactics and motivations. While this is also on display in edited packages in, say, pieces to camera, the live two-way appears – and confirmed by Marr, a former BBC journalist – to invite more sustained analysis and interpretation of the latest political events. The elevated status of live two-way reporters and their more forthright approach to interpreting politics over recent decades has also been observed by the current (at the time of writing) BBC political editor, Nick Robinson. In an interview with *Total Politics* (Dale 2012), his view of two-ways is worth quoting at length.

INTERVIEWER: When I interviewed Adam Boulton, he said there was a lot more opinion creeping into news reporting. If you're doing live two-ways, it seems almost inevitable.

NICK ROBINSON: It depends what you mean by opinion. There's more comment and analysis than there was. Sometimes I have to dig out old reports, and they're a reminder of how very straight reporting was 20 years ago. Occasionally people come along and change things. John Cole and Michael Brunson did it, and then Andy Marr. They rewrote the rules, and it became partly commentary, partly sketch and partly reporting. It's not opinion that says, "My view on Europe is A, and I'm now going to try and persuade you". It is comment and analysis that says, "I think that this hides the fact that the prime minister hasn't got an answer to A" or, "I think the Labour Party is struggling to find the resolution to B".

(Dale 2012)

The role of two-way reporters, in other words, has evolved over time, with senior journalists today given greater freedom to pass judgements about the policies and strategies of the main political parties. As previously acknowl-edged, while this is clearly a response to the professionalization of political culture – of increasingly savvy spin doctors and campaign managers shaping contemporary politics – broadcasters have responded to this asking journ-alists to interpret not just describe the actions and behaviour of politicians. Throughout the 1990s, for example, it became a top-down BBC cultural mission to enhance the editorial licence of journalists to emphasize their expertise (Born 2004). Two-ways appear to be reflective of this shift into the new mil-lennium. Conversely, politicians appearing in their natural habitat – debating in political institutions – have been downsized (see Table 5.3). Instead, repor-ters more routinely interview them individually, with the journalist's own line of questioning brought to the fore along with the reporter's appearance and personality.

Of course, the wider culture of journalism has changed over recent decades – as Chapter 1 explained – where political reporters move from one medium to the next to convey their views and verdicts. For broadcasters this may have once meant smartening up their appearance when moving from radio to television. But over more recent years political journalists not only have an on screen profile, they are regularly asked to blog and tweet their immediate thoughts and political verdicts. In doing so, making their voices stand out from the crowd arguably has had a systemic impact on reporters, encouraging them to offer something distinctive in an increasingly crowded blogosphere and opinionated world of Twitter. In short, it is almost an occupational necessity for political journalists to form clear, distinctive and authoritative judgements today – fuelled by the wider culture of journalism – and this is perhaps reflected in more interpretive live two-way conventions.

While relying to a greater extent on media rather than political actors is a measure of the mediatization of politics (Strömbäck 2008), it should not – as previous chapters have also concluded – be assumed to necessarily reflect a shift towards a commercial agenda, a market-driven ploy to cut costs or frame politics as a game. Of course, talk can be cheap to produce and there is evidence – notably from the US – that two-ways have been used largely in this capacity, with reporting emphasizing the personalities of politicians, promoting the horse-race aspects of politics, campaigning tactics or negativity of parties (Tuggle et al. 2010; Patterson 2000). Moreover, two-ways can be overused by editors – as Marr (2006) also conceded – or they can be reliant on inexperienced reporters to convey complex policy debates in, say health, crime or business coverage. As already explored, it is a critique launched primarily at continuous formats of news – on radio or rolling news channels – with hours and hours of airtime to fill. Indeed, the journalistic convention of two-ways – as the Andrew Gilligan affair famously exposed (Montgomery 2006) – can lead to serious journalistic malpractices when reporters cannot interpret the world of politics with the necessary precision or nuance.

But the majority of two-ways in evening bulletins – as shown in the 2012 study – were conveyed by relatively experienced political editors clearly well-informed by relevant political actors. While this perhaps reinforced the Westminster-prism of reporting politics, it also led to political issues being subjected to perhaps greater scrutiny than they would have otherwise been exposed to if reliant exclusively on edited reporting or, more specifically, relatively brief political soundbites. At times, this meant the game-frame of politics was brought to the fore – with the competing tactical positioning of the mainstream parties conveyed – but analysis appeared to be mostly mixed with deliberations about policy at the heart of live political two-way reporting. Two-ways, in other words, represented an interpretive form of journalism that potentially has normative qualities of informing viewers about the substantive issues in everyday politics and public affairs (Blumler and Cushion 2014). It is a conclusion similarly reached by Esser and Umbricht (2014) in their longitudinal cross-national study of newspapers. For they argued, "interpretive journalism which explained complicated 'policy' matters in ways that help broader publics to comprehend the world of politics is not only a defendable, but laudable, press practice" (Esser and Umbricht 2014: 243).

The evidence overall in this chapter thus points towards qualified support for the live two-way reporting of everyday politics. For live two-ways – delivered by experienced political editors and centred on understanding the competing policies of political parties – can bring important interventions in television news bulletins. How far they help in the understanding of and engagement with public affairs is taken up in the next chapter. It further considers whether two-ways and a generally more journalist-centred style of news reporting strengthens or weakens democratic culture.

Notes

1 See Ofcom's guidelines for local television news bulletins, available online at http:// stakeholders.ofcom.org.uk/broadcasting/radio/localness/localness-guidelines (accessed 23 May 2014).
2 Ofcom's "Due impartiality" guidelines are available online at http://stakeholders.of com.org.uk/broadcasting/broadcast-codes/broadcast-code/impartiality/ (accessed 25 June 2014).

Chapter 6

Interpreting the impact and consequences of the mediatization of news and politics

Introduction

The aim of *News and Politics* has been to understand the changing form, structure and style of evening television bulletins, considering how political reporting in particular has changed over recent decades and become distinctive from all news. For television news bulletins continue to be a permanent fixture in TV schedules and, in many advanced Western democracies, they remain the most popular format of news and influential source for citizens to learn about what is happening in the world. The resilience of the television news bulletin – a mainstay in broadcasting spanning over 60 years – is in spite of competition from online news and social media platforms over recent decades. Of course, television news bulletins have not maintained the vast audiences they once did decades ago when broadcasters were the monopoly supplier. After all, in the new media age of online, multi-channel television audiences have fragmented. But irrespective of the apparent choice and diversity of new information sources, the old-fashioned appointment to watch television news – tuning into a fixed time bulletin – has *not* been supplanted by receiving information at the flick of a switch or the tap of an app.

Although the format of the television news bulletin has withstood competition, the aim of this book has been to interpret whether its *raison d'être* – to bring viewers the day's news – has changed in light of the broader transformation of journalism, where news is delivered instantly on dedicated 24-hour news channels, online and social media platforms. Put another way, the book asked have television news bulletins adapted their format over recent decades to keep up with the pace and immediacy of contemporary journalism? In order to systematically and longitudinally examine the changing nature of television news bulletins over recent decades, the book drew on the concepts of mediatization and journalistic interventionism. By interpreting the mediatization of news and interventionist nature of different conventions, the goal was to consider if a systemic influence was evident in the format of evening bulletins. Had long-standing conventions and practices changed over time in order to reflect the journalistic thirst and pressure to bring viewers the latest news and instant analysis? This approach is consistent with Esser and Strömbäck's (2014a: 6; their emphasis) interpretation of mediatization in the context of politics, whereby the concept is used to understand a *"long-term process through which the importance of the media and their spill-over effects on political processes, institutions, organizations and actors have increased"*. In the context of this book's aim, the *"spill-over effects"* refer to the role and influence of rolling news logics (re)shaping the logic of fixed time bulletins.

But as the Introduction to the book explained, this analytical approach departs from conventional mediatization wisdom when interpreting the media influence on news and political reporting. For a singular logic in news media tends to be the accepted way of understanding the mediatization of politics (Strömbäck and Esser 2009), as opposed to a multiplicity of competing journalistic logics and different levels of journalistic interventionism. Not only that, it was argued that interpreting different logics amongst media outlets and systems prevents an understanding of how the media might mediatize itself. At first glance, this might appear a tautological proposition. But the aim was to ask if the broader values of contemporary journalism – enhancing the immediacy, pace and interpretive nature of news – was empirically apparent over time on the format of evening bulletins. Or, put another way, had a rolling news logic been increasingly subscribed to in fixed time bulletins?

This chapter begins by bringing together the key findings of the previous four chapters and considering them in light of ongoing debates informing the mediatization of politics. The first section summarizes the longitudinal examination of news coverage generally and political news specifically (Chapters 2 and 3), the cross-national comparative assessment of US, UK and Norwegian bulletins (Chapter 4), as well as the close textual understanding of the role of live two-ways and their value in conveying the world of politics (Chapter 5). This chapter then interprets the changes identified in the routine delivery of news from the perspective of viewers, reviewing the evidence about how audiences understand television news and the reporting of politics. The final section considers the future of mediatization debates, interpreting competing media logics and understanding the value of journalistic interventionism.

Enhancing the mediatization of news and journalistic interventionism: assessing longitudinal trends and differences between media systems

As Chapter 1 explored, television news evolved over many decades post World War II and, by the beginning of the 1980s, had entered into a period of maturity relying on a familiar set of routine conventions to shape an evening bulletin. To interpret any changes in the format of television news bulletins after this period – when dedicated news channels arrived – and assess how far they resembled rolling news practices, the book reinterpreted conventions as journalistic interventions. Broadly speaking, this relates to the "discretionary power" of journalists in reporting election campaigns (Semetko *et al.* 1991: 3). Since a greater degree of journalistic interventionism is seen to enhance the mediatization of politics (Strömbäck and Esser 2009), interpreting the "discretionary power" of journalists in routine conventions can reveal how far news is mediatized.

Moreover, the attempt in the studies drawn upon in this book was to theorize routine conventions and consider how interventionist they were according to a fixed or rolling news logic. So, for example, a fixed time logic privileges edited news, carefully scripted and produced, informed by multiple sources and subject to close editorial oversight. Rolling news logic, by comparison, delivers live news at a quicker pace, with live two-ways asking reporters to interpret ongoing events or make instant judgements without a script to hand. The book thus asked if a mediatization of bulletins was evident – a shift from a fixed to a rolling news logic – by assessing whether routine television news conventions have become more interventionist over time. More standardized measures of mediatization – such as soundbites or journalistic visibility – were more specifically examined in coverage of politics. The comparative and cross-national dimension to the book – with broadcasters operating under different public service obligations and market-driven pressures examined – meant the proposition that commercial media systems are more susceptible to mediatized influences could also be empirically tested (Strömbäck 2008).

Chapter 2 identified some clear longitudinal trends in the conventions of UK television news bulletins from 1991 to 2012. The pace of news delivery was enhanced, with a steady flow of shorter items narrated by television anchors a feature of today's evening bulletins. This was compounded by a reduction in edited packages and enhancement of live reporting. Live reporting – most strikingly in the use of two-ways – involved much shorter items compared to the sometimes lengthy edited packages. When different genres of news were isolated further, live coverage was found to be most prominently displayed in the reporting of politics. Live political reporting was also characterized as being more interpretive than other newsworthy topics, such as business or crime, with journalists routinely drawn upon to make sense of events and issues. Indeed, compared to edited news, live reporting relied far less on sources – whether political or business actors – to inform a story or make sense of it. Overall, it was suggested that the underlying logic of evening bulletins had changed, from covering the 'day's news' to reporting 'news as it happens' – a maxim familiar to the world of dedicated 24-hour news channels. While these trends can be interpreted as reflecting a mediatization of television news bulletins, they were not on display to a greater extent on the commercial broadcaster.

Indeed, the findings appeared to challenge some of the assumptions explaining the causes of mediatization, including technological, professional and commercial forces (Esser 2013a). For while evidence of changing technology and professional values was on display – with the ability to go live easier and deliver instant responses to news events and issues – it was argued that a shift in logic was not necessarily tantamount to market-driven influence. Moreover, the editorial decision to convey politics by the live two-way convention as opposed to editorial packages, for example, was arguably based on values associated with public service broadcasting aimed at raising viewers' understanding and knowledge about public affairs. Since ITV is a commercial public service broadcaster, it could be that the UK's hybrid broadcasting system is distinctive from other countries, such as the US, where market demands take greater precedence. Rather than viewing the mediatization of news as an adverse development, the chapter concluded that the interventionist role of journalists could serve to offer a more robust interpretation of issues, including the questioning and scrutiny of political actors.

To consider the mediatization of politics more systematically, Chapter 3 longitudinally traced whether all political news was distinctive from news generally between 1991 and 2013. It did so by drawing on well-established mediatized measures, as well as the type of journalistic interventions used, to report politics compared to all news. On the face of it, the study found some counter-intuitive findings, challenging trends more widely documented in political communication and journalism studies. So, for example, the length of soundbites or imagebites remained at the same level over successive decades. However, when live and edited political reporting was isolated and compared over time, some significant editorial changes were brought into sharper focus. While the form and style of edited news remained relatively similar, live news – as Chapter 2 established – substantially increased post millennium. Moreover, live news can be characterized as being far more interventionist than edited reporting, since political voices were less audible (relying on fewer soundbites) and journalists far more visible, routinely interpreting the latest issues and events. Put another way, journalists increasingly became more central actors in the reporting of politics, with the live two-way visually promoting the importance of the reporter's instant analysis.

In light of the distinctive role of live television news reporting, Chapter 3 concluded that studies about the mediatization of politics should place greater emphasis on the changing practice and culture of journalism. For mediatized measures tend to centre on the role of political actors – how they are sourced or appear in edited news – rather than on understanding how news is communicated about politics. As Chapter 2 argued, the character of evening bulletins appears to increasingly resemble a rolling news logic, injecting immediacy and interpretation into the routine reporting of politics. There was, once again, little to distinguish between broadcasters operating under different media systems. Indeed, it was the BBC – a wholesale public service broadcaster – that was the most mediatized, displaying a robustly interventionist approach to reporting politics. Equating mediatization with market logic – a commercial undercurrent – is thus open to challenge. As the previous chapter concluded, it could be that the market excesses of ITV – a commercial public service broadcaster – are restricted by its long-standing regulatory obligations. Turning to live two-way reporters to interpret the everyday world of politics, in other words, could reflect a public service desire to better enlighten viewers.

Chapter 4 offered a cross-national perspective to the comparative nature of television news, an increasingly important part of communication research. The aim was to systematically examine coverage on US, UK and Norwegian bulletins subject to different levels of public service obligations and market-driven pressures. But this comparative approach also meant evening bulletins could not only be compared between competing media systems, their form, structure and style could be examined in the context of different political identities and journalism cultures between each nation. Indeed, the study revealed the character of Norwegian bulletins – relying on pre-edited packaged news to convey the day's news – was distinctive from US and UK coverage, which relied more heavily on live conventions and interpretive reporting to convey what is happening in the world. The long-standing presence of 24-hour news channels in the latter two countries, it was suggested, could explain the greater resemblance to the rolling news coverage. For a dedicated Norwegian 24-hour news channel only began broadcasting in 2007, meaning the convergence between fixed and rolling news practices and conventions could still be in its infancy (Lund 2012).

The second part of Chapter 4 developed a more detailed follow-up comparative study of UK and US evening bulletins, including Channel 5 news, the least regulated public service broadcaster. The US has been singled out for having the most mediatized environment of political news, with a long history of independent journalism produced at arm's length from the government of the day. However, contrary to conventional mediatization wisdom, on a range of measures – from the visibility of journalists, reporters wrapping up news and interpreting it to a greater extent, to the more frequent use and length of imagebites – the UK exhibited a more interventionist approach to reporting routine politics. But the comparative dimension to the study revealed a greater degree of mediatization was present in political news produced by broadcasters with the greatest public service responsibilities. Considering the relative degree of mediatization, Channel 5 appeared to hover somewhere between US and UK coverage, perhaps reflecting the market-driven demands of US network news but also balancing the obligations inherent in the UK's public service framework. The conclusions thus challenged conventional mediatization wisdom that commercialism enhances interventionism or that a robust public service broadcasting system prevents it. Moreover, it was suggested that the type and nature of journalistic interventionism – such as lengthy two-ways or the visibility of reporters – should not be assumed to reflect a market logic but could deliver public service goals depending on the quality of communication.

The aim of Chapter 5 was to consider the value of mediatization more carefully by examining the role of live two-way reporting more qualitatively – a key transformation in television journalism established in previous chapters. Overall, the chapter concluded by offering qualified support for live two-way reporting of everyday politics. While talk can be cheap – a critique familiar to rolling news (Sambrook and McGuire 2014) or under-resourced newsrooms (Tuggle *et al.* 2010) – in UK evening bulletins two-ways were delivered by mostly experienced political editors. Indeed, both BBC and ITV political editors make up about 10 per cent of all news examined in 2012 – an amount that doubled when just live news was isolated. The role of Channel 5's political editor was even greater – representing a fifth of all news and over 40 per cent of all live news. In short, political editors occupy a significant proportion of airtime in contemporary evening bulletins.

In analysing more than 400 two-ways throughout this book, the game frame – where reporters consider the political personalities, party strategies and opinion polls shaping politics – was clearly part and parcel of routine two-way coverage. However, most two-ways mixed the game frame with an understanding of the mainstream party policies. It was argued this limited the ideological parameters of live two-way reporting, with politics understood largely through a Westminster-prism. Of course, strict impartiality requirements perhaps mitigated the freedom of reporters to move too far beyond the voices of elected representatives. But since political actors appear in edited packages that typically run immediately before a live two-way convention, reporters could – it was suggested – cast their interpretive nets wider and consider the broader ideological consequences from other information sources. Nevertheless, although the live two-way does appear to reinforce rather than extend the party-political dialogue of the mainstream parties, this type of journalistic intervention arguably subjects politics to greater scrutiny than edited news. After all, in the increasing professionalization of politics – where politicians deliver carefully scripted soundbites and remain on message – it was argued that live two-ways brought important journalistic interventions, making sense of party-political manoeuvring. Indeed, there was evidence to suggest – and supported by past and present political editors of the BBC (Marr 2006; Robinson 2012) – that live two-way reporters had become more interpretive into the new millennium, routinely delivering instant analysis and judgements about the actions and behaviour of parties and politicians.

In brief, live two-ways involving experienced political reporters were viewed as being able to potentially enlighten viewers about public affairs. The next section considers the evidence about viewers' experience and interpretation of live two-way reporting, before moving on to broader debates about the possible impact the mediatization of politics has on advancing people's knowledge and understanding of public affairs.

Live two-ways and the mediatization of politics: enhancing knowledge and understanding?

The shift towards a live and interventionist style of reporting in television news raises important questions about the changing information environment and how people understand contemporary politics (Blumler and Cushion 2014). After all, in most Western advanced democracies evening television bulletins continue to be the most watched format of news, despite the rise of online and social media platforms. However, there is a lack of audience research exploring how viewers' interpret and understand news according to different types of television news conventions. Studies have long established that viewers do not retain a huge amount of information after watching television news (Lewis 1991), but visuals – pictures or images – can enhance their recall of particular events (Graber 1990). Grabe and Bucy (2009) have more recently argued scholars still do not take images seriously in television news. They forensically examined how political actors appeared – such as imagebites, a measure of mediatization examined in previous chapters – in edited packages during TV coverage of US elections from 1992 to 2004. Tracking their longitudinal findings with election polling data, their evidence suggested viewers were influenced by visual framing – encouraging emotional responses – favouring Republican candidates in particular (Grabe and Bucy 2009).

While studies examining the visual cues and editing techniques of television news have increased over recent years, little sustained scholarly attention has been paid to how live images – in the form of two-ways, for example – shape viewers' understanding of political information (beyond questions of partisan bias) more generally. And yet, as the evidence in this book has shown, the longitudinal trends in television news suggest it is live – not edited – journalism that increasingly informs people about what is going on in the world.

Snoeijer et al.'s (2002) experimental study of 161 Dutch viewers offered a comparative assessment of the information recall of the live cross-talk convention (e.g. a live two-way) as opposed to an edited reporter package. The results were somewhat mixed. On the one hand, audience responses suggested live cross-talks were not as effective as field reports (e.g. edited packages) in the recall of political news (Snoeijer et al. 2002). On the other hand, audience appreciation of the story – measured by perceived importance, objectivity, attractiveness, understandability and immediacy – did not appear to be influenced by either a live or edited format. Given the limited scope, size and nature of the study – where just one story was compared in different format presentations – it would be hard to reach any definitive conclusions based on their research. Moreover, Snoeijer et al. (2002: 97) encouraged researchers to investigate the different formats of news further in order to "offer a more complete understanding of the informative and evaluative virtues of live reporting". So, for example, examining the informational recall and appreciation of conventions that operate in tandem, such as an edited package supplemented by a live two-way, where the reporter offers additional background and interpretation to a story.

However, crucial to enhancing viewers' understanding of television news is the quality of contextual information and how it is communicated. Tuggle *et al.*'s (2007) survey of attitudes towards live news reporting amongst 18–24 year olds is a case in point. Because of the emphasis of breaking news coverage in US local television news bulletins, they found many young people questioned the journalistic purpose and value of 'going live'. But even more source-driven journalism can bring knowledge gaps. Perhaps counter-intuitively, Jerit's (2009) analysis of US newspapers, for example, suggested the deployment of expert commentators reduced – rather than enhanced – people's understanding of a topic amongst the least knowledgeable. Expert commentary, in this context, referred to any specialized expert source quoted or paraphrased in an article, rather than a journalist supplying greater explanation to a story. Indeed, Jerit (2009) found the inclusion of contextual information – including additional social, economic or political background to a story – increased gaps in public knowledge. Her conclusions are instructive for communicating news in different formats:

> the findings suggest that modest changes in writing style (e.g., avoiding jargon, providing information about why or how events occurred and in what context) might go a long way toward erasing knowledge gaps. Likewise, it might be time to modify certain journalistic practices, such as the tendency to provide contextual information early on in the reporting of an event but not in subsequent news stories.
>
> (Jerit 2009: 454)

In the context of the rise of live two-way reporting, it could be that the contextual information supplied after an edited package – drawing attention to the crux of the story and interpreting it clearly – could help towards erasing the knowledge gaps Jerit identified. Examining Norwegian television news and newspapers during the 2009 election, for example, Grøttum and Aalberg (2012) suggested many readers and viewers found it difficult to understand the vocabulary of reporting or did not have the sufficient background understanding to make sense of the issues covered. In other words, political journalists assumed their audiences – and reporters on the public service broadcaster NRK were singled out – held the necessary knowledge to interpret what was being reported.

It is, of course, difficult to generalize the findings of these limited array of studies. Clearly, many are informed by media system level influences of specific countries – from the US's hypercommericalized market-driven environment to Norway's more closely regulated culture of public service broadcasting. But also the political environment could shape the comprehensiveness of reporting. More professionalized political cultures – where media management and spin doctors influence politicking – could enhance the game aspect of news, as reporters seek to de-spin their tactics and soundbites. How politics is routinely communicated and understood by viewers, in short, needs to be carefully considered in the context of the wider political culture as well as in the format and structure of television news coverage.

In respect of UK evening bulletins – the primary object of study in this book – the evidence revealed it was experienced political editors – not junior correspondents relied on in rolling news channels – who were central actors in communicating politics. Moreover, the UK's overarching public service frame-work has arguably shaped a broadcasting culture sensitive to raising public knowledge of its audience as well as maintaining journalistic independence by robustly scrutinizing the political class – a deep-rooted instinct to remain impartial that perhaps reinforces the Westminster-prism of reporting. This was encapsulated by an internal BBC review titled *Beyond the Soundbite* – a report published after the 2001 General Election which produced the lowest turnout in eighty years (Kevill 2002). The main public service broadcaster, in other words, felt personal responsibility to not just engage citizens but better inform them about politics by encouraging its reporters to interpret the beha-viour and actions of politicians. The rise of the live two-way, in this context, represents this twin mission – a point Andrew Marr (2006), former BBC poli-tical editor, has acknowledged. But how far this informalization or emotionality of broadcasting (Montgomery 2007) has contributed directly to re-engaging viewers in politics or enhancing understanding of public affairs remain open questions for future studies to address.

How do these conclusions more broadly inform debates about the relation-ship between audiences and an increasing mediatization of politics? As Witschge (2014: 344) has pointed out, in "empirical research into the mediati-zation of politics, there seems less attention for the audience and the focus is rather on the interplay between media and political actors". Broadly speaking, however, it is possible to detect a pessimistic mood amongst mediatization of politics scholars, a pejorative development in the worlds of politics and journalism – and ultimately democracy (Esser and Strömbäck 2014b: 225–26). But this broad-brush – and largely pernicious – assessment of the impact of mediatization is primarily concerned with the systemic relationship between politics and news media, rather than the reception of audiences and the wider influence on citizenship. Scholars make reference to effects literature such as priming, framing, content analysis or agenda-setting, but implicitly – as Witschge (2014) observed – the influence of mediatization tends to be characterized as promoting the strategic game frame or focusing on nega-tivity or personalization. And these trends – associated primarily with a market-driven logic – in turn create cynicism, disengaging citizens from poli-tical institutions and from participating in democracy and voting. While the relationship between news media coverage and audience consumption has been positively interpreted – creating a "virtuous circle" as Norris (2000) put it – potentially enhancing people's knowledge, engagement and participation in democratic politics in different contexts (Baum 2003), the effects literature tends to be overshadowed by the destructive role played by the mediatization of politics.

There is, of course, good reason to be pessimistic about some of the general trends established in literature about the mediatization of politics. For there is widespread evidence to suggest that the normative supply of information necessary to adequately inform citizens about politics and public affairs has diminished over recent decades (Cushion 2012a). However, as Esser and Matthes (2013) have cautioned, empirical analysis rather than systemic theories are needed to advance mediatization debates of the future. They write:

> Although it may be natural to ask whether mediatization improves or worsens the quality of democracy, in actual research this question needs to be broken down in more specific investigations. Does mediatization have a positive or negative influence on the structure and functioning of public communication?
>
> (Esser and Matthes 2013: 200)

To answer this question directly, the argument advanced in this book has been to offer qualified support for the mediatization of politics on *evening television news bulletins*. The various studies drawn upon established that the changing format of television news – enhancing the interventionist role of senior reporters delivering news in live contexts – could improve the quality of information for viewers. Put another way, a rolling news logic had reshaped the form, structure and style of fixed time bulletins in ways that might more meaningfully communicate and interpret political news for viewers. But as previously acknowledged, empirical research examining audience engagement with different news conventions is needed to assess how far this potential is fulfilled. To more precisely evaluate the normative value of mediatization of politics, there is thus a need for more specific case studies exploring the relationship between politics, news *and* audiences.

On the face of it, the concept of mediatization puts journalists centre stage in the reporting of politics. As de Vreese (2014) has argued, journalists have the power to frame politics, to make sense of fast-moving events and issues in ways that police the boundaries of audience understanding. Frames are thus important because

> they showcase how journalistic conventions and production processes translate political events into templates for news stories ... They can therefore be considered indicative of mediatization where journalism has the upper hand in determining not only what is covered but also how it is covered in

the news. The frames are also important because these templates make a real difference for the audience.

(de Vreese 2014: 148)

But while the evidence in this book has suggested political journalists have acquired greater "discretionary powers" over recent decades (Semetko *et al.* 1991: 3), audiences have arguably *indirectly* influenced how journalists interpret the world of politics. The rise of the live two-way, for example, could be interpreted in the context of broadcasters wanting to raise viewers' understanding and engagement with political affairs. Thus, moving beyond the soundbite – to paraphrase the BBC review cited earlier in this section (Kevill 2002) – was an attempt to de-spin the voices of politicians by changing the conventions from edited packages to live formats used to convey politics. For representative surveys have revealed the increasing disengagement of citizens from politics – measured not just in declining levels of voter turnouts (throughout the 1990s into the new millennium) but also in the public's suspicion towards, and the lack of trust in, their elected representatives.

Tolson (2011) has persuasively connected trust to an understanding of why journalists increasingly frame politics in live two-ways rather than in edited formats. He close textually examined the reporting of the UK budget – an annual Parliamentary event in April, where the chancellor of the exchequer allocates government resources – by comparing the conventions used in BBC television news bulletins in 1984, 2005 and 2009. In brief, Tolson (2011) identified a reduction in the length of airtime for politicians, leaving less space for them to articulate their positions. Consistent with the quantitative trends identified throughout this book, the reporting of budgets in 2005 and 2009 made greater use of live two-ways by political and business editors. Tolson's (2011) analysis drew attention to the issue of trust by focusing on how live reporters interpreted the politics of the budget by considering – or, more to the point, questioning – the integrity of what politicians say. He labelled this "'sceptical pragmatics'", a form of journalistic discourse that alludes to policies or ideologies and emphasizes the veracity of a politicians' statement or motivation. In Tolson's (2011: 70) words, "In sceptical pragmatics ... doubt about the quality of what someone is saying has become the norm, not the exception. In journalism of this kind, politics is characterised as a theatre of talk in which everyone is predisposed to be sceptical of what anyone might be saying".

Although adopting this "sceptical" position appears – according to Tolson – to represent an adverse development in political journalism, it might reflect what McNair (2000) would label a healthy adversarial reporting style. Chapter 5 suggested that, while there were moments when journalists focused on the candidates' character – promoting the game frame – matters of policy remained at the heart of live two-way reporting. Tolson (2011) did conclude, however, that in very recent years reporting had begun to focus on the ideological differences between parties (when the UK entered into coalition politics in 2010) rather than on political personalities. This draws attention to the reflexive process of mediatization – a term primarily used to capture the tug of war between journalists and politicians – but it could equally involve citizens' attitudes towards politics. During the 1990s and 2000s in the UK, for example, there was heightened suspicion of politicians' motives – most often associated with the rise of spin and sleaze of New Labour (McNair 2004) – perhaps culminating in the MPs expenses scandal in 2009. As a consequence, it could be journalists reorient their framing of news and interpretation of it according to both the changing political culture and the public's perception of politics.

The news media, of course, are not immune from the reflexive process of mediatization and journalists themselves routinely face public scorn and scrutiny. The level of trust invested in journalists can influence not just public attitudes towards politics generally, but which parties and policies they support and champion. The rise of cable news channels in the US – with Fox News being the operative example – has shown the ideological muscle journalists can flex when reporting matters of policy. Studies have revealed Fox can encourage viewers to understand particular policies – on immigration, the wars in Iraq and terrorism – which can promote right-wing agendas (Morris 2007). Moreover, without the regulatory requirement to remain impartial – rescinded in 1987 – surveys have shown US audiences increasingly turn to trusted partisan programming, with MSNBC acting as a less vociferous left-wing equivalent to Fox News. In doing so, an increasingly unregulated and partisan news environment can change the effect of mediatization – translating it into a powerful ideological force and working against the promotion of a reasoned and rational public sphere. Indeed, trust in television news is generally low in the US – a Gallup poll indicated just 18 per cent indicated they had a "great deal" or "quite a lot" of trust towards the medium – a finding that more than halved since the early 1990s (Dugan 2014).

However, the evening bulletins longitudinally examined in this book have been UK public service broadcasters, which are all subject to strict 'due impartiality' guidelines. This emphasis on impartiality makes broadcasting distinctive to other media, such as the loosely regulated newspaper market or the new world of online news and social media. As a consequence, the relationship audiences have with television news is different when compared to other sources of political news or indeed with political parties. While trust in media and political institutions has generally declined from the 1990s into the new millennium, a representative YouGov survey (Eaton 2012) revealed that the BBC still stands out as the most trusted information source (see Table 6.1). Moreover, it is broadcasters with the greatest public service obligations – the BBC and ITV – which respondents considered the most truthful in the communication of politics. Asked to name their most important news source – without prompting – another 2013 representative poll showed the BBC was chosen by the majority of respondents (58 per cent) – far higher than ITV (14 per cent) and other organizations (BBC 2013). Even during moments of 'crisis' – in the

Table 6.1 Media and political sources: Who do the British public trust to "tell the truth"?

BBC news journalists	44%
ITV news journalists	41%
Journalists on 'upmarket' papers (e.g. *Times, Telegraph, Guardian*)	38%
My local MP	37%
Leading Labour politicians	23%
Senior civil servants in Whitehall	21%
Leading Conservative politicians	19%
Journalists on 'mid-market' newspapers (e.g. *Mail, Express*)	18%
Leading Liberal Democrat politicians	16%
Senior officials in the European Union	13%
Journalists on red-top tabloid newspapers (e.g. *Sun, Mirror*)	10%

(Adapted from Eaton 2012)

aftermath of the Hutton Inquiry or the revelations about Jimmy Saville – the public consistently invested the most trust in the BBC when compared to rival broadcasters and other media competitors.

In light of the continued trust and value the public holds towards the BBC and public service broadcasters more generally, the rise of live and interpretive news in evening bulletins appears not to have diminished viewers' perceptions when compared to the voices and views of other political and media actors. Perhaps due to broadcasters' commitment towards impartiality and other regulatory safeguards, audiences trust the analysis and judgements of political reporters more so than tabloid journalists and politicians. Moreover, studies examining public knowledge show that understanding of politics and public affairs improves when people are exposed to news produced by public service broadcasters (Aalberg and Curran 2011; Cushion 2012b; Soroka *et al.* 2013). The conclusions of these studies are often based on the premise that public service broadcasters – in the UK and throughout much of Europe – deliver a more serious news agenda than the market-driven journalism prevalent in the US. But it could *also* be based on the more interpretive approach and style of television news conventions – identified throughout this book – that enhance viewers' knowledge and understanding of public affairs and politics. As already acknowledged, future studies examining how viewers learn about what is happening in the world should consider how news is conveyed on television – by different types of conventions – *in addition* to the information supplied.

Towards a mediatized future in news and political reporting? Understanding and interpreting new logics

Over the course of writing this book, debates about the concept and value of mediatization have intensified. Deacon and Stanyer (2014: 1032), for example, launched a wide-ranging critique of mediatization, asking whether it was worthy of being viewed as a "key concept" or if scholars had jumped on a "conceptual bandwagon". Interpreting mediatization debates generally, they highlighted three major issues. The first related to the media-centric nature of the concept. In their view, this emphasis potentially marginalizes other variables that could explain changes and developments under analysis. The second was the lack of research examining media over time, which meant historical changes were often presumed rather than empirically demonstrated. Part of this critique also included a lack of cross-national comparative studies examining mediatization. A third issue questioned the application of the concept, with mediatization often used in an abstract way, and constructed broadly and imprecisely. Deacon and Stanyer (2014: 1041) even accuse some scholars of not wanting

> to descend the ladder and carefully operationalize mediatization, preferring the comfortable generality of the world of no difference. In our view, the failure to develop discriminatory focus will mean that 'mediatization' remains little more than a tag which will inevitably mean that misgathering occurs and confusion reigns.

In short, the authors argued the design of much mediatization research is too media-driven, overly reliant on cross-sectional data and not methodologically rigorous about the changes being measured.

Each of these criticisms will be addressed in turn in the context of the approach taken in the book. First, the changing conventions and practices of television news specifically and political reporting generally were understood within broader historical and social developments. As acknowledged in the previous section, changes in political news – in respect of reporters questioning the integrity of politicians – were related to broader changing attitudes. So, for example, the scepticism of political journalists (Tolson 2011) was related to declining levels of public trust towards the political establishment and in society more generally. But other areas – from technological developments to regulatory requirements – were directly and indirectly connected to the changing character of television news. Second, most of the book examined television news longitudinally. While Chapter 1 provided the historical journey of evening bulletins – from their inception to their maturity into the 1980s – most of the remaining chapters sought to empirically examine, in detail, television news from the beginning of the 1990s to well over a decade into the new millennium. Although it was not possible to retrospectively obtain longitudinal data in the US or Norway, Chapter 4 did offer an insight into the cross-national differences between countries as well as broadcasters operating under different public and commercial systems. Further still, the book has drawn on a wider range of cross-national studies to interpret comparative trends. In this sense, the approach taken in the book supports Deacon and Stanyer's recommendation (2014: 1038) that since "mediatization is a concept that presupposes historical change, scholars that invoke it cannot afford to be incurious about charting its emergence and momentum". Third, and finally, the media and changes identified in previous chapters have not been explored generally or in an abstract way throughout the book. For not only was the early evening television bulletin the specific format of news under empirical inspection, the changing use of conventions were operationalized clearly, as well as other measures of mediatization, such as soundbites or imagebites, journalistic visibility or the type and nature of interpretation supplied by live reporters. Indeed, it was also suggested the form, structure and style of evening bulletins and the type of journalistic interventionism supplied was partly explained by the different political cultures, journalism traditions and regulatory oversight of bulletins broadcast under distinctive cross-national media systems. Generally speaking, then, the aim of *News and Politics* has been to interpret mediatization in the wider context of economic, political and cultural changes, and by developing a rigorous research design to analyse media over time.

While *News and Politics* is guilty of further popularizing the concept of mediatization, it would be difficult to argue the book has been a dedicated follower of fashion. For rather than simply jumping on the same conceptual bandwagon, the intention of the book has been to move specific mediatization of politics debates beyond whether political news conformed to either a media or political logic. In this conventional framework, journalists promoting a media logic are represented by whether the voices of politicians are reinterpreted by reporters, rather than allowing them to speak for themselves. This journalistic autonomy and power is measured mostly in mediatization studies at election time and has been labelled an *intervention* – a symbolic victory of media trumping political logic – at a critical battleground moment during the campaign. However, the scope of this book went beyond election campaigns and suggested a more media-specific framework could be developed that examined all news.

While acknowledging the tautology involved, the broader aim was to interpret the mediatization of news by theorizing competing media logics – of fixed time and rolling news platforms – and empirically testing whether they had converged over time on the format of evening bulletins. Or, put another way, trends of mediatization could be disentangled between media formats and according to dominant journalistic norms and routines. It was suggested operating with one media logic – as has been widely pointed out within the mediatization literature – means interpreting broad and generalized changes in journalism, including from sometimes radically different mediums and outlets. By making the object of study more precise – the evening television news bulletin – and developing specific content indicators measuring changing conventions and practices, it was argued a more nuanced framework could be established to understand the mediatization of news.

Comparing the underlying logics of fixed time and rolling news thus offered a more nuanced understanding of mediatization compared to the designs of many studies. As opposed to identifying changes within a format of news according to one overarching media logic, it was suggested these competing logics operate simultaneously – both within the culture of broadcast news and more broadly on online and social media platforms – where news is delivered instantly and on a rolling basis. By not understanding the self-reflexivity of media structures, forms and styles or how wider social, political and economic forces shape them, media logic can be homogenized and fail to capture the machinations shaping the process of mediatization. Moreover, mediatization scholars could extend their vocabulary and reconsider media logic as competing *journalism logics*, subject to changes over time and broader influences rather than viewing it as singular and uniform in scope. From changing technological possibilities, political conditions, cultural attitudes to issues of convergence, regulation, ownership and market pressures, by routinely making sense of journalism logics mediatization studies could more carefully interrogate changes within and between different media systems, platforms and cross-national cultures.

For the underlying logics of competing media – whether hyperlocal websites, dedicated 24-hour news channels or opinionated blogs – could be pushing and pulling competing journalisms in new and of course overlapping directions. After all, in the age of convergence – as Chapter 1 explored – journalists tend not to operate on one medium, but in multiple outlets, from tweeting the latest news to reporting in live radio spots or producing edited television packages, all with similar but somewhat distinctive logics. Klinger and Svensson (2014: 11) have recently argued, in this respect, a mass media logic operated differently according to "content production, information distrubition and media use" from a network media logic. They suggested these dimensions of network logic – epitomized by social media platforms such as YouTube, Facebook and Twitter – operate distinctively although not entirely separately from traditional mass media. As a consequence, they concluded, "it is the task of empirical studies to distinguish and measure the extent of mass media and network media logic in specific cases" (Klinger and Svensson 2014: 12).

Although this book has been primarily concerned with a traditional mass media format, it has from a different perspective followed Klinger and Svensson's (2014) suggestion to empirically disentangle the logics of competing old and new journalistic conventions and practices. Theorizing specific indicators measuring different media logics and then empirically testing them over time – as the studies informing this book have shown – can allow scholars to interpret the prevailing values shaping contemporary journalism. The more specific the object of study – the role of Twitter or YouTube, say, or a live blog – the more precise scholars could be in understanding the logics shaping it. So, for example, this book has suggested the rise of live, interpretive reporting on fixed time bulletins could be due to the systemic impact of the 24-hour news cycle. As this rolling news logic encouraged broadcasters to deliver news – notably from the world of politics – in a more instant and rolling format, it was suggested the underlying logic of fixed time news had changed accordingly. Taking this one step further, it could be that a fixed time logic is also distinctive according to the time it is broadcast and the wider influences that come with it. Put another way, a lunchtime or late evening bulletin – compared to the early evening one examined in this study – could convey news according to different logics. A lunchtime bulletin, for instance, might be able to bring the latest news or live action when institutional actors are in full swing – debating in Parliament or hosting press conferences – whereas a late night bulletin might be more reflective of the day's news, a time when the cycle of news produces less newsworthy events. The specific journalism logics shaping the production of news, in other words, should be interpreted in the context of the wider social, political and economic environment.

As media logics from the world of mass media and social media networks continue to evolve and intersect it is important to empirically trace how they do so in the future. As this book has shown, the journalistic logics of immediacy and interpretation – emblematic of new media values – have become important to the format of evening bulletins, a departure from the use of edited conventions towards more live reporters conveying what is happening in the world. How far live and edited news practices will continue to be balanced in fixed time bulletins remains an open question, but any reduction or enhancement in their use could reveal the dominant logics shaping television journalism. The concept of mediatization, in this context, could be used as a future yardstick to empirically measure the evolution of evening bulletins or other specific media formats over time.

Of course, in the network age the life span of fixed time bulletins appears to be coming to an end. The future of news tends to emphasize the participatory nature of its audiences – not the empowerment of journalists – diminishing their interventionist power and influence. When the *Huffington Post* launched "TV news for the Internet age" in 2012, for example, they asked: "If you were going to create the concept of TV news from scratch today, what would it look like? For starters, you wouldn't do it on a broadcast network" (Bercovici 2012). The initiative, in its words, "would be less linear and more on-demand than anything you can do on television. Above all, it would make full use of the web's two-way interactivity to turn viewers into participants" (Bercovici 2012). Once most households have Internet services that seamlessly converge with conventional television viewing – a process already underway in many Western countries – this increasingly live, visual and interactive approach to journalism could soon become a familiar reality for audiences.

Broadly speaking, enhancing the live news experience has been positively interpreted in previous chapters when used in the two-way convention. But this was qualified by the need for informative and engaging journalists to interpret and make sense of public affairs and politics. Put another way, while this book has argued the live two-way television experience has an important value and purpose for audiences, future interactivity should not be reduced to viewers picking and choosing between live streams and decontextualized images. After all, uploading more videos and raw footage might sound more democratic, but in the information blizzard it would no doubt produce, an experienced, knowledgeable and enlightening journalist would still be needed to consider the veracity of competing sources, to challenge and scrutinize political elites and to explain the wider significance of a story to viewers. Instead, the two-way interactivity of television news should be built on trust and establishing a bond with audiences, where journalists spend more time learning and understanding what viewers know – or don't know – about politics and public affairs. The future role of the fixed time bulletin, in other words, could be to bring greater assurance and stability for viewers against the backdrop of an increasingly frenetic and fragmented news culture. Television news bulletins could thus leave it to different media formats to deliver the latest visual images and concentrate on better explaining the news large swathes of people continue to tune into. Put simply, rather than simply mediating a steady stream of the latest news stories for evening consumption, the role of television journalists could be to step back from the pace of the news cycle and *mediatize* news in ways that more effectively communicate what is happening in the world.

The next chapter broadens the discussion beyond television news bulletins and the mediatization framework by exploring the future of news in the context of wider changes in society, communication and politics. The emergence of new content and social media platforms over recent years will be examined – Twitter and BuzzFeed in particular – considering their journalistic value and ability to effectively engage and inform citizens about politics and public affairs.

Chapter 7

Interpreting 24/7 journalism on new content and social media platforms

The online challenges and future directions of news and politics

Introduction

The book so far has focused primarily on evening television news bulletins, examining their changing practices and conventions in light of the wider influence of 24/7 news media over recent decades. In this final chapter the discussion will be broadened to include the value of new content and social media platforms, considering their journalistic merits and the role they play in 24-hour news culture. To help explain the arrival and increasing reliance on instant news and social media formats, the chapter begins by further broadening the scope of the book by examining the behaviour and lifestyles that shape people's media consumption habits today. It then explores how the 24-hour cycle of news has impacted on the actions and behaviour of politicians, since round-the-clock coverage puts pressure on elected representatives to react and respond in real time. The chapter thus examines the relationship 24/7 news has with society more broadly, considering people's everyday lifestyles, their use of media and the changing culture of politics.

To assess the journalistic value of instant news, information and social media formats in recent years, the chapter will focus on Twitter and BuzzFeed. Both platforms – and many more besides, such as Facebook, YouTube, Reddit, Dig, Instagram, Flickr, Snapchat and Vine – represent, in different ways, new methods of communicating information that challenge the one-way flow of power traditionally held by the mass media of the twentieth century. How Twitter is used by politicians, journalists and citizens will be critically examined along with the opportunities – and challenges – opened up by its instant and interactive format. For no longer is news predominately produced by professionally trained journalists; anyone can publish information – and call it 'news' – on new content platforms. Thus, since the arrival of new online and social media platforms, citizens have had an unprecedented amount of information at their fingertips. But in this blizzard of information produced by 24/7 instant formats, the chapter considers how the role of journalists should be understood and how news is communicated in an increasingly fragmented media culture. BuzzFeed, a content platform that splices together many different topics and features, represents a popular way many people now consume information, entertainment and news online. BuzzFeed's journalism will be put under the spotlight, assessing its use of sources, packaging of content and delivery of news between media devices. The chapter asks overall – how should the flow of online news on new content and social media platforms be interpreted? And considers, more broadly, to what extent do they strengthen or weaken democratic culture.

Reflecting the rhythms and routines of 24-hour society? Understanding the instant culture of news consumption

Needless to say, journalism does not operate in isolation from society. After all, it is a business that operates with the aim of reaching out to different people, routinely supplying news to a wide range of viewers, readers and listeners. To therefore understand how journalism has changed over recent times, it is necessary to consider how Western societies have evolved and behave in the twenty-first century. In doing so, the making, shaping and delivery of news can be interpreted in the context of people's everyday routines and lifestyles. In 2014, for example, a representative survey of UK media consumption habits found that, for the first time, in an average day people consumed media to a greater extent than sleeping (Ofcom 2014). To be more precise, whereas an average night's sleep was eight hours and 21 minutes, apparently people in the UK spent eight hours and 41 minutes a day on different media devices. At first glance, this might appear striking. Of course, most Western societies have long been voracious viewers of television. But whilst most people continue to be glued to their TV sets, it is the arrival of mobile technologies that have expanded media consumption habits. Picture a scene of people at a bus stop, a doctor's surgery or even queuing up at a supermarket, and it should involve at least some of them being mesmerized by their smartphones – the trusty companion to everyday life – whether texting, talking, typing, gaming, listening or watching (Miller 2014). Young people, in particular, are often singled out as being zombie-like figures, completely transfixed by the virtual world of social media and instant peer-to-peer communication.

But whilst it is understandable the young have embraced new technology to a greater extent – a trend repeated over many generations – the demand for instant media communication is not out of tune with the rhythms and routines of people's everyday consumer practices and experiences. Over recent decades it can be observed that many aspects of society operate at an accelerated 24-hour pace. Consider, for example, open-all-hours supermarkets or gas stations, round-the-clock banking or the wide range of services now available online. Rather than meeting people face to face or relying on the postal service, today governments increasingly ask its citizens to apply for services online, such as student loans, driving licences, passports or benefits. As a UK cabinet member enthusiastically claimed in 2010, "Online services are better for consumers and better for government, making services available in a convenient 24/7 format and reducing the costs of transactions" (cited in Asthana and McVeigh 2010). For the older generations not familiar with or connected to the information super-highway this development might not be welcomed. But generationally many Western societies are being socialized into using new media technologies and accepting the DIY culture of online communications.

This 'open-all-hours' cultural shift in society reflects the broader transformation of journalism over recent decades and is consistent with the faster-paced delivery of news in evening bulletins identified throughout the book. As previous chapters have explored, more sophisticated new technologies have brought many more platforms of instant and 24-hour formats of news. In making sense of the rise of rolling forms of journalism and the wider impact they have on society, scholars and journalists often refer to the emergence of a 24-hour news cycle, a continuous culture of news that expects – even demands – instant responses and immediate answers. As Rosenberg and Feldman (2008: 30) have colourfully put it, "The extreme speed of the Internet and 24-hour news … inevitably alters the behavior of those they cover. Their subjects develop siege mentalities and feel they have to move faster and faster and make decisions faster and faster to avoid being drubbed by media tormentors".

It is political actors, above all, who have had to adapt to this faster-paced media environment and learn how to deal with the pressures and demands of the 24-hour news cycle. Of course, since the US channel CNN began broadcasting 24 hours a day in 1980, over time the effect of always-on news has grown. So, for example, wars or conflicts – once kept conveniently away from the glare of the media spotlight – began to be fought in real time with the immediate humanitarian impact laid bare for television viewers. This coined the term "CNN-effect", a theory developed to demonstrate the immediate impact the first ever global rolling news channel was having on foreign policy making (Livingston 1997). While its tangible effects on governmental decision-making have been somewhat disputed (Robinson 2002), decades on political actors have complained about the effects the 24-hour news cycle has had on day-to-day governance. Tony Blair, the then UK prime minster, for example, used one of his last speeches in 2007 to decry the "feral beast" nature of political reporting due to "its sheer scale, weight and constant hyperactivity". More generally, scholars have evidenced how political actors and parties have sought to overcome the constant pressures of instant news and adapt to the rolling news age (Barnett and Gaber 2001; Dagnes 2010; Davis 2007, 2010; Franklin 2004; Wring 2004).

It is not only journalists who have benefited from new 24/7 media formats, different facets of society including politicians as well as ordinary citizens have been able to exploit new technologies to disseminate their messages and potentially communicate to a far greater constituency of people in the online world. The traditional gatekeepers of twentieth-century mass media – newspapers, radio and television – no longer hold a monopoly on the flow of information.

Where once the media environment was characterized as monological – a one-way communication exchange – today it is considered dialogical, since many people have the opportunity to participate, share and interact with one another. New sources of instant many-to-many peer communication have become globally popular, in particular YouTube, Facebook and Twitter, allowing information and images to be uploaded by individuals and immediately shared with the rest of the world. Taken together, the new media and communication landscape of the twenty-first century has not only broken down barriers of access, it has accelerated the speed at which messages can be spread around the globe.

The implications for news and politics are profound and far reaching. Journalism has been transformed since the arrival of the Internet and scholars have examined how, in different ways, new technologies have enormous potential in reshaping democratic structures and the distribution of power between citizens and political elites. At the same time, much of the optimism invested in the online world has been challenged from a variety of perspectives, since the potential for revolutionizing communications has not been fulfilled. Far from radically changing the information most people consume, for example, the top online sources of news continue to be well-established sources such as CNN, Fox News and NBC (Fenton 2010; Newman and Levy 2014). Moreover, many of the news items or messages people share on social media platforms tend to originate from these established sources or relate to 'old' media formats, such as television programmes or newspaper headlines. The gatekeepers of mass media in the twentieth century, in other words, have become increasingly dominant into the new millennium (Curran *et al.* 2012; McChesney 2013). But while 'new' media has not necessarily supplanted 'old' formats, there are new dialogical forms of media that have been exploited by politicians, journalists and citizens in ways that have reshaped the worlds of news and politics.

Consider Twitter, a micro blogging site allowing people to instantly send a 140-character message to fellow users (the US President Barack Obama has more than 45 million followers). Launched in 2006, it has quickly established itself as a vital information source, boasting more than 500 million worldwide users. Many politicians today have embraced this social media platform in order to compete with the collective power of mainstream media. While political elites have complained for many decades about the omnipotent gate-keeping role journalists play in defining the business of politics, Twitter is seen as a democratic counterweight, instantly allowing users to bypass the main-stream media to convey their own views, thoughts and ideas. All major political parties and candidates not only have Twitter accounts, they most probably have a team of advisors carefully orchestrating messages to appeal to key voters. The role played by social media platforms during Obama's successful presidential campaigns in 2008 and 2012, for example, was widely considered to be pioneering, used to reach out to demographics not necessarily engaged with mainstream media. Indeed, a picture of him and wife Michelle Obama in

November 2012 with a message "Four more years" was, at the time, the most retweeted message in history, shared by more than 400,000 users (McIntyre 2012). Building up a loyal army of followers can thus bring electoral advantages to politicians who can directly address voters or even answer individual tweets.

Further still, it has been claimed Twitter – and social media more generally – has become the key site for agenda setting, displacing other information sites as the most instant source of news. As Sambrook and McGuire (2014) have pointed out, "Twitter – and increasingly live blogs of breaking news events – consistently beat 24-hour TV channels". Moreover, according to Twitter's senior manager for government, news and social innovation, "The 24-hour news cycle has become a 140-character one", with the power to concisely set the political agenda, challenge it or change its direction. Of course, one tweet alone cannot set the Twittersphere alight, but trends can emerge and carry political momentum. So, for example, the rise of the hashtag – where messages have an abbreviated meaning and begin with a # – can collectively bring attention to shared concerns and topical issues. The most used hashtag in 2009 – #IranElection – helped shine a global light on people's disaffection with Iran's repressive government. It can more broadly alert people to political issues and debates. The tag #cdnpoli, for example, delivers immediate news about anything related to Canadian politics. According to Small (2011), it is a highly informative hashtag, a rich and diverse information source only made possible by users willing to share and extend their knowledge of Canadian political affairs.

Hashtags can not only inform, they can subtly influence political issues and widen policy debate. #Savethenhs – an inherent criticism of attempts made by the UK's Conservative-Liberal Democrat coalition to privatize the National Health Service – was considered to shape what Chris Mason (2012), a BBC political correspondent, calls "the political weather" of debates. Or, put another way, Twitter can set the background scenery to a political story, encouraging journalists to interpret the flavour of debate by the nature of tweets. Needless to say, this raises questions about the representativeness of the trends emanating from the Twittersphere and how journalists should interpret their significance. Are they, for example, simply an ephemeral backlash against a single issue, or do they reflect far deeper societal concerns that can – and should – be used to inform wider public debate? Lasorsa et al.'s (2012) comprehensive study of tweets from US journalists concluded the use of Twitter had quickly become normalized. In particular, they found that journalists routinely expressed their own opinions on topics – a trend exacerbating the more opinionated culture of US news and politics over recent decades (Cushion 2012b). Needless to say, journalists working for different outlets – on public service broadcasters, for example – might be less forthright about conveying their own views and remaining impartial. But Lasorsa et al. (2012) also concluded that Twitter opened up the possibility – although mainstream media outlets were less accepting of this – for greater interaction between users and journalists, and for being more accountable to reported stories by engaging in dialogue and discussion about topical issues and debates.

Beyond tweets from journalists, Twitter itself has become a routine source for news media outlets. For it can turn citizens into producers, expand the public sphere and act as the 'window on a world' for journalists unable to report on the ground. Bruno's (2012) study of international news coverage demonstrated the value of new real-time technology, such as Twitter. Considering the reporting of the 2010 Haiti earthquake, in particular, she argued, "a more open attitude toward social media enables faster and more accurate news-reporting and highlights geographical diversity by relying less on institutional sources" (Bruno 2012: 64). But social media can – as the study also conceded – perpetuate myths, since information and images can be difficult for news outlets to verify. In fast-moving events, remote locations or coverage of politically contentious issues, inaccurate or even fake news can spread like wildfire and be reported as 'fact'. While the value of Twitter is its rich supply of information sources, it can simultaneously deliver dubious nuggets of news that mislead rather than enlighten journalists or wider media audiences. As social media platforms have integrated further into news-gathering norms and routines, source verification has become a critical debating point in contemporary journalism.

However, when Twitter becomes a source for articulating ongoing political events or struggles, it is not the establishment of facts that becomes the focal point. Twitter can become a mass forum for articulating dissenting voices, organizing movements and challenging political decisions and policy outcomes. Consider the role of Twitter in the recent 2009 protests in Iran or in countries such as Tunisia and Egypt during the 2010/11 Arab Spring. In tightly controlled news environments, Twitter became a key democratic source for fellow citizens to communicate with each other and organize public revolts against government forces and wider media censorship. The impact of Twitter can also be observed in more routine domestic policy-making. So, for example, at the start of 2012 it has been claimed the Protect IP (PIPA) and Stop Online Piracy (SOPA) Acts in the US – legislation dealing with the protection of intellectual property – was undermined and effectively ended by an aggressive online campaign. While 7 million people had signed an online Google petition, 2.4 million tweets had apparently been sent to protest about the proposed legislation. According to the *Washington Post* (2012), although corporate lobbying played a role in raising the profile – and implications – of both acts, it "clearly was the millions of geeks (or people who identify with the geeks) that effectively killed PIPA and SOPA. And this exercise of power has produced a template for political action on a massive scale fuelled by social media". Twitter, viewed in this context, is more than just a source of news, but a site of democratic expression and resistance.

At the same time, it is important to remember that the forces that make Twitter – and social media more generally – a powerful platform both in the worlds of news and politics do not operate in isolation from the influence of competing rolling 24/7 news formats. As the argument developed throughout this book put forward, it was the broader journalistic culture of live and interpretive news over recent decades that influenced the nature and style of evening television bulletins. Put another way, the power of the 24-hour news cycle exists not when a powerful media outlet (aka CNN) flexes its considerable global muscle. Or by a lone tweet from a powerful politician. It is the *combined* forces and agency of contemporary media – from 24-hour news channels to conventional news bulletins, Twitter, Facebook and YouTube, to radio, newspapers, online services and the wider mediasphere – that act in tandem to shape the significance of an event or issue and help to determine the significance or meaning of it. Chadwick (2011), in this respect, has suggested the "24-hour news cycle" should be redefined as the "political information cycle". He rightly argued it is not only real-time speed that shapes the relationship between news and politics, but the interpretive frames both within and between 'old' and 'new' platforms that negotiate how people understand politics and public affairs. In Chadwick's own words:

> Political information cycles are partly dependent upon crossplatform iteration and recursion. These processes increase the likelihood that multiple, fragmented audiences will be exposed to political content and they arguably loosen the grip of journalistic and political elites by creating opportunity structures with greater scope for timely intervention by citizen activists.
> (Chadwick 2011: 40)

Rather than dissecting the influence of particular media formats, Chadwick offers a more holistic and systemic approach. For the "political information cycle" captures the rhythms and routines of people's everyday lives, the faster-paced infrastructure of communications and the wider culture of immediacy they promote both within journalism as well as other spheres of society, such as politics.

But while the political information cycle conveys the increasing hybridity of contemporary media and the need to recognize their collective power (Chadwick 2013), how can the quality of news and how it is communicated be evaluated? Put another way, in the information blizzard produced by the multiplicity of instant media formats, how can the value of news be understood in the context of better engaging and informing citizens in a democracy?

Communicating news on cross-media content platforms: interpreting the role and value of journalists in the online world

In an ever-expanding media marketplace, watching TV, flicking through the morning newspaper, browsing the Internet or keeping up with Facebook traffic can be both a daunting and overwhelming experience. Far from old media dying off, television and radio channels have expanded over recent years, while newspapers and magazines have not – as many predicted – been wiped out by the rise of online media. They have, in fact, further enhanced the size and scope of their formats. Not restricted by the same spatial limitations, needless to say it is the new media environment that is most celebrated for delivering an unprecedented amount of information online on a wide range of new platforms (iPads, smartphones, tablets, etc.). No wonder – as the Ofcom (2014) survey acknowledged earlier in the chapter – people in the UK appear more preoccupied by their media devices than sleeping at night.

But in a book about the relationship between news and politics, how should information-rich societies be more broadly interpreted? It could start with perhaps an obvious but important distinction between news and information. The latter, of course, could represent any manner of things from restaurant reviews, motorway directions, encyclopaedia entries to job vacancies, supermarket opening times and mortgage advice. News, by contrast, is typically produced by journalists, reporting recent events and issues of wider public interest (Harrison 2006). But this invites another distinction to be made – the difference between news and journalism. For new technologies have enabled – to paraphrase a US scholar – anyone to be journalists today, since news can be easily produced and distributed on a range of new media platforms. From this point what constitutes 'news' or being 'a journalist' becomes more subjective and contested. Consider WikiLeaks, a whistle-blowing organization that famously leaked sensitive documents about international diplomatic affairs. While some argue they represent nothing more than whistle-blowers manned by a loyal band of global citizens, according to WikiLeaks it is an online news source, staffed by an international army of global journalists. Journalists and journalism have thus become more fluid objects of study in the twenty-first century, an interesting debating point among practitioners and scholars about the very purpose of their role and value in society. Should journalists be defined by their professional training and status? Or can self-appointed bloggers covering public affairs be considered in the same standing?

Irrespective of whether an all-inclusive definition of journalists is accepted or not, what remains important in debates of this kind is the quality of news produced and the wider democratic implications of it. After all, while the Twittersphere or larger online world may well be packed full of wannabe journalists, how far do they inform most people about what is happening in the world? As this chapter already acknowledged, to a large extent many people continue to rely on news produced by mainstream news media and thus professionally trained journalists (Curran *et al.* 2012; Fenton 2010; Newman and Levy 2014). So, for example, while WikiLeaks might have been the *source* of the whistle-blowing, it was the elite newspapers, broadcasters and their respective online sites that picked over the documents, selected them according to their own news values and reinterpreted them in the context of their wider significance for international diplomatic affairs.

Since most citizens continue to turn to established suppliers of news for their primary understanding of the world, it can make sweeping statements about the apparent choice and diversity of today's rich media culture appear somewhat far-fetched. At the same time, much like the development of Twitter, there remain important new developments and trends that potentially enhance – or weaken – people's engagement with and understanding of politics and public affairs. Consider, for example, the rise of BuzzFeed, an online content platform launched in 2006 that delivers visually stimulating nuggets of news – most distinctively (although not exclusively) in the form of lists ("15 Things Twentysomething Taylor Swift Fans Are Tired Of Hearing" or "19 Things You'll Never Want To Hear Again After Freshers' Week"). It is, in this sense, difficult to distinguish between news and information. For BuzzFeed contains an assembly of headline-grabbing lists, quizzes, videos and pictures, addressing many themes from topical talking points ("12 Results Day Quotes For Every Eventuality") to entertainment ("The 'Saved By The Bell' Cast Looks Insanely Young In These 1989 Publicity Photos") and even political affairs ("Hamas Says 3 Of Its Senior Leaders Have Been Killed In An Air Strike In Gaza").

Compared to well-established elite sources – *The New York Times*, say, or *The Guardian* – BuzzFeed attracts more far online traffic (Preston 2014), approximately 150 million worldwide users per month (Isaac 2014). According to John Peretti, the founder of BuzzFeed, it was created "because people still want to be informed, entertained and inspired, but the way they consume media has dramatically shifted" (cited in Ponsford 2014). For much of its traffic is driven by social media, with links packaged to encourage people to share content between different platforms. The strategy, Peretti continued, reflects the "bored in line" generation, a reference – addressed at the beginning of this chapter – to how media is consumed, including the news (cited in Bacon 2014). For people consume news not only at home but on the move – in supermarkets, on trains and throughout the working day – on personal laptops, work stations or portable devices. In other words, as a supplier of all kinds of content, BuzzFeed has self-consciously sought to march to the beat of people's fast and fluid media consumption patterns.

While BuzzFeed started as a site predominantly fuelled by viral content, in very recent years it has received more investment, funding over 500 editorial staff to not only collate existing material, but to generate more serious content and breaking news stories. The configuration of its website (as of August 2014) demonstrates its dual agenda of serious and light-hearted content. Its left-hand column has a long list of content mixing news, information, quizzes and advertiser-funded material together (it makes money by publishing lists that are sponsored, e.g. "18 Ways To Survive Uni When You're Skint … Listen to NatWest [a commercial bank] and learn how to make your money stretch further"). On the right-hand side (excluding the top-10 list of pictures indicating what stories are trending on social media) under the caption "Big Stories" it has updates about national and international politics and public affairs. While many BuzzFeed staff have bylines, they are often based on repackaged stories taken predominantly from mainstream and elite sources. So, for example, in an August 2014 story with the headline "U.S. Launched Secret Operation In Syria To Rescue James Foley And Other American Hostages" the report was based on information and sources from *The New York Times*. At the bottom of the page a series of tweets from Marie Harf, the deputy spokesperson for the U.S. State Department, were collated without any additional reporting or context supplied from BuzzFeed's editorial team. Similarly, there are often rolling news blogs – covering, for example, the civil unrest in Missouri after an unarmed black youth was shot in 2014 – that bring together live updates with brief snippets of news, images and pictures plucked from BuzzFeed contributors but also from Twitter, YouTube and other assorted news and social media platforms. In other words, BuzzFeed acts as a conveyor belt for the latest news stories, but it remains reliant on external sources – from established news outlets to ordinary people uploading footage on the ground. How far this raw material is vetted and verified – as previously acknowledged – is an open question.

So how should BuzzFeed's recent surge in popularity as a source of news for tens of millions of people internationally be interpreted? Should it be celebrated for creatively tapping into the vast world of already existing information sources and viscerally weaving it together? Or should BuzzFeed be condemned for pillaging news from its original sources without supplying the necessary context about their significance? Former *Guardian* editor, Peter Preston (2014), admires this emerging platform – "You can make sense of all this if BuzzFeed is seen as the launching pad for millions of social messages, a referral resource rather than a coherent product" – but considers it to have limited democratic value. He condemned BuzzFeed because:

> There is no overall news vision. Anyone who wants to understand what's going on around them will need to scan a conventional paper or tune into proper TV or radio bulletins first. The Feed is extra. The Buzz is a blend of algorithms and gloriously mixed messages. Look at the top trending items and you won't find gritty seriousness making much of a show.
>
> (Preston 2014)

It would, in the latter sense, be a little unfair to single out BuzzFeed users as exclusively hunting down sensationalist stories. A quick glance at BBC News online and the most shared or read items typically involve quirky, human interest or salacious stories unlikely to be reported by their more highbrow TV or radio bulletins. BuzzFeed's amalgamation of the social media world and its expansion from entertainment-based news to more serious and broadsheet content could also provide what has long been understood as incidental learning (Blumler 1970). For rather than citizens picking and choosing their own content – clicking and largely sticking to Justin Bieber-like stories, for instance, or exclusively following his Twitter feed – BuzzFeed opens up a more diverse universe that could widen their news intake. Moreover, even some of its light-hearted coverage of politics ("Please Take A Moment To Look At This Picture Of Boris Johnson Battling A Hedge Trimmer") might even have what Baum (2003: 283) labels a "gateway effect", motivating citizens to investigate the story further, stimulating an interest and igniting social conversations in ways that might meaningfully enhance people's political knowledge, such as learning more about Boris's policy positions.

For today's media-savvy consumer, BuzzFeed appears a natural habitat, at home, work or on the move, its rolling format and visual content can be easily viewed and immediately shared across and between different content and social media platforms. But given all the *potential* and *indirect* democratic benefits of BuzzFeed, it would be hard not to conclude the value of BuzzFeed is as a supplement to rather than replacement for more traditional forms of journalism. For even scratching below the surface of its more serious content, its repackaging of information and combination of sources does little to expand the informative value of news or to diversify its content. Moreover, the emphasis on revealing the latest visual images or concise Twitter posts – from political elites to ordinary folk – can perhaps distract from rather than inform the context to a story or explain its wider significance.

As argued elsewhere, the democratic value of news should, above all, be the primary way of evaluating the quality of contemporary journalism (Cushion 2012a). If, as the old adage goes, information is power, then news can only be considered powerful if citizens learn about the key economic, political and social issues affecting them and their wider implications. In assessing whether the information age has enhanced people's understanding of politics and public affairs, consider Pew's (2007) longitudinal study of public knowledge in the US. Their representative surveys in 1989 and 2007 found people's knowledge and understanding of political leaders and current affairs had changed little despite the massive expansion of the news landscape. The report concluded that "changing news formats are not having a great deal of impact on how much the public knows about national and international affairs" (The Pew Research Center for the People and the Press 2007). Further still, Prior (2007) has argued that far from media choice enhancing US society's understanding of politics, it has led to inequalities of knowledge. For while those interested and engaged in political affairs have embraced the enlargement of news on rolling TV, radio and online formats, people who are not have been able to bypass serious news and turn exclusively to the world of entertainment. To put it another way, media choice has prevented incidental learning and involvement with politics, since even at election times citizens can avoid the network bulletins, radio programming and newspapers they once were exposed to (Prior 2007). Today's information environment, in other words, can both encourage and discourage democratic engagement according to the choices citizens make.

Of course, social media platforms have only become a familiar part of news and political culture in very recent years. But there is little to suggest they would have radically changed the pattern of media choice more than a decade into the new millennium. After all, 16 per cent of the US population use Twitter – and only half of that use it for news (Pew Research Center 2013). However, Twitter use does increase when young people are isolated. Further still, media consumption habits show many people are now moving more seamlessly between different platforms where information, entertainment and news intersect (Ofcom 2014). But it is perhaps too early to know whether social media platforms will become the primary hub of news for successive generations. Does BuzzFeed, for example, represent the future of news, or is it a passing technological fad soon to be replaced? Since the Buzzification of news is consistent with the wider supply of instant, visual, continuous and portable formats, it would at least appear to be the immediate future of journalism. Its distinctive lists of topical and quirky items, for example, have been emulated by more serious news platforms. Consider recent BBC News online items, such as "10 reasons chess may never make it as a spectator sport", "Scottish independence: Five unresolved questions" and "10 reasons why so many people are moving to Texas". Or a new regular feature entitled "10 things we didn't know last week". To put it mildly, these items have more than a faint whiff of BuzzFeed's journalism ("Sliced and diced", as the BBC puts it, "for your convenience"). If there is a wider Buzzification effect, it is in fanning the flames of the 24-hour news cycle so social media users – notably from Facebook – are perhaps more likely to feel the heat of major news stories and help raise their temperature by sharing them across different media platforms.

Much like the political information cycle, at this point it is worth reflecting on the wider landscape of news and considering how future political information environments can be cultivated in ways that deliver both an engaging and informative journalism as the twenty-first century deepens. Political information environments represent a "mediated public space through which political information flows" (Esser *et al.* 2012: 249). They tend to be constructed by national rather than international contexts, since most people continue to make sense of the world through a domestic media lens. Rather than considering the *demand* for news – of *individuals* using Twitter, say, or BuzzFeed – political information environments encourage us to think about the overall *supply* of news for audiences more generally (Aalberg and Curran 2011; Iyengar *et al.* 2009).

Needless to say, news does not magically appear online or on TV screens, but is a consequence of both government policies and market forces. Over recent decades, most Western societies have witnessed a deregulation of their media landscapes, allowing information sources to be privatively owned and shaped by largely commercial goals. Focusing in on consumer needs, the market has fed an appetite for infotainment-type news formats – including BuzzFeed – where the serious is spliced with the light-hearted. At the same time, with advertising revenue spread more thinly between an expanding media marketplace, the intense competition and concentration of corporate ownership has influenced the supply of news and the culture of journalism. Not least by the reduction of journalists asked to investigate, produce and convey the daily news agenda. In the US, for example, PR practitioners out-number journalists by a ratio of 5 to 1 and earn considerably more money (Williams 2014). Put another way, many information environments today are heavily dominated by and more lucratively reward those looking to spin the news rather than report it. Of course, not all PR practitioners promote evil causes or work for greedy corporate owners – consider Greenpeace, say, or Oxfam – but their supremacy in the world of communications reveals the limited resources journalism has to challenge and scrutinize their actions and behaviour.

Free from ownership and control, on the face of it new content and social media platforms play a role in countering political or corporate spin and represent a democratic force able to draw on the eyes, ears and views of millions of citizens worldwide. Moreover, the instant culture of news and the many formats to consume it now integrate into people's daily rhythms and routines. But as questioned throughout this chapter, how far can they amount to building an information environment where politics and public affairs can be meaningfully addressed and interpreted? So, for example, while BuzzFeed might have recently enhanced its editorial resources, it continues to pay a heavy journalistic price for its content. Its routine acceptance of sponsored stories – such as a paid Obama advert during the 2012 presidential campaign (Ellis 2012) – undermines journalistic independence (when it blurs with 'real' news) and reveals a continued reliance on elite power. Moreover, even BuzzFeed's more original editorial content relies on repackaging information from traditional news providers and – if alternative voices do feature – there is a limited degree of explanation about the sources drawn upon or the wider significance of their viewpoints. To put it more bluntly, dumping a multitude of sources into visually appealing cross-platform content – if that is the news of the future – does not appear a convincing blueprint for promoting high-quality journalism.

Amidst much of the hype and excitement about the latest technologies reshaping the new media landscape, it is important not to lose sight of 'old' media, which continue to exert their influence on most political information environments. Of course, the rise of cross-media and social media platforms over recent years have unquestionably enhanced the flow of information and further accelerated the pace of the 24-hour news cycle. But, as this chapter suggested, many of these mobile and convenient formats of news do not appear to exhibit strong newsgathering skills or sufficient editorial independence. Moreover, many lack the ability to robustly challenge elites or to meaningfully interpret the fast-moving world of politics and public affairs. Although many of these accusations could be levelled at old media outlets, for all their faults sustained exposure to TV, radio and newspapers continue to act as an important part of people's news diet. Despite predictions of their imminent demise or irrelevance to twenty-first century journalism, the disappearance of long-standing news formats – regular TV bulletins, say, or the mix of opinions and analysis in newspapers – would undoubtedly weaken democratic culture. As argued throughout this book, while the character of evening television bulletins has changed over recent decades, the enhanced use of live two-way reporting by public service broadcasters represents an old-fashioned – but still highly valuable – approach to better informing viewers. While technology might facilitate new conventions or create media platforms, there is no sub-stitution for well-resourced editorial teams, delivering accurate and balanced reporting from experienced journalists with the knowledge to interpret what is happening in the world.

References

Aalberg, Toril and Curran, James (2011) *How Media Inform Democracy: A Comparative Approach*. London: Routledge.

Aalberg, Toril, van Aelst, Peter and Curran, James (2010) "Media Systems and the Political Information Environment: A Cross-National Comparison", *International Journal of Press/Politics* 15(3): 255–71.

Aalberg, Toril, Strömbäck, Jesper and de Vreese, Claes H. (2012) "The Framing of Politics as Strategy and Game: A Review of Concepts, Operationalizations and Key Findings", *Journalism: Theory, Practice and Criticism* 13(2): 162–78.

Adotto, Kiku (1990) "Soundbite Democracy: Network Evening News Presidential Campaign Coverage (1968–88)", Research Paper R2, available online at http://shorensteincenter.org/wp-content/uploads/2012/03/r02_adatto.pdf (accessed 16 July 2014).

Altheide, David L. and Snow, Robert P. (1979) *Media Logic*. Beverly Hills, CA: Sage.

Asthana, Anushka and McVeigh, Tracey (2010) "Government Services to Be Online-Only", *The Guardian*, 20 November, available online at www.theguardian.com/society/2010/nov/20/government-services-online-only (accessed 28 August).

Bacon, Jonathan (2014) "Profile Interview: Jonah Peretti, Founder, BuzzFeed", *Marketing Week*, June 11, available online at www.marketingweek.co.uk/analysis/profiles/profile-interview-jonah-peretti-founder-buzzfeed/4010672.article (accessed 28 August).

Bainbridge, Jason and Bestwick, Jane (2010) "And Here's the News: Analysing the Evolution of the Marketed Newsreader", *Media Culture Society* 32(2): 205–23.

Barnett, Steven and Gaber, Ivor (2001) *Westminster Tales: The Twenty-First Century Crisis in Political Journalism*. London: Continuum.

Barnett, Steven, Ramsay, Gordon Neil and Gaber, Ivor (2012) *From Callaghan to Credit Crunch: Changing Trends in British Television News 1975–2009*. University of Westminster Publication, available online at www.westminster.ac.uk/ – data/assets/pdf_file/0009/124785/From-Callaghan-To-Credit-Crunch-Final-Report.pdf (accessed 14 July 2014).

Barnhurst, Kevin and Steele, Catherine A. (1997) "Image Bite News: The Visual Coverage of Elections in US Television News, 1968–88", *Harvard International Journal of Press Politics* 2(1): 40–58.

Baum, Matthew (2003) *Soft News Goes to War: Public Opinion and American Foreign Policy in the New Media Age*. Princeton, NJ: Princeton University Press.

BBC (2013) "Public Perceptions of the Impartiality and Trustworthiness of the BBC", May 2013, available online at http://downloads.bbc.co.uk/aboutthebbc/insidethebbc/howwework/reports/pdf/bbc_report_trust_and_impartiality_report_may_2013.pdf (accessed 14 July 2014).

Becker, Howard (1967) "Whose Side Are We On?", *Social Problems* 14(3): 239–47.

Bennett, Lance W. (1990) "Towards a Theory of Press-State Relations", *Journal of Communication* 40(2): 103–25.

Bennett, Lance W. and Entman, Robert M. (2001) *Mediated Politics: Communication in the Future of Democracy*. Cambridge: Cambridge University Press.

Bercovici, Jeff (2012) "Launching Today: HuffPost Live, TV News for the Internet Age", in *Forbes Business*, 13 August, available online at www.forbes.com/sites/jeffber covici/2012/08/13/launching-today-huffpost-live-tv-news-for-the-internet-age (accessed 16 July 2014).

Berry, Mike (2015) "The BBC and the Deficit Debate", forthcoming.

Blumenthal, Sidney (1980) *The Permanent Campaign*. Boston: Beacon Press.

Blumler, Jay (1970) "The Political Effects of Television", *The Political Effects of Television*, ed. Halloran, James D. London: Panther.

——(2012) "Foreword", in Esser, Frank and Hanitzsch, Thomas (eds), *Handbook of Comparative Communication Research*. London: Routledge.

——(2014) "Mediatization and Democracy", in Esser, Frank and Strömbäck, Jesper (eds), *Mediatization of Politics. Understanding the Transformation of Western Democracies*. Basingstoke: Palgrave Macmillan.

Blumler, Jay and Cushion, Stephen (2014) "Normative Perspectives on Journalism Studies: Stock-taking and Future Directions", *Journalism: Theory, Practice and Criticism* 15(3): 259–72.

Blumler, Jay and Gurevitch, Michael (1995) (eds) *The Crisis of Public Communication*. London: Routledge.

——(2001) "Americanization Reconsidered: UK-US Campaign Communication Comparisons across Time", in Bennett, Lance W. and Entman, Robert M., *Mediated Politics: Communication in the Future of Democracy*. Cambridge: Cambridge University Press.

Blumler, Jay and Kavanagh, Dennis (1999) "The Third Age of Political Communication: Influences and Features", *Political Communication* 16(3): 209–30.

Born, Georgina (2004) *Uncertain Vision: Birt, Dyke and the Reinvention of the BBC*. London: Secker & Warburg.

Brants, Kees, and van Praag, Philip (2006) "Signs of Media Logic. Half a Century of Political Communication in the Netherlands", *Javnost/The Public* 13(1): 25–40.

Bruno, Nicola (2012) *Tweet First, Verify Later? How Real-time Information Is Changing the Coverage of Worldwide Crisis Events*. Oxford: Reuters Institute for the Study of Journalism. Available online at http://reutersinstitute.politics.ox.ac.uk/sites/default/files/Tweet%20first%20%2C%20verify%20later%20How%20real-time%20information%20is%20changing%20the%20coverage%20of%20worldwide%20crisis%20events.pdf (accessed 28 August 2014).

Caldwell, John (1995) *Televisuality: Style, Crisis, and Authority in American Television*. New York: Rutgers University Press.

Casella, Peter (2013) "Breaking News or Broken News: Reporters and News Directors Clash on 'Black Hole' Live Shots", *Journalism Practice* 7(3): 362–72.

Chadwick, Andrew (2011) "Britain's First Live Televised Party Leaders' Debate: From the News Cycle to the Political Information Cycle", *Parliamentary Affairs* 64(1): 24–44.

——(2013) *The Hybrid Media System: Politics and Power*. New York: Oxford University Press.

Chalaby, Jean (1996) "Journalism as an Anglo-American Invention: A Comparison of the Development of French and Anglo-American Journalism, 1830s–1920s", *European Journal of Communication* 11(3): 303–26.

Cohen, Jeffrey (2008) *The Presidency in the Era of 24-Hour News*. Princeton, NJ: Princeton University Press.

Coleman, Stephen (ed.) (2010) *Leaders in the Living Room – the Prime Ministerial Debates of 2010: Evidence, Evaluation and Some Recommendations*, Oxford: Reuters Institute for the Study of Journalism.

Conlan, Tara (2010) "Channel 5 Plans Revamp of News Programmes". *The Media Guardian*, available online at www.guardian.co.uk/media/2010/nov/23/channel-5-plans-news-revamp (accessed July 5 2013).

Conway, Mike (2007) "A Guest in Our Living Room: The Television Newscaster before the Rise of the Dominant Anchor", *Journal of Broadcasting and Electronic Media* 51(3): 457–78.

——(2009) *The Origins of Television News in America: The Visualizers of CBS in the 1940s*. New York: Peter Lang.

Cottle, Simon and Rai, Mugdha (2008) "Global 24/7 News Providers: Emissaries of Global Dominance or Global Public Sphere?", in *Global Media and Communication* 4(2): 157–81.

Couldry, Nick (2008) "Mediatization or Mediation? Alternative Understandings of the Emergent Space of Digital Storytelling", *New Media & Society* 10(3), 373–91.

——(2012) *Media, Society, World: Social Theory and Digital Media Practice*. Cambridge: Polity Press.

Couldry, Nick and Hepp, Andreas (2013) "Editorial: Conceptualizing Mediatization: Contexts, Traditions, Arguments", *Communication Theory* 23(3): 191–202.

Crisell, Andrew (2002) *An Introductory History of British Broadcasting*. London: Routledge.

——(2012) *Liveness and Recording in the Media*. Basingstoke: Palgrave Macmillan.

Curran, James and Park, Myung-Jin (2000) *De-Westernizing Media Studies*. London: Routledge.

Curran, James, Fenton, Natalie and Freedman, Des (2012) *Misunderstanding the Internet*. London: Routledge.

Cushion, Stephen (2010) "Three Phases of the 24-hour Television News Genre", in Cushion, Stephen and Lewis, Justin, *The Rise of 24-Hour News: Global Perspectives*. New York: Peter Lang.

——(2012a) *The Democratic Value of News: Why Public Service Media Matter*. Basingstoke: Palgrave Macmillan.

——(2012b) *Television Journalism*. London: Sage.

——(2014a) "Injecting Immediacy into Media Logic: Re(Interpreting) the Mediatizaton of Politics on UK Television Newscasts 1991–2013", *Javnost/The Public* 21(3): 39–54.

——(2014b) "Journalism and Current Affairs", in Conboy, Martin and Steel, John, *The Routledge Companion to British Media History*. London: Routledge.

——(2014c) "Assessing, Measuring and Applying 'Public Value Tests' beyond New Media: Interpreting Impartiality and Plurality in Debates about Journalism Standards", in Barkho, Leon, *From Theory to Practice: How to Assess and Apply Impartiality in News and Current Affairs*. Chicago: University of Chicago Press.

Cushion, Stephen, Aalberg, Toril and Thomas, Richard (2014) "Towards a Rolling News Logic in Fixed Time Bulletins? A Comparative Analysis of Journalistic Interventions in the US, UK and Norway", *The European Journal of Communication* 29(1): 100–109.

Cushion, Stephen and Lewis, Justin (2009) "Towards a 'Foxification' of 24-Hour News Channels in Britain? An Analysis of Market Driven and Publicly Funded News Coverage", *Journalism: Theory, Practice and Criticism* 10(2): 131–53.

Cushion, Stephen and Lewis, Justin (eds) (2010) *The Rise of 24-Hour News Television: Global Perspectives*. New York: Peter Lang.

Cushion, Stephen and Thomas, Richard (2013) "The Mediatization of Politics: Interpreting the Value of Live vs. Edited Journalistic Interventions in UK Television News Bulletins", *The International Journal of Press/Politics* 18(3): 360–80.

Cushion, Stephen, Lewis, Justin and Gordon, Neil (2012) "The Impact of Interventionist Regulation in Reshaping News Agendas: A Comparative Analysis of Public and Commercially Funded Television Journalism", *Journalism* 13(7): 831–49.

Cushion, Stephen, Lewis, Justin and Groves, Chris (2009a) "Reflecting the Four Nations? An Analysis of Reporting Devolution on UK Network News Media", *Journalism Studies* 10(5): 1–17.

——(2009b) "Prioritizing Hand-Shaking over Policy-Making: A Study of How the 2007 Devolved Elections Was Reported on BBC UK Network Coverage", *Cyfrwng: Media Wales Journal* 6.

Cushion, Stephen, Lewis, Rachel and Roger, Hugh (2014) "Adopting or Resisting 24-hour News Logic on Evening Bulletins? The Mediatization of UK Television News 1991–2012", *Journalism: Theory, Practice and Criticism*, iFirst.

Cushion, Stephen, Roger, Hugh and Lewis, Rachel (2014) "Comparing Levels of Mediatization in Television Journalism: An Analysis of Political Reporting on US and UK Evening News Bulletins", *International Communication Gazette* 76(6): 443–463.

Dagnes, Alison (2010) *Politics on Demand: The Effects of 24-Hour News on American Politics*. Santa Barbara, CA: Praeger.

Dale, Ian (2012) "In Conversation with … Nick Robinson", in *Total Politics*, available online at www.totalpolitics.com/print/284832/in-conversation-with-nick-robinson.thtml (accessed 16 July 2014).

Davis, Aeron (2007) *The Mediation of Power*. London: Routledge.

——(2010) *Political Communication and Social Theory*. London: Routledge.

Dayan, Daniel and Katz, Elihu (1994) *Media Events: The Live Broadcasting of History*. Cambridge, MA and London: Harvard University Press.

Deacon, David and Stanyer, James (2014) "Mediatization: Key Concept or Conceptual Bandwagon", in *Media, Culture and Society* 36(7): 1032–1044.

de Vreese, Claes (2001) "Election Coverage – New Directions for Public Broadcasting: The Netherlands and Beyond", *European Journal of Communication* 16(2), 155–79.

——(2014) "Mediatization of News: The Role of Journalistic Framing", in Esser, Frank and Strömbäck, Jesper (eds), *Mediatization of Politics. Understanding the Transformation of Western Democracies*. Basingstoke: Palgrave Macmillan.

Dimitrova, Daniela and Strömbäck, Jesper (2010) "Exploring Semi-Structural Differences in Television News between the United States and Sweden", *International Communication Gazette* 72(6): 487–502.

Djerf-Pierre, Monika, Ekström, Matts, Håkansson, Nicklas and Johansson, Bengt (2014) "The Mediatization of Political Accountability. Politics, the News Media Logic and Industrial Crises in the 1980s and 2000s", *Journalism Studies* 15(3): 321–38.

Dugan, Andrew (2014) "Americans' Confidence in News Media Remains Low", in Gallup Politics, 19 June, available online at www.gallup.com/poll/171740/americans-confidence-news-media-remains-low.aspx (accessed 14 July 2014).

Eaton, George (2012) "The BBC Is Still the Most Trusted Media Organisation", *New Statesman*, 13 November, available online at www.newstatesman.com/broadcast/2012/11/bbc-still-most-trusted-media-organisation (accessed 14 July 2014).

Economist (2011) "Bulletins from the Future", *Economist*, 11 July available online at www.economist.com/node/18904136 (accessed 15 July 2014).

Ekström, Mats (2000) "Information, Story-telling and Attractions: TV Journalism in Three Modes of Communication", *Media, Culture and Society* 22: 343–70.

Eldridge, John (1993) (ed.) *Getting the Message: News, Truth and Power*. London: Routledge.

Elliott, Larry and Atkinson, Dan (2012) *Going South: Why Britain Will Have a Third World Economy by 2014*. Basingstoke: Palgrave.

Ellis, John (2000) *Seeing Things: Television in the Age of Uncertainty*. London: I.B. Tauris.

Ellis, Justin (2012) "BuzzFeed Adapts Its Branded Content Approach to Political Advertising, and Obama's In", *Neiman Journalism Lab*, October 24, available online at www.niemanlab.org/2012/10/buzzfeed-adapts-its-branded-content-approach-to-political-advertising-and-obamas-in (accessed 28 August 2014).

Esser, Frank (2008) "Dimensions of Political News Cultures: Sound Bite and Image Bite News in France, Germany, Great Britain and the United States", *The International Journal of Press/Politics* 13(4): 401–28.

——(2013a) "Mediatization as a Challenge", in Kriesi, Hanspeter, Bochsler, Daniel, Matthes, Jörg, Lavenex, Sandra, Bühlmann, Marc, Esser, Frank, *Democracy in the Age of Globalization and Mediatization*. Basingstoke: Palgrave Macmillan.

——(2013b) "The Emerging Paradigm of Comparative Communication Enquiry: Advancing Cross-National Research in Times of Globalization", *International Journal of Communication* 7: 113–28.

Esser, Frank and Hanitzsch, Thomas (eds) (2012) *Handbook of Comparative Communication Research*. London: Routledge.

Esser, Frank and Matthes, Jörg (2013) "Mediatization Effects on Political News, Political Actors, Political Decisions, and Political Audiences", in Kriesi, Hanspeter, Bochsler, Daniel, Matthes, Jörg, Lavenex, Sandra, Bühlmann, Marc, Esser, Frank, *Democracy in the Age of Globalization and Mediatization*. Basingstoke: Palgrave Macmillan.

Esser, Frank and Strömbäck, Jesper (eds) (2014a) *Mediatization of Politics. Understanding the Transformation of Western Democracies*. Basingstoke: Palgrave Macmillan.

Esser, Frank and Strömbäck, Jesper (2014b) "A Paradigm in the Making: Lessons for the Future of Mediatization Research", in Esser, Frank and Strömbäck, Jesper (eds), *Mediatization of Politics. Understanding the Transformation of Western Democracies*. Basingstoke: Palgrave Macmillan.

Esser, Frank and Umbricht, Andrea (2014) "The Evolution of Objective and Interpretative Journalism in the Western Press. Comparing Six News Systems since the 1960s", *Journalism & Mass Communication Quarterly* 91(3): 229–49.

Esser, Frank, de Vreese, Claes H., Strömbäck, Jesper, Aelst, Peter van, Aalberg, Toril, Stanyer, James, Lengauer, Günther, Berganza, Rosa, Legnante, Guido, Papathanassopoulos, Stylianos, Salgado, Susana, Sheafer, Tamir and Reinemann, Carsten (2012) "Political Information Opportunities in Europe: A Longitudinal and Comparative

Study of Thirteen Television Systems", *The International Journal of Press/Politics* 17(3): 247–74.

Fairclough, Norman (1994) "Conversationalization of Public Discourse and the Authority of the Consumer", in Keat, Russell, Whiteley, Nigel and Abercrombie, Nicholas, *The Authority of the Consumer*. London: Routledge.

Farnsworth, Stephen and Lichter, Robert (2006) *The Mediated Presidency: Television News and Presidential Governance*. Lanham, MD: Rowman & Littlefield.

——(2007) *The Nightly News Nightmare: Network Television's Coverage of US Presidential Elections, 1988–2004*. Lanham, MD: Rowman & Littlefield.

Fenton, Natalie (2010) (ed.) *New Media, Old News: Journalism and Democracy in the Digital Age*. London: Sage.

Fink, Katherine and Schudson, Michael (2013) "The Rise of Contextual Journalism, 1950s–2000s", *Journalism* ifirst, published 17 February 2013.

Franklin, Bob (1999) *Newszak and News Media*. London: Routledge.

——(2004) *Packaging Politics: Political Communications in Britain's Media Democracy*. London: Arnold.

Frisch, Karl (2010) "Obama: '24/7 media … exposes us to all kinds of arguments, some of which don't always rank that high on the truth meter'" in *Media Matters*, 9 May, available online at http://mediamatters.org/mobile/blog/2010/05/09/obama-247-med iaexposes-us-to-all-kinds-of-argum/164426 (accessed 21 November 2014).

Glyn, Kevin (2000) *Tabloid Culture: Trash Taste, Popular Power, and the Transformation of American Television*. Durham, NC: Duke University Press.

Grabe, Maria E. and Bucy, Eric. P (2009) *Image Bite Politics: News and the Visual Framing of Elections*. New York: Oxford University Press.

Graber, Doris A. (1990) "Seeing Is Remembering: How Visuals Contribute to Learning from Television News", *Journal of Communication* 40: 134–55.

Grøttum, Eva-Therese and Aalberg, Toril (2012) "Incomprehensible News. How Pre-knowledge Requirements and Expert Sources Make Political News Coverage Incomprehensive", *Norsk Statsvitenskapelig Tidsskrift* 1: 3–23.

Gurevitch, Michael and Blumler, Jay (2004) "State of the Art of Comparative Political Communication Research: Poised for Maturity?", in Esser, Frank and Pfetsch, Barbara (eds), *Comparing Political Communication: Theories, Cases, and Challenges*. Cambridge: Cambridge University Press.

Hallin, Daniel (1992a) "Sound Bite News: Television Coverage of Elections, 1968–88", *Journal of Communication* 42(2): 5–24.

——(1992b) "Sound Bite Democracy", in *WQ Spring*, available online at http://archive.wilsonquarterly.com/sites/default/files/articles/WQ_VOL16_SP_1992_Article_01_2.pdf (accessed 16 July 2014).

——(1994) *We Keep America on Top of the World: Television Journalism and the Public Sphere*. New York: Routledge.

Hallin, Daniel and Mancini, Paolo (2004) *Comparing Media Systems: Three Models of Media and Politics*. Cambridge: Cambridge University Press.

——(2012) *Comparing Media Systems beyond the Western World* (eds) Cambridge: Cambridge University Press.

Hanitzsch, Thomas (2007) "Deconstructing Journalism Culture: Toward a Universal Theory", *Communication Theory* 17: 367–85.

The Hansard Society (2014) *Tuned in or Turned off? Public attitudes to Prime Minister's Questions*. London: Hansard Society.

Harrison, Jackie (2000) *Terrestrial TV News in Britain: The Culture of Production*. Manchester: Manchester University Press.
——(2006) *News*. London: Routledge.
Hartley, John (1982) *Understanding News*. London: Routledge.
Heffernan, Richard (2001) *New Labour and Thatcherism: Political Change in Britain*. Basingstoke: Palgrave.
Hepp, Andreas (2013a) *Cultures of Mediatization*. Cambridge: Polity Press.
——(2013b) "The Communicative Figurations of Mediatized Worlds: Mediatization Research in Times of the 'Mediatization of Everything'", *European Journal of Communication* 28(6): 378–81.
Higgins, Michael and Smith, Angela (2012) "Strategy, Evasion and Performance in the Live Two-way: Kate Adie Reporting from Iraq for the BBC", *Journal of War and Culture Studies* 5(2): 203–18.
Hjarvard, Stig (2008) "The Mediatization of Society: A Theory of the Media as Agents of Social and Cultural Change", *Nordicom Review* 29(2): 105–34.
——(2013) *The Mediatization of Culture and Society*. London: Routledge.
Hopmann, Dennis and Strömbäck, Jesper (2010) "The Rise of Media Punditocracy? Journalists and Media Pundits in Danish Election News 1994–2007", *Media, Culture and Society* 32(6): 943–60.
Hutchby, Ian (2006) *Media Talk: Conversation Analysis and the Study of Broadcasting*. Berkshire: Open University Press.
Isaac, Mike (2014) "50 Million New Reasons BuzzFeed Wants to Take Its Content Far Beyond Lists", *The New York Times*, 10 August, available online at www.nytimes.com/2014/08/11/technology/a-move-to-go-beyond-lists-for-content-at-buzzfeed.html?_r=0 (accessed 28 August 2014).
Iyengar, Shanto, Hahn, Kyu S., Bonfadelli, Heinz and Marr, Mirko (2009) "'Dark Areas of Ignorance' Revisited: Comparing International Affairs Knowledge in Switzerland and the United States", *Communication Research* 36(3): 341–58.
Jerit, Jennifer (2009) "Understanding the Knowledge Gap: The Role of Experts and Journalists", *Journal of Politics* 71(2): 1–15.
Journalism Practice special edition (2014) *Mediatization of Politics: Facets of Media Logic* 8(3).
Journalism Studies Special edition (2014) *Mediatization of Politics: Theoretical and Empirical Perspectives* 15(3).
Kalina, Paul and Murfett, Andrew (2012) "Headline Success for News", in *The Sydney Morning Herald*, November 22, available online at www.smh.com.au/entertainment/tv-and-radio/headline-success-for-news-20121121-29op2.html (accessed 15 July 2014).
Kammer, Aske (2013) "The Mediatization of Journalism", in *Journal of Media and Communication Research*, *Mediakultur* 54: 141–58.
Kepplinger, Hans Mathias (2002) "Mediatization of Politics: Theory and Data", *Journal of Communication* 54(2): 972–86.
——(2007) "Reciprocal Effects: Toward a Theory of Mass Media Effects on Decision Makers", *Harvard International Journal of Press/Politics* 12(2): 3–23.
Kevill, Sian (2002) *Beyond the Soundbite: BBC Research into Public Disillusion with Politics*. London: BBC publication.
Klinger, Ulrike and Svensson, Jakob (2014) "The Emergence of Network Media Logic in Political Communication: A Theoretical Approach", in *New Media and Society*, iFirst.

Landerer, Nino (2013) "Rethinking the Logics: A Conceptual Framework for the Mediatization of Politics", *Communication Theory* 23(3): 239–58.

Lasorsa, Dominic L., Lewis, Seth C. and Holton, Avery (2012) "Normalizing Twitter: Journalism Practice in an Emerging Communication Space", *Journalism Studies* 13(1): 19–36.

Lewis, Justin (1991) *The Ideological Octopus: An Exploration of Television and Its Audience*. New York: Routledge.

——(2001) *Constructing Public Opinion*. New York: Columbia University Press.

Lewis, Justin and Cushion, Stephen (2009) "The Thirst to Be First: An Analysis of Breaking News Stories and Their Impact on the Quality of 24-Hour News Coverage in the UK", *Journalism Practice* 3(3): 304–18.

Lewis, Justin, Inthorn, Sanna and Wahl-Jorgensen, Karin (2005) *Citizens or Consumers: The Media and the Decline of Political Participation*. London: Open University Press.

Livingston, Steven (1997) *Clarifying the CNN Effect: An Examination of Media Effects According to Type of Military Intervention*. John F. Kennedy School of Government's Joan Shorenstein Center on the Press, Politics and Public Policy at Harvard University.

Livingston, Steven and Cooper, Kurtis (2001) "The Changing Nature of CNN 'Live Events' Coverage and the Consequences for International Affairs". Paper presented at the International Studies Association, Chicago.

Livingstone, Sonia (2009) "On the Mediation of Everything", *Journal of Communication* 59(1): 1–18.

Lund, Maria K. (2012) "More News for Less: How the Professional Values of 24/7 Journalism Reshaped Norway's TV2 Newsroom", *Journalism Studies* 6(2): 201–16.

Lundby, Knut (2009a) "Media Logic: Looking for Social Interaction", in Lundby, Knut, *Mediatization: Concept, Changes and Consequences*. New York: Peter Lang.

——(2009b) *Mediatization: Concept, Changes and Consequences*. New York: Peter Lang.

MacGregor, Brent (1997) *Live, Direct and Biased: Making Television News in the Satellite Age*. London: Arnold.

Marr, Andrew (2006) *My Trade: A Short History of British Journalism*. London: Pam.

Marriott, Stephanie (2007) *Live Television: Time, Space and the Broadcast Event*. London: Sage.

Mason, Chris (2012) "Twitter Effect: How the Hashtag Has Shaped Political Debate", *BBC News*, 25 April, available online at www.bbc.co.uk/news/uk-politics-17824255 (accessed 28 August 2014).

Mazzoleni, Gianpietro (1987) "Media Logic and Party Logic in Campaign Coverage: The Italian General Election of 1983", *European Journal of Communication* 2(1): 81–103.

——(2008) "Mediatization of Politics", in Donsbach, Wolfgang (ed.), *The International Encyclopaedia of Communication*. Malden, MA: Blackwell.

Mazzoleni, Gianpietro and Schulz, Winfried (1999) "'Mediatization of Politics': A Challenge for Democracy?", *Political Communication* 16(3): 247–61.

McChesney, Robert W. (2013) *Digital Disconnect: How Capitalism Is Turning the Internet against Democracy*. New York: The New Press.

McIntyre, Marina (2012) "Barack Obama Victory Tweet Becomes Most Retweeted Ever", *The Guardian*, 7 November, available online at www.theguardian.com/world/2012/nov/07/how-barack-obama-celebrated-twitter (accessed 28 August 2014).

McNair, Brian (2000) *Journalism and Democracy: An Evaluation of the Political Public Sphere*. London: Routledge.

——(2004) "PR Must Die: Spin, Anti-spin and Political Public Relations in the UK, 1997–2004", *Journalism Studies* 5(3): 325–38.

McNair, Brian, Hibberd, Matthew and Schlesinger, Philip (2003) *Mediated Access: Broadcasting and Democratic Participation*. Luton: University of Luton Press.

McQuail, Dennis (1987) *Mass Communication Theory*. 2nd ed. London: Sage.

Medienorge/TNS Gallup (2012) "Min viktigste nyhetskilde", available online at www. med ienorge.uib.no/?cat=statistikk&medium=it&queryID=374 (accessed 19 October 2012).

Meltzer, Kimberly (2010) *TV News Anchors and Journalistic Tradition: How Journalists Adapt to Technology*. New York: Peter Lang.

Miller, Joe (2014) "Britons Spend More Time on Tech than Asleep, Study Suggests", *BBC News*, available online at www.bbc.co.uk/news/technology-28677674 (accessed 28 August 2014).

Montgomery, Martin (2006) "Broadcast News, the Live 'Two-way' and the Case of Andrew Gilligan", *Media, Culture and Society* 28(2): 233–59.

——(2007) *The Discourse of Broadcast News: A Linguistic Approach*. London: Routledge.

Morris, Jonathan (2007) "Slanted Objectivity? Perceived Media Bias, Cable News Exposure, and Political Attitudes", in *Social Science Quarterly* 88(3): 707–28.

Nacos, Brigitte (2003) "Terrorism as Breaking News: Attack on America", *Political Science Quarterly* 11(1): 23–52.

——(2007) *Mass-mediated Terrorism: The Central Role of the Media in Terrorism and Counterterrorism*. Lanham, MD: Rowman & Littlefield.

Newman, Nic and Levy, David (2014) (eds) *Reuters Institute Digital News Report 2014*. Oxford: Reuters Institute. Available online at https://reutersinstitute.politics.ox.ac. uk/sites/default/files/Reuters%20Institute%20Digital%20News%20Report%202014.pdf (accessed 28 August 2014).

New York Times (2004) "*The Times* and Iraq", 26 May, available online at http:// www.nytimes.com/2004/05/26/international/middleeast/26FTE_NOTE.html (accessed 16 July 2014).

Norris, Pippa (2000) *A Virtuous Circle? Political Communications in Post-Industrial Democracies*. Cambridge: Cambridge University Press.

Ofcom (2007) *New News, Future News*. London: Ofcom.

——(2012) *Licensing of Channel 3 and Channel 5*. London: Ofcom.

——(2013) *News Consumption in the UK*. London: Ofcom.

——(2014) *The Communications Market 2014* (August). London: Ofcom. Available online at http://stakeholders.ofcom.org.uk/market-data-research/market-data/commu nications-market-reports/cmr14/ (accessed 28 August 2014).

Patrona, Marianna (2012) "Journalists on the News: The Structured Panel Discussion as a Form of Broadcast Talk", *Discourse and Society* 23(2): 145–62.

Patterson, Thomas (1993) *Out of Order*. New York: Vintage.

——(1996) "Bad News, Bad Governance", in *Annals of the American Academy of Political and Social Science* 546: 97–108.

——(1997) 'The News Media: An Effective Political Actor?', *Political Communication* 14: 445–55.

——(2000) *Doing Well and Doing Good: How Soft News and Critical Journalism Are Shrinking the News Audience and Weakening Democracy – And What News Outlets Can Do About It*. Cambridge, MA: John F. Kennedy School of Government, Harvard University.

——(2002) "The Vanishing Voter: Why Are the Voting Booths So Empty?", *National Civic Review* 91(4): 367–78, available online at www.uvm.edu/~dguber/POLS125/articles/patterson.htm (accessed 3 August 2014).

Pew Research Center (2013) *News Use across Social Media Platforms*, 14 November, available online at www.journalism.org/files/2013/11/News-Use-Across-Social-Media-Platforms1.pdf (accessed 28 August 2014).

The Pew Research Center for the People and the Press (2007) "Public Knowledge of Current Affairs Little Changed by News and Information Revolutions", April 15, available online at www.people-press.org/2007/04/15/public-knowledge-of-current-aff airs-little-changed-by-news-and-information-revolutions (accessed 28 August 2014).

The Pew Research Center's Project for Excellence in Journalism (2012) *The State of the News Media 2012: An Annual Report on American Journalism*, available online at http://stateofthemedia.org/2012/overview-5/key-findings (accessed 15 July 2014).

——(2013) *The State of the News Media 2013: An Annual Report on American Journalism*, available online at http://stateofthemedia.org/2013/overview-5/key-findings (accessed 15 July 2014).

Philo, Greg and Berry, Mike (2004) *Bad News from Israel*. London: Pluto Press.

Pollard, Nick (2009) "Non-stop Deadlines: 24-hour News", in Owen, John and Purdley, Heather, *International News Reporting: Frontlines and Deadlines*, Malden, MA: Wiley-Blackwell.

Ponsford, Dominic (2014) "BuzzFeed Uses $50m New Investment to Expand News, Lifestyle and Video Content", *Press Gazette*, 11 August, available online at www.pressgazette.co.uk/buzzfeed-uses-50m-new-investment-expand-news-lifestyle-and-video-content (accessed 28 August 2014).

Preston, Peter (2014) "BuzzFeed: We Report News Differently Now – But Is It Better?", *The Observer*, 17 August, available online at www.theguardian.com/media/2014/aug/17/buzzfeed-internet-expansion-way-report-news-coverage-changing (accessed 28 August 2014).

Prior, Marcus (2007) *Post-Broadcast Democracy: How Media Choice Increases Inequality in Political Involvement and Polarizes Elections*. Cambridge: Cambridge University Press.

Ray, Vin (2003) *The Television News Handbook: An Insider's Guide to Being a Great Journalist*. London: Macmillan.

Raymond, Geoffrey (2000) "The Voice of Authority: The Local Accomplishment of Authoritative Discourse in Live News Broadcasts", *Discourse Studies* 2(3): 354–79.

Reid, Alasdair (1999) "Are Traditional Peaktime News Bulletins Outdated? One-third of UK Television Viewers Can Access News Coverage Whenever Suits Them Best. So Now that ITV's Stalwart, News at Ten, Has Rung Its Final Bong, Is It Time to Face up to the Fact That [sic]", *Campaign*, 12 March, available online at www.campaignlive.co.uk/news/22294 (accessed 20 July 2014).

Reynolds, Amy and Barnett, Brooke (2003) "This Just In … How National TV News Handled the Breaking 'Live' Coverage of September 11", *Journalism and Mass Communications Quarterly* 80(3): 689–703.

Reynolds, John (2014) "ITV and Channel 5 Forced to Show UKIP Parliamentary Election Broadcasts", *Media Guardian*, 3 March, available online at www.theguardian.com/media/2014/mar/03/itv-channel-5-to-show-ukip-election-broadcasts (accessed 16 July 2014).

Robertson, Alexa (2010) *Mediated Cosmopolitanism: The World of Television News*. Cambridge: Polity Press.

Robinson, Nick (2012) *Live from Downing Street: The Inside Story of Politics, Power and the Media*. London: Bantam Press.

Robinson, Piers (2002) *The CNN Effect: The Myth of News Media, Foreign Policy and Intervention*. London: Routledge.

Rosenbaum, Martin (1997) *From Soapbox to Soundbite: Party Political Campaigning in Britain since 1945*. Basingstoke: McMillan.

Rosenberg, Howard and Feldman, Charles (2008) *No Time To Think: The Menace of Media Speed and the 24-hour News Cycle*. New York: Continuum.

Salgado, Susan and Strömbäck, Jesper (2012) "Interpretive Journalism: A Review of Concepts, Operationalizations and Key Findings", *Journalism* 13(2): 144–61.

Sambrook, Richard (2004) "Tragedy in the Fog of War", *British Journalism Review* 15(3): 7–13.

——(2012) *Delivering Trust: Impartiality and Objectivity in the Digital Age*. Working paper. Oxford: Reuters Institute for the Study of Journalism, University of Oxford.

——(2013) "TV Bulletins Still on Top for Big International News", 24 April, BBC College of Journalism, available online at www.bbc.co.uk/blogs/blogcollegeofjournalism/posts/TV-bulletins-still-on-top-for-big-international-news (accessed 15 July 2014).

Sambrook, Richard and McGuire, Sean (2014) "Have 24-hour TV News Channels Had their Day?", in *Media Guardian*, 3 February, available online at www.theguardian.com/media/2014/feb/03/tv-24-hour-news-channels-bbc-rolling (accessed 15 July 2014).

Sampert, Shannon, Trimble, Linda, Wagner, Angelia and Gerrits, Bailey (2014) "Jumping the Shark. Mediatization of Canadian Party Leadership Contests, 1975–2012", *Journalism Practice* 8(3): 279–94.

Schudson, Michael (2001) "The Objectivity Norm in American Journalism", *Journalism: Theory, Practice and Criticism* 2(2): 149–70.

Schulz, Winfried (2004) "Reconstructing Mediatization as an Analytical Concept", *European Journal of Communication* 19(1): 87–101.

Seethaler, Josef and Melischek, Gabrielle (2014) *Phases of Mediatization. Empirical Evidence from Austrian Election Campaigns since 1970, Journalism Practice* 8(3): 258–78.

Seib, Philip (2001) *Going Live: Getting the News Right in a Real-Time, Online World*. Lanham, MD: Rowman & Littlefield.

Semetko, Holli A., Blumler, Jay G., Gurevitch, Michael, Weaver, David H. and Barkin, Steve (1991) *The Formation of Campaign Agendas: A Comparative Analysis of Party and Media Roles in Recent American and British Elections*. Hillsdale, NJ: Erlbaum.

Sergeant, John (2001) *Give Me Ten Seconds*. London: Pam Books.

Siebert, Fredrick S., Peterson, Theodore and Schramm, Wilbur (1956) *Four Theories of the Press: The Authoritarian, Libertarian, Social Responsibility, and Soviet Communist Concepts of What the Press Should Be and Do*. Urbana and Chicago: University of Illinois Press.

Small, Tamara (2011) "What the Hashtag? A Content Analysis of Canadian Politics on Twitter", *Information, Communication & Society* 14(6): 872–95.

Snoeijer, Roland, de Vreese, Claes H. and Semetko, Holli A. (2002) "Reporting on Recall and Appreciation of Political News", *European Journal of Communication* 17(1): 85–101.

Soroka, Stuart, Blake, Andrew, Aalberg, Toril, Iyengar, Shanto, Curran, James, Coen, Sharon, Hayashi, Kaori, Jones, Paul, Mazzoleni, Gianpetro, Woong Rhee, June,

Rowe, David and Tiffen, Rod (2013) "Auntie Knows Best? Public Broadcasters and Current Affairs Knowledge", *British Journal of Political Science* 43(4): 719–39.

Steele, Catherine and Barnhurst, Kevin (1996) "The Journalism of Opinion: Network Coverage in US Presidential Campaigns, 1968–88", *Critical Studies in Mass Communication* 13(3): 187–209.

Strömbäck, Jesper (2008) "Four Phases of Mediatization: An Analysis of the Mediatization of Politics", *The International Journal of Press/Politics* 13(3): 228–46.

Strömbäck, Jesper and Dimitrova, Daniella (2011) "Mediatization and Media Interventionism: A Comparative Analysis of Sweden and the United States", *The International Journal of Press/Politics* 16(1): 30–49.

Strömbäck, Jesper and Esser, Frank (2009) "Shaping Politics: Mediatization and Media Interventionism", in Lundby, Knut (ed.) *Mediatization: Concept, Changes, Consequences*. New York: Peter Lang.

——(2014a) "Mediatization of Politics: Towards a Theoretical Framework", in Esser, Frank and Strömbäck, Jesper (eds), *Mediatization of Politics. Understanding the Transformation of Western Democracies*. Basingstoke: Palgrave Macmillan.

——(2014b) "Introduction: Making Sense of the Mediatization of Politics", in *Journalism Practice* 8(3): 245–57.

Strömbäck, Jesper, Negrine, Ralph, Hopmann, Dennis N., Maier, Michaela, Jalali, Carlos, Berganza, Rosa, Seeber, Gilig U. H., Seceleanu, Andra, Volek, Jaromir, Dobek-Ostrowska, Boguslawa, Mykkänen, Juri, Belluait, Marinella and Róka, Jolan (2011) "The Mediatization and Framing of European Parliamentary Election Campaigns", in Maier, Michaela, Strömbäck, Jesper and Kaid, Lynda Lee (eds), *Political Communication in European Parliamentary Elections*. Aldershot: Ashgate.

Takens, Janet, van Atteveldt, Wouter, van Hoof, Anita and Kleinnijenhuis, Jan (2013) "Media Logic in Election Campaign Coverage", *European Journal of Communication* 28(3): 225–40.

Tolson, Andrew (2006) *Media Talk: Spoken Discourse on TV and Radio*. Edinburgh: Edinburgh University Press.

——(2011) "Political Discourse in TV News: Conversational Presentation and the Politics of 'Trust'", in Ekström, Mats and Patrona, Marianna (eds), *Talking Politics in Broadcast Media*. Amsterdam: Benjamins.

Tuggle, C.A. and Huffman, Suzanne (2001) "Live Reporting in Television News: Breaking News or Black Holes?", *Journal of Broadcasting and Electronic Media* 45(2): 335–44.

Tuggle, C.A., Casella, Peter and Huffman, Suzanne (2010) "Live, Late-Breaking, and Broken: TV News and the Challenge of Live Reporting in America", in Cushion, Stephen and Lewis, Justin (eds), *The Rise of 24-Hour News Television. Global Perspectives*. New York: Peter Lang.

Tuggle, C. A., Huffman, Suzanne, and Rosengard, Dana (2007) "Reporting Live from the Scene: Enough to Attract the 18–24 Audience?", *Journal of Broadcasting & Electronic Media* 51(1): 58–72.

Unger, Arthur (1987) "Network Difficulties. Fast changing channels. The Future of TV News. Part 1", *The Christian Science Monitor*, 30 November, available online at http://m.csmonitor.com/1987/1130/ltv1.html (accessed 18 December 2013).

Wahl-Jorgensen, Karin, Sambrook, Richard, Berry, Mike, Moore, Kerry, Bennett, Lucy, Cable, Jonathan, Garcia-Blanco, Inaki, Kidd, Jenny, Dencik, Lina and Hintz, Arne (2013) *BBC Breadth of Opinion Review: Content Analysis*. BBC Trust publication.

Available online at http://downloads.bbc.co.uk/bbctrust/assets/files/pdf/our_work/breadth_opinion/content_analysis.pdf (accessed 16 July 2014).

Washbourne, Neil (2010) *Mediating Politics: Newspapers, Radio, Television and the Internet*. Maidenhead: Open University Press.

The Washington Post (2012) "Social Media's Role in Politics", *Washington Post: Innovations*, 25 January, available online at www.washingtonpost.com/national/on-innovations/social-medias-role-in-politics/2012/01/25/gIQAQvZgdQ_story.html (accessed 28 August).

Williams, Alex (2014) "The Growing Pay Gap between Journalism and Public Relations", Pew Research Center, 11 August, available online at www.pewresearch.org/fact-tank/2014/08/11/the-growing-pay-gap-between-journalism-and-public-relations/ (accessed 28 August 2014).

Winston, Brian (2002) "Towards Tabloidization? Glasgow Revisited, 1975–2001", *Journalism Studies* 3(1): 5–20.

Witschge, Tamara (2014) "Passive Accomplice or Active Disruptor? The Role of Audiences in the Mediatization of Politics", *Journalism Practice* 8(3): 342–56.

Wring, Dominic (2004) *The Politics of Marketing the Labour Party*. Basingstoke: Palgrave Macmillan.

Zeh, Reimar and Hopmann, Dennis (2013) "Indicating Mediatization? Two Decades of Election Campaign Television Coverage", *European Journal of Communication* 28(3): 225–40.

Zelizer, Barbara and Allan, Stuart (2002) *Journalism after September 11*. London: Routledge.

Index

Note: page numbers in **bold** indicate a table; page numbers in *italic* indicate a figure.